Demystifying Strategy

This book is dedicated to Thomas who lives in my heart throughout its writing. May we be reunited again.

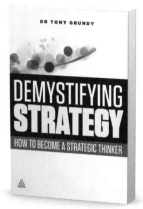

Demystifying Strategy
How to become
a strategic thinker

Tony Grundy

KoganPage

LONDON PHILADELPHIA NEW DELHI

First published in Great Britain and the United States in 2012 by Kogan Page Limited

120 Pentonville Road	1518 Walnut Street, Suite 1100	4737/23 Ansari Road
London N1 9JN	Philadelphia PA 19102	Daryaganj
United Kingdom	USA	New Delhi 110002
www.koganpage.com		India

© Tony Grundy, 2012

ISBN   978 0 7494 6568 1
E-ISBN   978 0 7494 6569 8

British Library Cataloguing-in-Publication Data

A CIP record for this book is available from the British Library.

Library of Congress Cataloging-in-Publication Data

Grundy, Tony, 1954-
   Demystifying strategy : how to become a strategic thinker / Tony Grundy.
      p. cm.
   ISBN 978-0-7494-6568-1 – ISBN 978-0-7494-6569-8   1. Strategic planning.   I. Title.
   HD30.28.G783 2012
   658.4'012–dc23

                                                                                    2012014138

Typeset by Graphicraft Limited, Hong Kong
Printed and bound in India by Replika Press Pvt Ltd

CONTENTS

Opening the doorway to strategy

Introduction

Why did I write this book? Let's explore...

When I first began to have an interest in strategy in the late 1970s and early 1980s the discipline was relatively simple and straightforward. At that time there were the embryonic germs of later thinking – in terms of having a longer-term planning process, understanding competitive positioning and also the relative attractiveness of different markets and industries.

Since then, strategy has become a lot more complex and arguably far too much so: making it hard for the layperson – who might even be a CEO – to get their head around. Also, many, though not all, strategy professors and consultants often over-conceptualize it, and cloud it in unnecessary jargon. Even books that start off in a reasonably simple and straightforward way rapidly become increasingly weighed down by complexity – as if the writers cannot fail to become intoxicated by the ornate nature of the discipline. I will be avoiding that.

In my view, strategy – such a simple term – has become entangled with conceptual overgrowth. As a result, end users of the language of strategy end up saying things in real business situations without much real meaning at all. Do you, as the reader, recognize that, for example when someone says something about the strategy and you simply don't get it?

To paraphrase Christopher Robin in the first chapter of the first book of Winnie-the-Pooh stories: 'I wish there was a better way, if only I could think of it.' This book is therefore based on three main premises:

1 that strategy can and must be demystified in order for it to add real insight and value;

2 that instead of strategy being the domain of a few masters located in the esoteric towers of business schools, or in some impressive and palatial London West End office block, most of us can unlock the power of strategic thinking that lies as a potential within us;

3 that a single book can equip you with the reference points and flagpoles that you will refer back to over many years in order to turn difficult strategic situations into simple and successful strategies to lift your career.

I felt – to answer my opening question – that the existing books on strategy underemphasized the practical nature of the subject and didn't really engage the reader as practitioner sufficiently to cause a real shift in thinking and one that was reflected in changed management activity. Also, by and large, they fail to express its core principles in as simple a way as possible.

My dream was that I could distil the wisdom of strategy in a sufficiently transparent way to get my readers to appreciate its essence – in a way similar to how I was opened up to it over the past 30 years. The difference is that having got to this point, I can help you to get there much faster than it took me, particularly in developing your strategic thinking capability. I aim to open up a new voice in your head – one that you might feel as being, as it were, your 'strategic conscience' – that will kick in when you are approaching a problem or an issue in too tactical a way.

This book's main audience are practising managers who want to get inside strategy and learn about strategic thinking without taking a long course, or as a refresher. These will be managers, probably in senior positions, with responsibility for developing the strategy, or implementing it.

A secondary group of people are those who would have liked to have done an MBA but practicalities or cost precluded it – the 'MBA bypass' segment. Then there are those who completed an MBA but feel a need for the strategy piece to come more together, or to be related to their practice.

Finally there might be MBA students who find the conventional books too dry and want to have a lot more on 'how to do it'. They will probably find that this book is refreshingly different and that it helps to facilitate learning through the emphasis on demystification.

In this first chapter on 'opening the doorway to strategy' we now look at:

- What will the book do for you?
- What is entailed in reading it?
- What is strategy and why is this important?
- How do we discover the strategy guru hidden inside us?
- Looking forward to the world of strategy.
- Lessons so far.

What will the book do for you?

This book will help you in eight key ways:

- Give you a refreshingly simple understanding of the key ideas and concepts in strategy.

- Help you learn the language of strategy without getting lost in it – and show you how it can often be translated into everyday words that will lose people or leave them cold.
- Help you to become a strategic thinker, and make you more deeply thoughtful, too.
- Explain to you the value of these ideas and highlight any drawbacks or limitations.
- Illustrate this with practical examples.
- Give you concrete help in managing the strategy process.
- Give you self-help exercises to apply the ideas to things you have direct experience of.
- Give you probably the most complete system of strategic thinking that currently exists.

We will now expand on these individual points.

Keeping strategy simple

First of all, there is no reason why strategy shouldn't be kept as simple as possible; indeed, our very mission to demystify it is based on the premise that it doesn't have to be, and shouldn't be, so esoteric.

As an illustration of this, I was once teaching strategy at a major business school as part of a bigger team and I introduced a relatively simple tool called the strategic option grid (a technique that we will learn and grow to love, for appraising strategic options) to around 160 MBA students. The senior strategy professor under whom I had been working came up to me the next day and, waving the grid in an accusing fashion, said to me, 'Who has been introducing this grid to the students?', clearly horrified for some reason. Apparently he was very concerned because this technique appeared to reduce strategy – making it into just five key variables. As he was a purist, he was objecting that in his view 'that is far too simplistic and we don't want to be making it too easy for students'.

I felt somewhat bruised by this encounter, but hundreds of senior executives outside the business school had found this 'simplistic tool' incredibly useful and it had been rolled out, for example, by the retailer Tesco and many others. I had felt that the students would really benefit from something that gave them a far more 'helicopter' overview of the issues.

A few days later, an MBA student came up to me, waving the same piece of paper and saying, 'Who introduced this grid?' By this time I was rather sensitive about the whole thing and slightly meekly admitted that it was me. He then went on to shock and surprise me by saying that it was brilliant and that 'this is the first time that I have actually understood how to evaluate a strategy'.

While no one would suggest that, given today's business complexity, strategy can be easily boiled down to just a few ideas, I do think – and I feel that this view is shared by CEOs and senior executives – that it need not be made any more complex than it really is. The moral of this story is that there is great virtue in simplicity, particularly as the technique in question facilitated cognitive understanding of strategy without obviously oversimplifying it. The strategic option grid, although it boils decision making down into just five key criteria, raises a lot of further questions and is anything but over-simplistic. We will be seeing a lot of this grid.

The strategic option grid is particularly useful in technology markets because it ensures the quick communication of complexity. This is essential in organizations with high information overload, operating in a turbulent environment.

Defining your language

The complex and abstract language so often used by strategy professionals is another major factor that we will be addressing. There are possibly over a hundred terms or more that are used when discussing strategy. Some are useful and generally clear terms, such as 'competitive advantage' and 'growth drivers', but some carry wide and possibly too general and vague connotations, such as 'mission' and 'vision'.

The number and ambiguity of these terms make strategy hard to follow. Also, it is hard to understand how these terms and concepts interrelate with one another. Even terms such as 'strategy' and 'tactics' still get confused with one another – which might be surprising to some. A common vocabulary helps you to save time and reduce errors, as all too often strategy words are open to interpretation.

But no baby is born with a prior understanding of language generally, let alone the language of strategy, and thus we all need to learn it at some stage. But even today, most managers lack any formal training in strategy, and even those who have this training have still been exposed to the way that these terms are used in practice – which is essentially confusing. So, as I was taught at university, if 'the meaning of a word is its actual use' (from the philosopher Wittgenstein), then using a strategy word to mean quite diverse and different things will lead to much confusion of meaning, especially for busy managers on the hoof. And so it is in strategy.

So we will be teaching in straightforward terms what these words actually mean, through defining and explaining every term that we introduce, especially in the first three chapters. Please bear with us on that.

Helping you to do strategic thinking – and to make you more deeply thoughtful, too

In this book we will be giving you many tips on how to do strategic thinking. We look at the number of different perspectives on strategy and strategic thinking – including the conceptual, the cognitive, the emotional, influencing and politics, and implementation (Chapters 2 and 3), and the economic (Chapter 4). We devote a chapter to options (Chapter 6), to implementation (Chapter 7) and to the strategy process (Chapter 8).

In doing all of that – and through the strategic exercises – we will try to get you to be far more deeply thoughtful than you might have been previously, for example in asking the question 'why', in stepping outside of existing mind-sets, in challenging assumptions and in seeing things from a very fresh and bigger-picture perspective. This will feel like some effort, but it is both enjoyable and fruitful. We hope that you can shift more and more into that habit.

Capturing its value and avoiding the downsides

The value of strategic thinking resides in:

- more effective strategic decisions that add real economic value;
- avoiding making strategic constraints;
- avoiding time wasted getting there;
- avoiding unnecessary difficulties and politics;
- influencing key stakeholders and building ownership;
- at an everyday level, going back to your strategy constantly to help resolve operational dilemmas, and thus having a frame of reference;
- greater confidence and proactivity;
- far less anxiety about things like 'Are we deciding to do the right things?', 'Will I look silly suggesting this is an option?' etc.

In addition, we will be looking at how these ideals, concepts and tools are actually used – and at their value and their limitations. Even simple tools like SWOT (strengths, weaknesses, opportunities and threats) have many subtleties, and if used naively can actually be very dangerous. This will come mainly in Chapter 4 onwards. We will be integrating this within the strategic thinking process.

These tools are used for a variety of reasons. A good reason for using them is that they allow managers to make sense of complex business realities without oversimplifying them. Another is that they make it easier to untangle dilemmas and make difficult choices, even though they lack certain information. They facilitate debate on inevitably political issues without abandoning reason. They encourage greater detachment and objectivity. Also, they allow strategy to be communicated in a clearer and more transparent way.

But sometimes they are attractive for perhaps the wrong reasons. For instance, these tools are often used as what was once described as 'uncertainty sponges' – to make managers more comfortable in committing to a particular (often preconceived) direction.

We will be showing you how to use these tools according to best practice. We will do this by careful explanation in a way that assumes you are starting without necessarily knowing what they are and what they mean and by looking at practical examples throughout, so that you get the sense that strategy is essentially experiential. The theory only really makes sense when we can use it in a direct, specific way, rather than it transcending everyday management experience.

Using everyday examples

Everyday experiences are often a good way of developing one's understanding of strategy. We will be drawing examples from those experiences to demystify strategy. We would encourage the reader, especially over the course of the few weeks when they will probably read this book, to use every shopping expedition, every advert that they see as they travel to work or on TV, every website that they look up, as experiences for reflection and learning. There are countless opportunities for strategic thinking in everyday life.

For example, when I was writing this I was on a visit to the London Dungeon, which is run by Merlin Entertainments, a large leisure group that I might fancy doing some strategy work with one day. Merlin owns a plethora of venues, including theme parks like Alton Towers, Chessington and Thorpe Park in the UK, and Sea-World, Madame Tussauds and the London Dungeon, and is also developing globally. Its longer-term aim is to challenge Disney.

Merlin Group seeks to maximize revenue streams at each and every turn. It appears to have an 'umbrella strategy' which defines its overall shape and competitive focus and has added some bolt-on strategies incrementally. For example, since the group acquired these businesses they have introduced a number of strategic innovations. For instance, there is an annual pass to all of its sites, which costs over £140 per individual or £96 per person for a family. A visit to a single attraction can be from £18 to £40. But an extra strategy which produces a secondary revenue stream has been put in place as well. This rather clever strategy is to offer discounts to customers at the London Dungeon (eg for Madame Tussauds) in order to generate incremental revenue.

After visiting the London Dungeon experience, including having a simulation of being hanged which is a bit too realistic, the crowds pour into an enormous gift shop where there seems to be no way out – by which time their kids have spent at least another £10. And there's an enticing picture of being hanged for another £7 on top!

You can see Merlin's strategy at work here as you enjoy the Merlin experience, especially during your waiting time: amusingly I named this bolt-on strategy, on the way back from the venue at London Bridge, a 'value suction strategy', to signify that the aim is to suck all the economic value from a customer by hooking them emotionally to a linked set of experiences. This is often an ingredient of successful strategies (where the customer is entirely engaged through the emotional experience) which can be replicated in other contexts, for example in your business.

As a compulsive strategic thinker, there is no actual or imagined purchase that is made without looking at the situation in a strategic light.

We will also be getting you, our reader, to do some work on your own issues as we go along, so that there is an element of interactivity in the process. This is intended to awaken the sleeping strategy guru within you. It is very easy to lapse into reading a book at a passive level only. My goal is to do a lot more than that with your consciousness of strategy so that, if we were ever to meet, I could detect that you had in some degree been, as one client once called it, 'Tony-ized'. This would mean that the strategy guru inside your head is switched on, and even though you may not have all the answers, you have been asking the right questions.

Throughout the book I will be using some case study examples, like the one above in Merlin Entertainments, to illustrate the points. Major case studies are those of the funerals industry in Chapter 4, the development of a global yoga business at Bikram Yoga and Pfizer's wonder drug Viagra in Chapter 5, searching for new options at Virgin Galactic in Chapter 6 and managing the strategy process at Legal Complaints in Chapter 9. I will also be referring more briefly to organizations such as Amazon, Dell, Facebook, Ryanair and Tesco at other points in our journey. This isn't a text top heavy with case studies, as I devote much space to you actually doing quite a number of strategic exercises yourselves.

Managing the process

While managers may be unclear about much of the language and concepts of strategy, they are often even more unclear about how to manage the strategy process itself. How should they set about developing or adapting a strategy to arrive at one that is challenging yet robust, comprehensive but straightforward – and within a reasonable time period? These are often questions that they don't really know the answer to before embarking on a strategy process. Through many years of consulting experience these will be mapped out for you in this book – avoiding painful and unguided experimentation. Without doubt, if you invest sufficient time in the book and in doing the many strategic exercises, you will emerge as a far more effective strategic thinker.

Doing the process yourselves

The book is unique, with emphasis on do-it-yourself exercises (see later). This is really important as if you don't get to practise, your understanding will be more superficial and you won't retain that more conceptual knowledge for very long. Also, you will certainly be far less motivated to experiment with the tools in everyday life and this will mean that any learning will decay and much of it will be temporary.

This is a complete thinking system and can be used to transform the way you manage – as it has done already for thousands of managers to whom I have taught it. (At one business school, managers were paying, at today's prices, around £3,000 for the experience – and getting their colleagues to come on it after them – so there must be real value in it!)

So is this the most complete system – and why?

I am an eclectic by nature and continually monitor the market for new approaches and models. To date, I really haven't found many comprehensive systems, and certainly not ones that take the best from everything. Typically texts tend to make a lot of some aspects according to the philosophies of their writers, rather than try to unify these in a coherent whole. Almost all fail to deal with implementation, and also don't address how you actually use the tools in practice.

My strategic thinking process is designed to deal both with the external environment and its uncertainties and with developing strategies equally well – and as a creative and inventive process, and at every conceivable level. It gives help in deciding what to use which tools on and how, and how to deal with the results. It also gives similar attention to conducting this as a process. So my claim that this is the most 'complete' process is not based on thin air. The process is also extremely well tested, as evidenced in the experiences of major corporations such as the drinks company Diageo, HSBC, Microsoft and Tesco who have taken it on board in the past. The strategic option grid process described in Chapter 6 was developed for Diageo.

What is entailed in reading it?

This book can be read a number of ways:

- skim-read: to pick up the key messages from the summaries and from the introductions;
- as a conventional and sequential read;
- as a source of checklists;
- as a programmed sequence of real strategic exercises.

On reading this book

As a skim-read: when I look at a book in a bookshop to see if it might be worth buying I typically skim-read the whole thing at a high level in about two to three minutes. This will typically involve reading the opening and closing parts of each chapter to get their essential messages. I will also run through the pictures and illustrations to see both what the author already recognizes and whether there seems to be anything novel or interesting about them, and also any new ones. I will then do a little random sampling of the clarity and interest of a few paragraphs.

Following a similar process allows one to get a rough grasp of the flavour of a book. One can also prepare oneself for a more detailed read and this facilitates absorbing the knowledge and makes reading the book far easier, too. This process should, of course, be repeated when one has finished reading the book, and ideally a few weeks later, to finalize the blending of existing and old knowledge.

As a conventional read: I have sometimes wondered whether managers ever have time to read all the books they buy, given their work and lifestyle. I never see them doing it at work, so, as they work long hours, when do they do it outside work? (Reading in the car is dangerous – don't try that!) What percentage of books do they actually finish, and what proportion of these actually gets read?

If the answers to both these questions are 'low', that invites the question: 'Do authors and publishers actually know this?' Perhaps many management books are impulse or 'feel good' or even 'look good' purchases? Such purchase patterns do have a real role: HR directors usually have a few cerebral-looking books dotted around, but one wonders whether these have been read.

It might go without saying that it is strongly hoped that you do read all of this book, even if your pattern of reading is to read it over a period of time – say a chapter a week, or a couple of chapters on each business flight. It is written without padding, so that the collective wisdom that I have been able to draw from both experiences and learnings is presented in a compact but digestible form. So even if you do decide to skip a few things, make a mental or physical note to go back to them again.

In terms of making notes, there are a number of ways to do it. The bold approach is to write your thoughts on the book or to underline passages or to put a mark in the margin. I don't really mind you doing that: it is your book, you have bought it, and you are not spoiling it by doing that. If anyone else picks it up, it makes you look more intelligent and thoughtful, not less.

A softer approach is to stick some yellow Post-its at the front and write down the page numbers of particularly good points, with some succinct comment on these. This is good not only to extract the learning points but also to be able to revisit these points and to access things later on. Who knows – with electronic versions you should be able to make comments and track these: if this isn't already happening, it will be soonish. Now that's an example of a fresh strategic thought, perhaps?

As a wider thing to remember, it is also important to record your strategic ideas and thoughts on an everyday basis, otherwise these will be quickly forgotten and not developed further; write these down anywhere convenient, such as in your diary. Personally I am in the habit of texting myself an idea, particularly an opportunity, so that I won't forget it and will see it the next day – that works for me. Having, somewhat embarrassingly, just got my first smartphone, there must be a way of making notes somewhere – although my Samsung just tried to charge me for that; again the strategic extras!

As a source of checklists: at frequent intervals we will be providing you with checklists in the form of key questions that you can use to diagnose your issues. The book can thus be used in an ongoing way to look up key sections and thus to prompt you in real time to stretch your thinking.

Learning through the exercises

As a programmed series of strategic exercises: ideally this should be done as you go along. This means that rather than thinking 'oh, I will just read this chapter now and that will take 20 minutes or so', you should do a quick skim-read ahead and adjust your estimate by, for example, adding on between 5 and 15 minutes' thinking time for the exercises. There are 61 exercises in all.

I know that it is so very tempting just to read on and pass over the exercises. But you may well not get full value out of the book unless you take some reflective space out – and invest in that. I would advise you to get a small strategic notebook for that.

In terms of expectations, the emphasis of the book will very much be on 'value-added thinking', which we will call VAT. VAT is an essential ingredient of all management. It implies taking a management issue and then putting it at some distance, objectifying it as it were, and then looking at it from a variety of perspectives. In doing this the aim is to add some real value to it, so that it is targeted economically. Strategic thinking is highly value added.

As you can tell, I hope to write in a lively style so that you have no chance of falling asleep: why do strategy gurus seem to have to make this all so heavy and serious? Strategy has got to be stimulating and fun!

Besides the many case studies, both short and long, I will also be making use of my everyday experiences of a strategic nature that I have had both during the writing of this book and before. I believe that these will help you see how strategy can be used to interpret everyday experiences and to generate ideas directly from that. This should also encourage you to do likewise. These experiences also frequently have a humorous element which will assist in the concentration process and lighten the areas where we need to be a little more conceptual.

So let's begin the process by looking at 'What is strategy?' Stay with me – it will be worth it...

What is strategy?

'Strategy' has many possible definitions and this in itself can be highly confusing. I have always tried to take a pragmatic approach here, and rather than get into long sentences with concepts like 'matching the environment' or 'inimitable competitive advantage' that can quickly put people to sleep, I will give you the first of my three useful definitions (Grundy, 1995): 'Strategy is how you get from where you are now to where you want to be – and with real competitive advantage.'

There are just five ingredients to this definition:

- Knowing where you are now.
- Knowing where you want to be.
- Knowing how you will get there.
- The 'how' is based on competitive advantage.
- This is real and not just in your head.

Simple stuff, right? But all five ingredients need to be there to begin to stand a chance of getting value out of strategy. And quite a lot is entailed in that definition.

Number one, you need to have a very clear idea as to where you actually are. This means asking key questions:

1 What is going on in the environment around your industry/market: the economy, technology, social trends, regulation etc?

2 How much competitive pressure is there, and is it changing within your market and its dynamics?

3 How do customers see your business, what value does it add relative to the competition, and what are the strengths of your customer base?

4 What is the relative strength of, and threat of, competitors?

5 What are your distinctive skills and other strategic assets (and weaknesses, too)?

Notice here that these points are posed as questions: questions open up the mind a lot more than mere checklists, as they get you to think. A strategy without thought is a delusion.

Using value-added SWOT analysis

A classic device to establish strategic position is to do a four-cornered box figure of a SWOT analysis, for:

- strengths;
- weaknesses;

- opportunities;
- threats.

The advantages of SWOT analysis are:

- It is easy to use.
- It is familiar to most managers.
- It puts issues into categories.
- It is evaluative: strengths and opportunities are positive but weaknesses and threats are negative.
- It is powerfully visually.
- If used incisively, it can cut through the strategic mist.

Its disadvantages and drawbacks are potentially:

- It is often superficial, especially if not accompanied by, for example, Porter's five forces (Chapter 4) and competitive benchmarking (Chapter 5).
- It can be dangerously incomplete.
- It can be biased.
- It can lack sufficient evidence.
- It is normally not prioritized.
- It is not critically thought about – the 'so what?' implications are not extracted.
- It is not used to develop options.

Thus it is highly dangerous if used on its own. I see its use as being not so much a central tool but: a) to kick-start early stage thinking; b) to use as a vehicle for learning as other issues come up and other data is gathered and interpreted; and c) as a means for presenting a final overview of the current position, along with the 'so what?' implications.

To get more out of it, it should also be prioritized – either by asterisking the most important elements or through colouring them. Alternatively, each of its elements can be prioritized more systematically in terms of a) their relative positivity/negativity multiplied by b) their degree of importance or possible impact.

Also, the implications of SWOT need addressing by looking at:

- What patterns are there in the SWOT's broad themes, for example has the company lost its way competitively? Is it too slow and unresponsive? Is it unbalanced in some way, or is there a fault line around its leadership, culture and mindset?
- Are some of the threats areas of major weakness, increasing the company's vulnerability?
- Are there specific opportunities where it is particularly strong, which might be candidates for breakthroughs?

One can therefore start to look at the interdependencies between the four segments of the SWOT. The basic SWOT analysis can thus be extended to be more powerful as SWOT plus options, or 'SWOTO' analysis, where there is also a box for all the options coming out of the SWOT.

But coming back to the main theme of strategy, I would like to pose the question: 'Does strategy actually matter?' My answer to that is: 'Yes, it most certainly does.' For example, BMW made the strategic mistake of buying Rover Group and nearly lost its independence as a result. Both Shell and then BP made blunders with strategic consequences that severely damaged shareholder value and corporate reputation. IBM got complacent in the 1990s and fell from grace, and took over 10 years to reposition itself fully.

Newer companies whose strategies work backwards from the customer and forwards by cunning innovation, such as Google, Facebook, Apple and Amazon, are on the ascendency, with better, fresher and future-looking strategies, and the results for shareholders have been mouth-watering.

But coming back to our first point above, I have always maintained that often companies think they know where they are now, but they don't. So when you are reviewing or setting strategy you do need to spend sufficient time to ensure that you are not suffering any strategic delusions. Quite often, especially where a company has lost its way, one might have to spend up to two-thirds of one's time in anchoring the strategic position into business reality. This can amount to as much as 50 per cent of the time in the strategy process if the current position is unclear.

That said, with a business that has a really good understanding of these five key questions this ought to take no more than 20 per cent of the time – it depends.

Just a quick note on question 2: we will be explaining competitive pressure in more depth in Chapter 4 as Porter's five forces. For the present, we should think of it as being: 'The intensity of competitive forces that influence how you compete and what rewards you get'; we will keep that simple, although there is a lot more to learn underneath that.

Next, let's look at the third question, on where you might want to be in the future.

Thinking your future and time horizons

One of the distinctive benefits of strategy as an idea is that it encourages us a lot more to think future. Much of what goes on in everyday management is focused on the immediate: this meeting, today's tasks, this week. For many managers next week is 'strategic'. So it is important that we stretch our time horizons further ahead.

As was once said by someone asked about why the future is so important, 'It is because we are going to spend the rest of our lives in it', which highlights that the vast majority of management discussions are rooted in either the past or the present. Where it does focus on the future, this is typically very short term.

So strategy serves a very real purpose by getting us to think about the future environment, future options, future competitive advantage etc. It takes us outside our more normal, introverted perspective.

Also, the future itself is an important variable and we need here to think about what time horizons we should be thinking of. This could be as short as a day or even as long as 25 years. But it is important not necessarily to assume that this must be seen as very long term. Strategy was popularized in the 1960s and 1970s as 'long-range planning' and has since perhaps become too closely associated with the very long term. There might be many other shorter-term occasions when you might need to work out where you are now, where you want to be and how to get there, with real competitive advantage....

Typical time horizons could be:

- a fashion company: the next 3 to 6 months;
- a major retailer: 2 to 3 years;
- a bank: 5 years;
- a pharmaceutical company: 15 years;
- an oil company: 20 years;
- the nuclear industry: 30 years.

Where we want to go is not just an average place to be but one that is determined by some imaginative and possibly stretching strategic goals. We return to that in our second definition of strategy, coming soon. This means that strategy should have both ambition and intent – it must have real purpose. And this can be framed in a variety of ways, which may include some positioning in your competitive space, a level of distinctive ability, an attractive stream of cash etc. So it needs to be broken down into distinctive, if interrelated, strategic goals. Strategic thinking thus means being able to travel imaginatively through time in the future.

Another key feature of strategic thinking is that it is about posing strategic hypotheses. We will explore this in Chapter 8 on the strategic process.

Strategy as being the how

The strategy itself is to be found primarily not in these goals but in the how itself. Any strategy needs to have form and colour and we must be able to describe it in specific terms. Often it is believed that strategy is inevitably broad, said by Mintzberg (1994) to be an 'umbrella strategy', as at Merlin Entertainments, or one that is a broad direction, or even something about 'what business(es) we are in'. That might be the case sometimes, but generally speaking it should be the exception: it is more commonly unhealthy to leave it that broad and ambiguous unless that is labelled 'strategic intent', which isn't quite the same thing.

For example, MBA students working on case studies are asked to come up with strategies for a particular business. When looking at options they often come up with possible strategies like 'acquisitions' or 'alliances', which they proceed to evaluate and conclude on. Yet they have not said a thing about what they are going to buy or who they are going to have an alliance with, what they are actually going to do and what it is going to cost to do that. On lectures to drive the point home I will say: 'That is as absurd as saying should I go out for a date with someone tonight without a clue of who it is, what they are like, what we will do and where it will lead to in the most abstract of terms.'

Managers are sometimes confused by this, however. They will challenge: 'But that is about implementation, which I always thought was operational and tactical.'

In response I would say that it would be a very odd thing if one could say how a strategy would be implemented without saying something about operational action. For me, strategy does need to be specific and tangible, otherwise how do we achieve it and how will we know if it ever happened?

Applying the big test: do we have sustainable competitive advantage?

This now leads us back to the search for a decent strategy, which must be one 'with real competitive advantage'. Here we aren't looking for average strategies but ones which are distinctive in some way. For what is the point of having the average plan, which is probably what at least 60 per cent of most companies' strategies actually are? It would be a very real surprise if this were going to give us anything above average returns. Probably 80 per cent of companies do not have significant competitive advantage or a cunning strategy.

Companies which have achieved a very real competitive advantage in more modern times include Amazon, Facebook and Google, and this has been achieved not just through technology but through a deep appreciation of the emotional value that is generated, as well as giving customers what they 'really-really want' – and at a reasonable cost.

Competitive advantage is now defined as 'giving customers distinctive value relative to internal costs that are either or both better than other competitors'.

This distinctive value can be both real and perceived, but the proof of the pudding is in what customers think these are, and not what the company thinks. So that means we must understand the world of value of products and services from the customer's point of view – and not from our own.

Think about the last time that you were impressed by the way that distinctive value was given – and without waste of resources: was it when you sat down to watch a premiership football game in 3D with BSkyB and it didn't cost an arm or a leg? Was it at an Indian restaurant where they cooked you a dish that you had suggested to them yourself? Or was it when you had a wonderful experience with your estate agents who moved mountains to get your sale through, despite snail-like solicitors? (Amazingly, that actually happened to me!) Competitive advantage gained in these kinds of ways is unfortunately rarer than we would like. Herein lie oceans of opportunities strategically.

Unfortunately, too many companies seem to be hell-bent on creating competitive disadvantage. If only they could avoid that, as other competitors are typically trapped in that mode. For instance, today it took me an hour and a quarter in an RBS branch to do a transfer in Croydon. The branch was like a funeral parlour with so few staff and an enormous area of empty space – wasted resources. This had been my first visit to a branch for 10 years – they have so few branches in England that I think I will be a convert to internet banking!

So strategic thinking inevitably involves taking a variety of mindsets – customers, competitors, ourselves – and the ability to look at the world through different perspectives. And it is thus agile in nature.

Back to our definition: in terms of cost, this doesn't mean price, as price is a measure of economic value. Also, we say here that it is about either superior value or costs, or both, so it is possible to achieve competitive advantage just by differentiating value, or through having a disproportionately low cost base. Finally it is a question always of relative competitive advantage – and this needs to be benchmarked, not just through generalized comparison, for example 'we are ahead of most of our competitors on this', but 'we have a specific competitive advantage over this specific competitor'. So when doing a SWOT analysis, to say that something is a 'competitive strength' is to suggest that it is an area of measurable edge over competitors, and isn't just an average capability.

Next, we talked about having 'real' competitive advantage, and this means for a start that it is measurable in some way – or at least it can be observed. How this can be done is the focus of Chapter 5. Also, we need to have some confidence that it is lasting, or more technically 'sustainable'. This is an important test as we need to have some assurance that our current edge isn't going to be simply eroded overnight. So now we have to think about how this edge can be protected, and who might try to erode that edge, and how, or even leapfrog over it. This test is absolutely crucial.

For example, for some years I was a non-executive director of a chain of health clubs in the UK. We had set up a new business of budget health clubs – there were a lot of cunning ingredients in this plan. But I needed to play the role of the CEO's strategic conscience and ask him: 'So how long will it be before we are threatened by imitation and what are we going to do about that – both before it happens, and when it happens?'

The advantage of this first definition above is that it helps us to think around a strategy in a very sound, analytical and clinical way. But a disadvantage is that it isn't perhaps terribly exciting, or inspiring. No definition of strategy is perfect, so we need more, which is coming soon. But first it is your turn to do some thinking by addressing the first exercise which you will be doing in parallel.

STRATEGIC EXERCISE 1.1 How clear is your strategy? A
mini 'strategy audit' – 5 minutes

Thinking about one of the strategies in your organization, based on the structure that we have already gone through, score it in terms of the clarity with which you understand its key ingredients as follows (in doing this you will need to think about all the factors that we described earlier – try not to do this at too unsophisticated a level):

	Very clear indeed 5	Very clear 4	Quite clear 3	Not so clear 2	Unclear 1
Current positioning – environment					
Current positioning – competitive advantage					
Future goals					
How you will implement it					
What's the competitive advantage of the 'how'?					
Total score out of 25:					

What does that tell you about where you need to focus or investigate more?

So what did you learn from doing that strategy: that you had a very clear idea of your strategy, or that you have areas where you could work on it further? You *did* do that exercise, didn't you? If you skip all or most of the exercises, you won't get the full value from this book.

Strategic thinking thus means having the capacity to be highly objective, and to be able to take a fresh and detached perspective on your strategy and position.

Strategy as being 'what we really-really want'

So if our earlier definition of strategy gets us started, let us move on to a second definition which might be somewhat more inspirational (they are all of some value). This is one that takes a more visionary perspective on it as being: 'Strategy is what we really-really-really want.'

This takes us on to the domain of true imaginary stretch. Some may remember echoes here of the once-famous British girl group called the 'Spice Girls' who sang that song. In the realm of strategy this is a helpful definition because it tells us to imagine a future world with strategic possibilities and where we can realize an exciting dream. It says to us: 'We are definitely not going to have a strategy where we are anything remotely like average, but whatever our chosen market or niche we are going to establish a strong and exciting position in it – and full of further potential.' The 'Spice Girl' definition of strategy comes into its own when managers have got entrenched in their existing position and the mindset that goes with that.

What is good about this definition is that it can give a lift to expectations about what can be credibly achievable. The downside can be that it may not be grounded in competitive reality and may be delusional. To work well with a 'Spice Girl' strategy requires a deep understanding of its alignment factors: what are all the things external or internal to the business that have to line up to deliver it? Provided that we have identified all of these, the Spice Girl perspective can be most fruitful.

The wishbone analysis tool in Chapter 7 on implementation is a practical way of using this idea to visualize the necessary and sufficient conditions needed for a successful strategy.

Strategy as the cunning plan

Our third and final definition is that of 'strategy is the cunning plan'. We define this as follows:

- It works backwards from the result.
- It is fundamentally simple.
- It achieves its goals by a combination of obvious, and less than obvious, ideas.
- And it isn't particularly easy to imitate.

In the television comedy series *Blackadder* – a comedy set in historical times – there featured a character, known as Blackadder, renowned for getting into all kinds of scrapes. His companion, a most scruffy and disgusting character called Baldrick, often used to help him try to get out of these scrapes, usually with disastrously funny results. But a constant theme of this immortal series was that they would usually come back to the cunning plan to rescue them. While this was a humorous comedy invention, it also inspired me in my long quest to demystify strategy.

I had for many years been frustrated that managers seemed content with more or less any kind of strategic plan, whether it was a cunning one or not. The fact that it looked 'strategic' was satisfying – even though it might have been no better than average, and often they were just happy to have a plan, full stop. So I latched onto the idea that I should stress to them that average plans, or even slightly above average ones, simply wouldn't do: what we really-really wanted was the cunning plan.

I impressed on them obsessively the need to search for a cunning plan. They would then typically go away and come back with some more stretching aims, such as 'to achieve £100m sales in this market', with at best a slightly better plan for how to get there. So all they had succeeded in accomplishing was to widen the strategic gap.

To paraphrase Blackadder, 'on my giddy aunt's smelly underclothes that have gone off in a pile on a hot summer's day, that's about as cunning as asking a great White Shark that is just going to bite all of your limbs off for a snack that he should kindly open a can of sardines for you while you swim away' – my rendition (apologies to Ben Elton, writer of *Blackadder*).

So, regardless of this simple concept of being 'cunning', I decided that as perhaps most managers typically don't see themselves as being innovative, let alone cunning, they need a lot more help to get their heads inside what one might think is a simple and very appealing idea. I would expose them to the story of the Millennium episode called 'Back and Forth' where Blackadder and Baldrick invent a time machine so that they can go back into the past and steal things that can be sold as expensive items – like Nelson's boot – and also change the course of history in their favour. They think they have a cunning plan but they don't actually implement it very well at all. In fact, Baldrick falls by accident on the time controls and they get sent back in time, but can't get back to the present because they have no idea what setting 'now' is on. This is the first example in this story of the need always – when doing strategic thinking – to ask oneself the question: 'What is the one big thing we've forgotten?'

They then arrive in Roman times and find that they have been reincarnated as Roman soldiers standing on top of Hadrian's wall in Scotland. Unfortunately, the wall is only three feet high, which is a metaphor in strategy for the importance of not spreading yourself too thinly. A key lesson of strategy is that you must choose, and this frequently means saying 'no' to options.

The Roman general arrives to boost morale by announcing a retreat back to Rome – just as Blackadder and Baldrick spot something in the distance. The Roman general's assistant says: 'Is that an orange hedge moving toward us?' And then seconds later his lieutenant says: 'No, it's the Scots!' A hoard of crazed Scots with nasty-looking weapons overwhelm the wall and surround the time machine where Blackadder and Baldrick have taken refuge. This is another important metaphor for the need in strategy to monitor signals in the environment.

There is another reminder in this part of the story about 'what's the one big thing that we have forgotten', too. When the Roman general appears on the scene he is almost fully armoured except down below, where all he has got on is his underpants! – echoing the story of the emperor's clothes.

At this point it is useful to reflect on what the options actually are for our two anti-heroes to be able to find out the setting on the time controls. Working backwards from the result one might, for example, get:

- some kind of truth drug;
- deep hypnosis;
- torture methods;
- shocks.

So here there are a range of options that need separate evaluation. But the really cunning one is yet to come....

After many attempts at going up and down in time to try to get back to the present, Blackadder begins to show real frustration and reflects: 'So I am going to be cursed to spend the rest of my life being in a small wooden box with the most stupidest man in the world.'

Then Baldrick shows an unusual flash of intelligence: 'My lord, I think that I have a cunning plan: well you know that if you are at the moment of death that your life flashes before your eyes? Well, if we were to drown you we could take you back to the moment in your life when I feel on the time controls and just at that moment of death you would see the controls on the time machine, and then we would bring you back to life and we would all get back to the present' – with a clever-looking grin on his face.

Whereupon Blackadder looks very thoughtful and then says: 'Well, Baldrick, that is quite a cunning plan, but I think that I have got an even better one.' And with that word he punches Baldrick unconscious and the next thing that we see is Baldrick's head being pushed down a loo to drown him – held by his legs. Each time he surfaces, spluttering, he gets closer to remembering and finally sees in his head the control settings, saying: 'I've got it!' and then, as he stops spluttering, 'I wish that we had flushed the loo!' – or, 'What's the one big thing that we forgot?'

So there are a number of most important learnings about strategy that come out of this story:

- However good a strategy is, it will fail if implementation is bad.
- Always ask yourself: 'What's the one big thing that you forgot?'
- Don't spread yourself too thinly: and strategy is about saying 'no'.
- Sense and interpret signals from the environment.
- Strategy is about options.
- We should seek out the cunning plan.
- And even when it is cunning, see if it can be further refined with a last ingredient – to be the 'stunning' plan.

Coming back to the idea of the cunning plan in the *Blackadder* case, this was most certainly arrived at by thinking about how one might remember something that one had forgotten: under what conditions might this actually happen?

Having established that, it then became easier for Baldrick and Blackadder to work out the cunning plan in terms of taking the near-death experience as a vehicle, and working out exactly how this could be done in a controlled way, so it didn't turn into a real death. While this plan had some elegant simplicity, it wouldn't be that easy to imitate – QED.

STRATEGIC EXERCISE 1.2 What is your cunning/stunning plan? – 10 minutes

For the same strategy that you worked on in Exercise 1.1, let's now see if you can improve it by working in your cunning plan:

- What do you really-really want to achieve out of it?

- Working backwards from the future, what steps might you have taken to get there?

- How has that exploited not just one but several interrelated and real competitive advantages?

- Where these are customer facing, to what extent do they appear irresistible?

- How easily and quickly and well can that be imitated by competitors, and how can you discourage that process?

- What's the 'one big thing' that you have missed to take the strategy up a final level (the stunning plan)?

This second exercise is very worthwhile – so please don't give into temptation and skip it.

Here we are beginning to bring in some of the thought processes that we will see in the 'cunning checklists' later on – to lift the thinking from the average to the more inventive. The glue for this is strategic thinking, to which we turn next. In the next subsection I will be illustrating the practical nature of strategy – with which we started this book – through some experiences in everyday life, where one is developing and implementing and learning from strategies all the time.

Some cunning plans in everyday life

Coming back to one of the strategic gems from *Blackadder*, which you should etch into your mind, always asking the question: 'What's the one big thing that we have forgotten?', a very simple example from everyday life which occurred recently underlines this – and is worth exploring. My (then to be) wife number three was making the major strategic decision of what kind of wedding dress to buy.

Her cunning plan was to go to a number of specialist shops and try on some dresses to get some ideas and to see what really looked good on her. Then she would buy hers on the internet – getting the same quality at probably a third of the price. With wedding dresses (as the ladies will know), measurement is all-important: a critical success factor. So, most carefully, she measured herself....

The dress was duly delivered and the trying-on and viewing process occurred in secret behind closed doors. After numerous debates the dress had to be altered. The reason? Not that the measurements had been taken wrongly – no, not at all! No, they had been taken at the wrong time of the month – not around the middle when our wedding was scheduled. My (then) fiancée has a different bust size mid-month to what it was when she was measured! It seems that, like the economy, if less so, her bust size moves through cycles – although fortunately not by as much!

The one big thing that she forgot...

Always ask, too, 'What's the second thing that we forgot?' In this case she forgot to factor in that she was going to lose a couple of pounds before the wedding day – which led to her saying to me: 'Look, Baby, I have shrunk a bit! Is that alright?' Although this may seem to some readers to be a tactical issue, I can assure you that from her perspective and in the context of a wedding – it was strategic! A further lesson here is that 'strategic' can have a different perspective according to the varying perspective of different stakeholders.

But before we leave the cunning plan for the time being, a slightly humorous illustration of this idea was when I was on the dating market a few years ago. After the disappointments of two unsuccessful marital strategies (yes, we strategists get things wrong, too; as there are complex and uncertain variables in choosing the right partner, I had 60 criteria the third time), I began the most important strategic project of acquiring a new, sustainable and stable partner with whom I would be happy (my four key strategic goals). Naturally I decided to see if this could be done with a cunning plan. The planks of this strategy were:

- a detailed assessment of my current strategic assets and constraints;
- a segmentation analysis of the market: age, profession, geography, family situation, personality type, stability, geographic location and core common interests;
- a distribution strategy: prioritizing adverts in national newspapers, the internet, dating evenings, general socializing, through friends etc – quite complex;

- marketing and branding strategy: how to position myself and how that fitted the segmentation analysis;
- acquisition criteria: these were along the lines of the strategic option grid – except that I tailored it to produce 12 categories (not just 4) with 5 subcategories in each, which made the 60 above. This was used to qualify prospects, to track them through the dating period and afterwards to see how it was all going....

Sorry if this sounds a bit too clinical, but I found that the process did prove very effective. For instance, I had a false start with someone who appeared almost ideal at first and, using the criteria, scored 83 per cent, but after major difficulties at the six-month mark she scored 45 per cent – which was a 'fail'.

The most cunning and perhaps most humorous aspect of the plan lay in developing a distribution strategy. I found that *The Times*, the *Guardian* and the *Telegraph* all had dating pages – *The Times* twice a week. So I put an advert in each – with some good results. It then occurred to me that I was really interested in several segments of the market. Also, I had a number of different positionings that I could advertise, but given the small number of words you could only do a subset in one advert. So I put more than one advert in each paper, each looking for something slightly different (and with different recorded messages that people could listen to). Interestingly, over that period I had only one person who heard multiple recordings of my recorded message from different adverts of mine and who said 'Oh, it's you again!'

So my emergent competitive strategy became a deliberate one. At the peak I had no fewer than five adverts on the same page of *The Times* Encounters! That's a market share of around 5 per cent of the whole page! As it happens, it was internet dating that won out eventually... so in strategy, beware doing the wrong thing really well....

The above example is a classic case of strategic thinking as practised in everyday life. More generally, this whole discussion of strategy as the cunning plan highlights that strategic thinking should be innovative and creative.

So, having defined strategy in a number of ways, let's now turn to the topic of the mysterious concept of strategic thinking itself.

What is strategic thinking?

Strategic thinking is our next concept to define and demystify. First, one might challenge the very notion that this is something that actually goes on much at all. In the words of Lord Thurso, the then CEO of Champneys, a leading and deluxe chain of spa resorts: 'Ah, strategic thinking,... well it is such a good thing to see managers actually thinking, let alone strategic thinking...', as if the occurrence of strategic thinking was such a rarity that one should be happy with evidence of some thinking – full stop.

So we can now define strategic thinking as 'all the thinking processes that look at any complex situation from a variety of angles, and seeks out options and evaluates them and their implications – from differing perspectives, in a novel way'. Its key ingredients are therefore:

- Thinking: this a structured process which takes into account causality, the degrees of freedom and the constraints and weighs the pros and cons of alternative decisions. It is also innovative and creative.

- Complexity: this usually occurs where there are many interdependent variables with uncertain dynamics.

- Different angles: this can be from external and internal perspectives, over short-, medium- and longer-term time horizons, from different stakeholders' points of view, with different sets of assumptions etc.

- Options: it distils possible choices into discrete and specific options.

- Evaluates them: it uses multiple criteria founded on evidence and judgement.

- Implications: it looks at things like the investment required, the implementation needs, the influencing of key stakeholders and the intended and not intended consequences.

- In a novel way: the end goal is to come up with some cunning (if not stunning) ideas; also, the actual process for arriving at these ideas might itself be novel – for example, considering what a competitor might do with the same opportunity.

One aspect of strategic thinking here is that of activating one's strategic radar. Here one uses the environmental analysis tools that we will meet in the form of Porter's five forces (see Chapter 4) and also towards the end of this chapter.

Asking the right questions

Arriving at a novel way of looking at things often happens not by analysis or deduction but by simply asking the right questions. In many ways this is more powerful than in evaluating position and obvious opportunities. For instance, fruitful strategic questions might be:

- Are we in too many businesses?

- How do we turn weaknesses into strengths and threats into opportunities?

- If we were a new entrant to our industry or a competitor, what would we do here?

- How can we attack competitors where they are weak and would find it difficult to respond?
- How can we achieve a truly dominant competitive position in this particular market?
- What would we do if we had no position in this market at all and were a fresh entrant?
- What are our strategic assets and how might we exploit them in new ways, and where?
- If we hadn't got into this market, would we not regret it, and if we were to want to get out of it, how could we do this?

Strategy and helicopter thinking

Associated with this definition is the need to remember that it is particularly important when doing strategic thinking to hang on to the big picture – and to avoid getting lost in the detail. Strategic thinking has sometimes been likened, metaphorically, to 'helicopter thinking'. Helicopter thinking means to have a stream of thought that is as agile as a helicopter, which:

- can lift up from the ground to see the big picture of what's going on;
- can land on, or hover over, an important feature or detail;
- has agility: to go forwards, sideways, upwards and downwards;
- has speed;
- has surprise and the advantages of concealment;
- is powerful: being able to attack in different ways, eg rockets, bombs, missiles, machine guns;
- has flexibility: performing different roles such as attack, carrying troops, rescue missions, reconnaissance.

There are many parallels for all of these roles specifically for strategic thinking. But most important is the 'feel' of the thinking: does it seem to have that kind of dynamic or is it ponderous and bitty – do we ever get any sense of the whole issue or problem, or just glimpses of parts of it?

Strategic thinking isn't just something that we should do when developing corporate strategy but at all kinds of levels, even – and especially – including the everyday. For example, I and my then wife-to-be (number three!) were talking about the problem that her daughter's (Frannie's) GCSE exam results had not come through the post. We reached the conclusion that this was due to the fact that we had redirected our post to where we were living from where we had been renting, but had not redirected her post.

We couldn't ask the school as it was the holidays and over the summer the buildings are unattended as teachers disappear from all contact – however urgent. The website advised waiting until the school reopened – meanwhile, all Frannie's friends would have their results while she didn't.

I kept asking what the options were for finding out: did anyone have the mobile number of her teacher so that the teacher could look up on a school computer if they happened to be popping in? Although we hadn't cracked the problem, at some deeper, unconscious level we were both still thinking about it. (Incidentally, strategic thinking often takes place at that deeper level as we may be doing something else.) The thought on my mind was that of 'the joy of constraints', one of my many ways of being cunning (see later in the book) which continually challenges one to think, and the more constrained the situation the more one tries to see new angles in it.

We were just about to meet an old friend of mine in Croydon and Carolina suddenly said: 'After we have had a drink with your old friend we could just go and see if our last house has got anyone in it – and ask for Frannie's letter.' We had lived in that house for a year and, when we left, the owner was going to redevelop it. We had passed it recently and it had looked empty for months.

I said it was worth a try and so we went up the garden in the dark – the garden had grown a few feet of weeds and it was very spooky. Carolina knocked on the door with predictably no reply, took the front door key out of her bag and we went in! (The landlord had never bothered asking for it back as the house was going to be left empty and then knocked down.) And there was Frannie's envelope in a massive pile! She was so pleased to find unexpectedly that she had got an 'A' in Physics.

After that, we did think about holding our wedding party for free there... from the cunning plan to the stunning plan! But we thought that might be going too far.

Returning to strategic thinking more generally, I have often found it helpful to contrast strategic thinking with that which is more operational in its focus. I developed this many years ago during a workshop with some senior managers of an insurance company. They seemed to be struggling to make the shift from more operational to strategic thinking, so I drew the shifts that this necessitated as I saw them – after three days of our work, and they went very quiet and said, simply: 'Why did you not show us that earlier?'

Consider the following comparison:

Operational thinking	Strategic thinking
● Linear	● Iterative and unpredictable
● Deductive	● Inductive and intuitive
● Pre-programmed	● Creative
● Clear boundaries	● Ambiguous and fuzzy boundaries
● Safe	● Anxiety provoking

While operational thinking seems to be step by step (linear) and deductive (one thing follows from the other), strategic thinking frequently revisits its starting point (it is iterative) and its trajectory is less predictable, typically. Also, operational thinking can be pre-planned while strategic thinking must have a creative spark. There are also much fuzzier boundaries with strategic thinking.

Finally, while the experience of operational thinking is usually low anxiety and feels safe, strategic thinking – especially for beginners – can feel quite scary. If a lot of anxiety is being experienced, this will make the thinking process very difficult as cognition will be impaired. Also, when managers discuss the issues, this underlying anxiety can easily give rise to confusion, frustration and conflict. That is one of the good reasons to have some facilitation on the process, besides some structured process (which we will be coming on to, too), as well.

STRATEGIC EXERCISE 1.3 Strategic thinking – 10 minutes

Pick an issue either in your organization or perhaps in your everyday life generally that is quite complex and at least to some extent uncertain, and where there may be dilemmas or choices. This could be, for example, that sales of a business area are down year on year, or communication is poor or one is threatened by new entrants to the market. Or it could be that you are worried that a dinner party that you are organizing with friends will not go well! First try the approach of more operational thinking, for example to structure it as:

Problem – objectives – solution – detailed plan

Recognize that deductive, linear, bounded process of thinking?

- Problem – what is it?

- Objectives – your preconceived aims.

- Solution: a suitable fix.

- Detailed plan: tactics to get there.

Now try to take a more strategic perspective:

Problem – diagnose causes – understand context/degrees of freedom/angles on the issue – generate options – evaluate plan

Here we see more stages and better formed ones. Not only do we look in more depth at the diagnosis phase (through examining the root causes) but we also consider the wider context and the extent of possible choices that we may have (the 'degrees of freedom') before generating options and evaluating them in detail.

Now start again with the same issue and follow the extended, second process above – and try to extend your awareness of the problem, its context, the different ways of looking at it, and to develop less average options. Ideally you should also have some quite specific criteria in your mind. Make sure that you write all this down as you go, so that you can make the reflective part of the process more 'hands free'.

Was a little more effort needed to do this? Probably, but wasn't there a better result? Almost certainly!

So what did that exercise feel like as a somewhat different type of thought process? Probably it felt more demanding and difficult at first, but then once you started to jot your ideas down the reflective process became activated and built on itself. Your brain will have been operating quite differently and in the later phases you are very likely to have felt stimulated, as the strategic thinking process will have released endorphins!

Before we move on to tell you more about what we will be coming on to in the rest of this book, let us round up our discussion of strategic thinking with what was a most topical series of events that happened in the UK in August 2011. We will use this to illustrate a first use of scenarios.

Introducing scenarios: riots in England – the end of society as we know it?

In August 2011 riots broke out in Tottenham, in northeast London, after a member of the public allegedly carrying a gun was shot dead by police.

In a matter of days the riots had spread to Clapham, Peckham, areas of west London and out as far as Croydon where we live in south London. I was coming back from a meeting in the Midlands and went through East Croydon station at about 6.40 pm on Monday evening, 8 August. I passed through about 15 minutes before the action started. I had just got home and all that one could hear all evening were the sirens of police cars and, later on, endless circling helicopters. A big pall of smoke rose over west Croydon and drifted over us to the east. We watched, gripped, as the television showed Croydon going up in smoke – a furniture store had gone up in flames. (We ended up buying a bed from them afterwards, from a makeshift office, as we were in sympathy with them – apparently business is booming after their distress, so they now have an emotional competitive advantage.)

Rioters, who appeared to be well organized and mobile, had swept into Croydon from Thornton Heath in the north, attacking the less well-policed and vulnerable peripheral shopping areas in west and south Croydon. Their Blitzkrieg went on, taking out all the attractive shops on London Road with things like DVDs, alcohol, bikes and cigarettes. They went as far as Purley to the south and towards Addiscombe to the east with a right hook. All around London there were violent outbreaks and looting. The pattern replicated itself elsewhere, with three people killed by a car when they tried to protect their premises in Birmingham.

Naturally this was a most disgusting and worrying chain of events which undermines one's sense of safety and of order – was this the beginning of the end of society as we know it? But from a strategic point of view it was of some interest, if only because these riots were enabled by social networking and by mobile telephony and appeared well planned, mobilized and coordinated. Facebook was used by the rioters as well as BlackBerry mobile phones which enabled messages to be spread around a network very quickly indeed. This gave them at least a comparable system to the police – and without a formal hierarchy to slow things up. This offered the rioters the additional possibilities (competitive advantages), relative to those in past riots and to the police, of:

- coordination;
- planning;
- mobility;
- speed;
- flexibility;
- concentration of force;
- surprise;
- targeting where to attack;
- sequencing of moves;
- reinforcements: as new rioters were attracted by the fun to join in.

These were the hallmark more of the famous ancient Chinese writer Sun Szu (on the art of war) than of a conventional mob.

It would appear that the police, at least initially, had more of a set-piece strategy which might have worked a lot better against a less organized and less mobile group of rioters. They also had to operate through a formal hierarchy, which meant less speed and responsiveness, and needed to work within policy constraints.

To be fair to the police, who appeared somewhat overwhelmed by the scale, given the surprise and the unprecedented speed and coordination of these attacks it would have been incredibly difficult to have done much better than they did. But that was given the fact that they were operating according to existing tactics and rules of engagement, which meant that they weren't ever going to be fully effective in this very new scenario. While I have never been a police officer, I have worked on strategic issues with three different police forces, and it did seem to me that a different modus operandi might have been more resilient in that context.

As an example of strategic thinking, some possible elements of a more cunning future strategy might be:

- Emergency measures could be put in force in exceptional circumstances to black out mobile phone transmissions in an area.
- Early-warning monitoring of such unusual traffic (if legal/technically possible).

- Mobile response teams rather than set-piece officers on foot tackling an existing crowd.
- The obvious point – much discussed in the media afterwards – was the use of water cannons to disperse rioters.
- On the second night of any violence, a curfew could be put in place, perhaps just for certain urban areas.

But one idea of a process nature was that the police could do some scenario development to simulate future riots. This could be done by setting up a simulation with one or more groups of police imagining that they are rioters in separate rooms from the room where some police actually imagine that they really are the police (a scary thought?). The role-playing rioters could be dressed with hoodies on – to help them to get into the part – and have to work out how to out-manoeuvre the police even more dramatically than seemed to occur in Croydon. For example, learning from the lessons of the 2011 riots, they make sure that as they get to an area of intended action they all change into other clothes so that the CCTV cameras can't be used to match what rioters are wearing with CCTV pictures of them getting off the tram going to the riots. Or at least they wouldn't be travelling by public transport. (Obviously this might limit their capacity to carry the swag!)

In one simulation they get some old vans and use police-like tactics of having these reinforcements hidden round the corner, just as the police do themselves. They also decide to stage decoy attacks on spurious targets to draw police resources and attention there. It goes without saying that their tactics are pre-rehearsed and planned out, just like the old-fashioned bank robbers used to do in films.

The mass of would-be rioters are then sent to their chosen targets by means of coded messages sent via BlackBerry. After surgical attacks on their targets, as with the Croydon furniture store, the rioters then quickly melt away, or re-form where the police are not expecting them.

By simulating the results of this gaming and in the context of what the police actually do in deploying and redeploying their forces, the police could be one step ahead of the rioters next time, rather than just having a plan that reacts to what the rioters did last time. Notice here, besides the fact that there are possibly more cunning elements in the strategy than before, the fact that by using a cunning process (scenarios and role-playing situations), this in itself led to a far richer and more inspired outcome. The lesson here is: 'Often the process in strategy is more important than the content.'

Note: the suggestion of using strategic thinking along these lines was actually put to one of the major forces in the UK involved in the riots – I am still waiting to hear from them.

This brief case is an example of scenario storytelling that we will pick up again in Chapter 8 within 'Scenarios and uncertainty'.

In conclusion, strategic thinking can be informative when looking at major national events and analysing them in novel ways.

Overview of the book

Looking forward now to what is to come, the main part of this book looks at a number of dimensions of strategy:

- Embracing the strategic world: looking at the different perspectives on strategy, such as the conceptual, the cognitive, the emotional, the political, the process, and the implementation perspective.
- Economic analysis and where it comes in.
- Dynamic competitive positioning: looking at how relative competitive advantage changes over time and its impact, and also how to see inside the heads of competitors.
- Breakthrough thinking and how that can be created, for example through scenario storytelling and being far more cunning.
- How to implement strategy and the challenges and hurdles that that poses.
- Hints and guidelines for managing the strategy process.
- Nurturing the strategic mind: learning to think strategically and in a more agile way.
- Applying the tools and processes practically – awakening your strategic consciousness on an everyday basis.

The core processes are now set out in Figure 1.1 to give you a more pictorial overview of the book.

FIGURE 1.1   The structure of the book

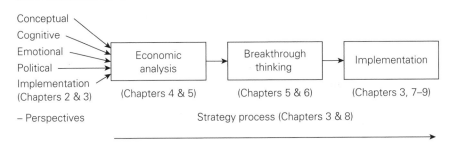

Key insights from the chapter

We end this introduction with a summary of the insights of value, and will repeat that process for reinforcement and for easy reference throughout all the chapters of this book:

- Strategy should be kept as simple and as practical as possible – at all times.
- Keep the language clear and transparent – and define any terms. Don't assume meaning.
- Beware using strategy tools too naively and avoid the traps.
- Observe everyday situations in a strategic way to gather insights – and ask the right questions.
- Switch on the 'inner strategic light' in your head.
- Always write down any strategic ideas – for later reflection.
- Strategy entails knowing where you are now, where you want to be in the future, and how to get there with real competitive advantage.
- Where you are now may be quite complex: analyse this both externally and internally.
- Gaining real competitive advantage isn't easy, as you need to be doing something that others would find it hard to do well.
- Often in a complacent competitive market some competitive advantage can be gained simply by avoiding the competitive disadvantages of others.
- Think about 'what you really-really-really want' in determining where you want to go.
- The future can have a range of time horizons, and strategies can be short and medium term.
- Goals can be broken down into a number of strategic objectives.
- A strategy mustn't be just average, it must be cunning.
- 'Cunning' can be discovered both in what you choose to analyse and thus its 'content' or in how you set about thinking from it – ie in the 'process'.
- Always ask: 'what is the one big question we forgot?' – and 'what is the second big question we forgot to ask?'
- Often in strategy the process is more important than the content.

These are the most valuable thoughts to go back to again when you have finished reading this book, and periodically afterwards.

Embracing the strategic world – part 1

Introduction

In our second and third chapters we look at six key perspectives which shed much light on strategy. For ease of digestion these have been grouped into two main chapters:

- Chapter 2:
  - Conceptual: how strategy gets understood through concepts, frameworks and tools.
  - Cognitive: how mindsets and thought styles can shape and predetermine the thought process.
  - Emotional: how feelings can influence how we think (and vice versa) and behave strategically and reflect this through stakeholder agendas.
- Chapter 3:
  - The influencing and the political: how these twin processes can be managed to channel strategic decisions and the urge to make and to implement these.
  - Processes: the way in which the management process is supported and coordinated and made inventive rather than run of the mill.
  - Implementation: for example through projects, change management and other interventions and processes.

To position this: these two chapters have a lot of important material, including different theories, further definitions, explanations of the various processes, illustrations and, of course, exercises for you to do. Please, however tempted you are, try not to skip them. Once we have got beyond this meaty content, we will be able to deal in Chapter 4 and beyond with the strategy tools themselves, and some longer and more complex case studies.

Also, I want to make a very important and educative point here. Almost all strategy books are two-dimensional in that they are conceptual and process based – only two of the perspectives, and often they are imbalanced towards one of these perspectives.

For example, while Porter's work is almost exclusively conceptual (1980, 1985), Mintzberg (1994) is primarily about strategy process. But few books do each of these two justice. Tovstiga (2010), which is excellent on dynamic strategy, deals well with the conceptual and the cognitive, the latter really well, and the most balanced that one can probably find is Mintzberg *et al's Strategy Safari* (1998), which deals with the conceptual, the cognitive, the political and influencing – four out of six. But, sadly, there is not a lot there about the emotional and the implementation aspects, despite their practical importance.

Indeed, there are very few books that do address the implementation perspective – full stop. From a practising manager's perspective, that is just not good enough.

So my book attempts to be far more complete than others. That means that you will have to expand your mental awareness to take all of that in – as I will be interrelating all the really key linkages between the six, both in these two chapters and as we move through the book. So while the book is called *Demystifying Strategy*, there is no pretence that it is simpler than it really is.

We begin therefore with the cognitive perspective, which is clearly of major importance to strategic thinking.

The conceptual perspective

The conceptual perspective, as was said earlier, is about the concepts, frameworks and tools that we use to understand strategy. It is a perspective thus closely linked to the cognitive.

A strategic concept is something that enables us to make sense of, and to categorize, our strategic ideas. For example, 'market attractiveness' means 'the structural and dynamic features within a market which lead to above average, average or below average returns in that market: relative to other markets'.

When defining a concept it is always useful to define what we don't mean by a term. For example, what we don't mean by 'market attractiveness' is 'a market which appears particularly attractive to us', because this is something conditioned by our biases and by our existing competitive advantage, which is quite a separate thing.

Another example of a strategic concept is that of a strength, as opposed to a weakness – within a SWOT analysis. One could, for example, say that a strength is something we are simply good at. But that would probably not be good enough to be of much real use in later analysis, for such capabilities might simply be a prerequisite of competing within this particular market. Identifying such things as 'strengths' introduces a lot of background noise into strategic positioning and distorts the picture.

A tighter definition would be to say, possibly: 'A "strength" is some strategic asset or skill which adds real value to the business, and is one genuinely a level above our competitors.' Here we are emphasizing the isolation of the really key factors that make a competitive difference and so this is all about assessing relative competitive advantage.

We can also illustrate the concept of competitive advantage from our previous one in Chapter 1 as: '"Competitive advantage" is "giving customers distinctive value relative to internal costs that are either, or both, better than other competitors"'.' This distinctive value can be both real and perceived, which means that we must understand the world of value of products and services from the customer's point of view and not from our own.

'... it is about either or both superior value or costs so it is possible to achieve competitive advantage just by differentiating value or through having a disproportionately low cost base. Finally it is a question always of relative competitive advantage – and this needs to be benchmarked as... "we have a specific competitive advantage over this specific competitor".'

In my view (Grundy, 2002b), competitive advantage breaks into two key elements. The first are the 'motivator factors' (the things that you feel you really can't get easily from elsewhere and are a 'turn-on' in added value). These are certainly distinctive. The second are the 'hygiene factors' that are not met (ie the things that you expect a supplier to get right but they don't, and if they don't this destroys a lot of value). Motivator factors are thus a good way of turning a resource-based theory of competitive advantage into something very tangible and meaningful.

An example of a motivator factor was my estate agents that I used to sell my old house in 2011 in tough market conditions. I have had many bad experiences of estate agents over the years and fortunately had an amazingly good one on this occasion with Gibbs Gillespie, Ruislip, who:

- listened to me when I wanted not to drop my price too soon and by too much: I estimate that this was worth between £5,000 and £10,000, and my lectures on Porter's five forces and how they are shaped by the urgency to do a transaction;

- operated as a seamless team between the two key agents who worked different hours over the week so that the ball was passed with perfection – like Barcelona football team on a good day;

- man-marked my lethargic solicitors to eventually get them to be slightly more proactive than their default mode in the process of exchanging contracts, which was one that could best be characterized as 'lethargic';

- personally intervened through a friend in Uxbridge planning department to get a document copied from the vaults in half an hour that might have taken days and days;

- gave something akin to psychotherapy to my nervous buyer who was concerned that a garden wall had a millimetre gap in it – and I had to do building works;

- came over as always honest and direct;

- were always bouncy and bright to talk to and could enjoy my strange sense of humour.

I have been through nine previous house deals and estate agents are not my favourite people, but they managed to score 100 per cent: and what a list of motivator factors!

By comparison, the experience of doing a bank transfer in Croydon (let's spare naming the bank again) destroyed value in many ways:

- At a quiet time of the day I had to stand up queuing for 10 minutes.

- The teller had not wanted to help me because the transfer would take too long: for half of the time I was in the bank she was doing nothing.

- The adviser told me that as the money from my overnight funds wasn't in yet I would have to come in again when it did (telephone banking had told me that that was no problem).

- He didn't know when that would be.

- After an argument when I said ('Spice Girl' strategy) that this was not what I really-really-really wanted, he decided that he would give it a try.

- Eventually we tracked down someone in the vaults of the bank who could send the money from overnight into my account.

- It then took 20 minutes to get it authorized!

I think I will switch banks after 15 years with them. Do you have many stories like this one of contrasting competitive advantage?

STRATEGIC EXERCISE 2.1 Competitive advantage – 10 minutes

Think of one area of your business:

- How would customers say (if at all) that they got distinctive value from your business?

- How important is it to them – and what value do they get?

- How certain are you that there aren't competitors who could do more or less the same?

- Are there any areas in which you feel that you have distinctively low costs and that these are areas that competitors can't match?

This series of questions should weed out your list of strengths down to relative strengths – as opposed to more general competences. It provides a useful structure for your strategic thinking about your current position.

So let's just run through some definitions of other key strategic concepts that might be useful to you, our reader. These include:

- assumptions;
- critical success factors;
- economic value;
- gap analysis;
- life cycles;
- mission;
- objective;
- option;
- scenario;
- stakeholders;
- strategy;
- sweet spot;
- vision.

Obviously, if you think you know these already, you can skim-read these or just pick out those that you wish to be clearer on.

Assumptions

'A strategic assumption is the condition or value of any variable which will have a big role in determining future strategic position and financial performance.'

A condition might be the state of a market or it might be a level of competence internally: as a 'softer' factor. As a 'harder' factor it could be a value such as relative market share, or a particular rate of growth, or an assumed shift in share price or profitability etc.

Critical success factors

'Something that we must get right, or avoid doing wrong, to achieve our strategies and goals.'

A critical success factor (CSF) is thus something quite tangible that we need to achieve, such as, for a consultancy, to penetrate a particular number of quality, new key accounts, or to avoid losing any. These should be listed, usually during strategy development for each specific business one is looking at: it can't be done through having just a general and preconceived list. It is important that in defining the CSFs there shouldn't be too many of these – one needs to be selective.

A CSF might be, for example, getting to a very low level of costs, having a distinctive brand, being able to respond to rapid market and competitive change etc.

STRATEGIC EXERCISE 2.2 Critical success factors –
10 minutes

In this next exercise, identify for an area of the market or for your business some of the CSFs for getting this right and those for avoiding getting them wrong, listing these against some general challenges down the left-hand side, for example price competition, innovation, customer service etc.

Challenges: CSFs – do right	CSFs – not do wrong
1.	
2.	
3.	
4.	
5.	

From your review of changing market and competitive conditions (eg competitors' and new entrants' future strategies), what is your list of key competitive challenges that you are facing?

For each of these key challenges, what will you have to do right – or avoid getting wrong – to achieve strategic success?

Economic value

Economic value is a more financial concept. It can be defined as 'the present value of future cash streams from present and future strategies having reflected the amount of investment needed and its cost of capital'.

Economic value thus takes into account the changing value of money over time, the likely cash flows given assumed strategic positioning and over time, and similarly the underlying competitive advantage. It is thus arrived at by both competitive and economic analysis, and is very dependent on the assumptions – see above.

Gap analysis

The gap is 'the difference between where we want to be and where we are likely to be, under present strategies'. Gap analysis is an essential way of framing the degree of stretch that the organization wishes to set itself, before doing any strategic option evaluation.

Gap analysis is typically framed in terms of some performance metrics, the most typical being:

- sales;
- profit.

But we could add to that:

- economic profit;
- relative market share;
- gaps between us and specific competitors;
- unit costs;
- capability.

With regard to capability, this can be split down into different variables which lend themselves to the from–to (or FT) analysis that we will see in Chapter 7 on implementation. Also, competitor profiling (Chapter 5 on dynamic competitive positioning) can be used to do competitor gap analysis.

Gap analysis is a way of assessing either a) the difference between where you are and where you want to be (snapshot), or b) where you are likely to be on current plans, and where you want to be (future gap) based on projected future performance. Here your projected future performance (without new breakthrough strategies), is a function of:

- present position;
- current breakthroughs and continuous improvements;
- plus any environmental upsides, such as improvements in the economy generally/other factors helping the growth drivers/reducing competitive pressure;

- minus any environmental downsides, such as economic downturn/ other factors including increased competitive pressure, moves and general improvements generally, increased customer expectations/ price pressure etc and negative longer-term life-cycle effects.

Or, as an equation:

$$G = O - (P + U - D + CS) \text{ (before new strategic breakthroughs)}$$

Where:

$$G = (O - [CS + U - D - CP])$$

G is the gap
O is future objectives
P is pressure
U is upsides
D is downsides
And CS is current strategies.

Once one has come up with some additional and new breakthrough strategies (BS), the gap becomes:

$$G = (O - [CS + U - D - CP]) \text{ (after new strategic breakthroughs)}$$

where the impact of the strategic breakthroughs is bigger, the smaller the gap becomes, or indeed, may be negative.

A quick and simplified example of this, in terms of the sales gap for a single-year planning period, is:

- current sales: £10 million;
- currently projected upsides: £300,000 (general market growth);
- currently projected downsides: minus £500,000 (increased competitive aggression etc);
- effects of existing breakthroughs: positive £400,000;
- future objective: £10.8 million (8% growth).

$$
\begin{aligned}
G &= £10.8m - (£10m + £300k - £500k + £400k) \\
&= £10.8 - £10.2m \\
&= \text{a £600k residual gap}
\end{aligned}
$$

At any stage of the planning process there might still be a gap. Instead of choosing to pretend that there isn't one, this can be managed by, for example:

- listing the 'lines of enquiry' that may well make it possible to close the strategic gap, that is, it is 'work in progress';
- engaging top management in the process to see if they feel that the strategy might be developed in a particular direction – so that the constraints can be alleviated;

- explaining to top management (upward management) why the situation is more difficult than expected; for example, use Porter's five forces to help explain why margins in this particular business are inferior to those in the rest of the group, and/or compare the external competitive forces (Porter – Chapter 4) now versus in the past, using an FT analysis (Chapter 7).

So we cannot assume that the present position is in a steady state. Indeed, in maturity the norm will be for the present position to show a trend of decline, which means that we have to run harder to stand still. The position of Tesco in the in the UK in 2011/12, as also for its rivals, for example, would be very much in that kind of situation. At that time it was facing a market with virtually unprecedented pressure on real consumer incomes – with inflation higher than wage rises, and increased taxes, so that it was having to do even more than it had in the past to maintain its strategic momentum.

Gap analysis is an essential strategic thinking tool – in my view, more important than SWOT analysis, as we need to keep track of the value of our strategic options and their contribution to the assumed shifts in strategic performance, otherwise we may not meet our strategic goals.

Obviously, it is important that the strategic objectives that have been set are ones which are not competitively unrealistic. Unfortunately, this can often be the case. Top managers frequently set an artificial stretch on the levels of managers below – and without giving them the training and time, support and coaching to come up with strategies that will actually deliver the gap (sounds familiar?).

This dysfunction of strategic behaviour is compounded when managing plans in a large group, where it is not unusual to find that the top-down targets really are not feasible. By putting so much pressure on managers one succeeds only in building anxiety levels to a point where they can't function imaginatively any longer: the result is a set of artificial numbers without robust underlying plans. The consequence is that the business always delivers less than expected and this increases top-down pressure to deliver, reinforcing the game, or what has been called 'strategic droop' – never quite realizing expectations. Behavioural issues like this are probably the biggest constraints in getting the potential value out of strategy.

This was depicted in a classic cartoon featuring a manager with his hair standing on end, with the caption: 'Five Minutes to Find A Plan – the Deadline Nobody Wanted! – send for Thomson!' I used to use this for every workshop and then one day one of the managers said to me: 'How the hell do you know that?' I said: 'Know what?' He replied: 'That I am actually called Thomson – and I'm the strategic planner!' I hadn't known that at all, but it was so funny that it had happened: clearly he felt exactly that – the victim of the wrong kind of gap analysis in an inadequate planning process. Continuing with this theme, all too often managers thus turn 'GAP analysis' into what I have called 'CRAP analysis', where 'CRAP' means 'creating artificial plans'.

To combat these inherent problems with managing the strategic gap, my suggestions are:

- To top management: not to set too definitive targets straight away but broader aspirations – based on their best thinking about the possible prospects of a business unit; they should think about that themselves first.

- This should be framed not in terms of straight-line projected numbers but in terms of the key variables of my gap analysis equation above.

- The evolution of detailed strategic options should follow the 'challenge and build' process that we describe in Chapter 6 on strategic options, which we will see at Diageo who rolled out our processes.

- There should be sufficient strategic thinking tools used and especially the strategic option grid, with 'deep-dive' techniques (see Chapter 6), rich and relevant data collection, and cunning reflection so that the future strategies are inventive and fill the strategic gap – and even more.

- There needs to be a truly creative process with sufficient space to do that.

Returning now to our definitions:

Life cycle

'The stage of evolution of the market, its competitive structure and intensity, of products, or of the company as a whole': often characterized as, for example, embryonic, growth, maturity, or decline.

Mission

'The overarching purpose of the organization and the kind it wants to be, what businesses it wants to be in, and its guiding philosophy.'

In defining a useful mission it is vital that it has some grounding in robust assumptions about its present and potential strategic position and is distinctive in some way. It is important here that we are able, from seeing the mission statement, to work backwards and be able to identify the specific organization that we are looking at here.

Objective

'A "strategic objective" is a goal of our strategy.'

Thus it isn't to be confused with the strategy itself and is an output – and a very specific one at that. These strategic objectives can be, and should be, broken down into, for example, compound sales growth, changes in relative market share or other measures of relative competitive position, development of key capabilities, and successful strategic breakthroughs. Also, it might look at return on sales, return on capital, compound growth in profitability, economic value added etc.

Option

'A "strategic option" is a way in which a strategy can be formulated such that it could actually be implemented.'

This means that it needs to be sufficiently specific not only in terms of being able to evaluate it, but also being clear about how it will be implemented. It mustn't be so general that if the people who created it were to suddenly die we would struggle to understand it and actually do it. For example, a strategic option 'to grow by acquisition' would not count as it would be far too vague. You do need to be relatively specific here. See Chapter 6 on strategic options for more.

Scenario

'A plausible and coherent storyline of the competitive and/or organizational future.' A scenario must thus have an internal dynamic of an interdependent series of events set within a background of possible environmental conditions and their likely changes.

A scenario isn't the same thing as a strategic forecast – as its concern isn't to predict, but to anticipate the possible. (We return to scenarios in Chapter 8.)

Stakeholders

Stakeholders are individuals or a group of individuals who: 'are anyone inside or outside the organization with an influence either directly or indirectly over what strategic decisions are made, or over their implementation (the how), or who may be impacted on by these strategies and/or their implementation'.

This definition thus captures a large domain of potential stakeholders and investigates their attitude and influence on the strategy(ies). Their attitude and influence will vary over the different strategic issues and decisions, and will also change over time. This picture is thus complex and changing – see Chapter 3 on the political and influencing perspective, and Chapter 7 on implementation for more on stakeholders.

Strategy

Strategy is 'a cunning plan which will add economic value'. A strategy is essentially one or more strategic options (that are closely related) that have actually been chosen. Again, like strategic options, this must be quite specific and not too general.

Sweet spot

This is 'an area of competitive space where we satisfy customer value needs and which is not served well at all by other competitors'.

The idea of a sweet spot can be a useful focus of strategic analysis and strategy formulation because it helps us to isolate not only that small number of areas of competing with most leverage but also adds a more tangible way of identifying real competitive advantage. It is also a useful concept to guide thinking about the cunning plan, for example with its focus on economic value processes deep within customers (how do they recognize it?), and also locates areas of potential edge specifically. (We look at this more in Chapter 5.)

A 'sweet spot' is a niche – but obviously a positive one.

Vision

We define vision as being 'a picture of either the environment, and of our fit within it, or just of ourselves – at some stage in the future'. Here it is possible for the focus thus to include, on an equal basis, the context of the organization alongside the state of success of the business, or to have this as just a model of the organization and how it is. If this is approached in the latter way, it is still very important to address the environmental context within that thinking.

STRATEGIC EXERCISE 2.3 Mission, objectives, gap, vision, strategies, critical success factors – 15 minutes

---

This exercise is to help you to organize a clear logical structure of your strategy. This may not be quite the order in which you talked about the issues, as you might, for example, have talked about the CSFs before determining your strategies.

The point of the exercise is to trace the linkages between the concepts:

- Mission:
  - What is your big-picture view of what the purpose of the organization is?
  - What scope of business activities does this imply and how you are choosing to compete?
- Objectives:
  - What does the organization seek to achieve in terms of growth, size and shape, financial performance etc?
  - How consistent with the mission are these goals?
- Gap:
  - What is the gap between the performance expected from the current strategy and the strategic objectives?
- Vision:
  - What will the organization need to change, having addressed that gap, to deliver the strategic objectives?
- Strategies:
  - What strategies will close that gap and bring about the vision?
- Critical success factors:
  - What are the critical success factors that if not met might cause the strategy to fail?

Next, let us take a quick look at some frameworks which are then explained individually. We can define a strategic framework as a broader way of making sense of strategy.

For example, a number of strategic frameworks which help to structure strategic thinking that might be helpful are those of:

● breakthrough thinking;
● competitive strategy;
● resource-based theory of competitive advantage;
● project management;
● strategic cost management;
● change management;
● value;
● strategic planning.

Breakthrough thinking

The main element in breakthrough thinking (Grundy, 1995) is that one should narrow down the most important elements of the strategy and give them paramount focus in terms of resource allocation, concentration of effort, and also in communication through the organization. This implies that one cannot just decide to do too many options which are relatively stretching and difficult.

Breakthrough thinking comes from Japanese management philosophy in terms of managing the evolution of a business. In Japan it is called simply *Hoshin*, which means 'breakthrough' – and this complements its sister concept of *Kaizen*, which is often better known and means 'continuous improvement'. In Japanese management philosophy the successful business evolves through a combination of *Kaizen* and *Hoshin*.

I first heard of *Hoshin* at Texas Instruments in 1990, and the focus it gave to their strategy development – particularly in technological advancement – was impressive. I found it occasionally in other Western companies such as GSK, but it doesn't seem to have been assimilated into that thinking as much as one would have expected (despite my own efforts – see my earlier book *Breakthrough Strategies for Growth*, 1995). This is a surprise, particularly as I developed an incredibly successful short course called 'Breakthrough Strategic Thinking' attended by over 1,000 managers in 12 years: we had to wait-list senior executives and run with crazy numbers to go on it. So obviously managers as individuals, if not as groups, saw very clearly the relevance of the idea of breakthroughs to their own personal management situation. (Perhaps it didn't help in the difficulty of popularizing this simple idea that some of the key texts on *Hoshin* at the time hadn't been translated from Japanese!)

Hoshin, in essence, suggests that:

- Within a particular part of the organization there should be only one to three breakthroughs attempted within a particular phase.
- Over time one can then roll out other breakthroughs: so, for example, if the organization is very nimble then the maximum number of breakthroughs in, say, a two-year period would be two times three, or six.

An example of breakthrough thinking is that of Tesco plc, now an international retailer with sales of over £67 billion in 2010/11 and profits of £3.8 billion. In the mid-1990s when I first worked with Tesco, it was almost entirely a UK company and in 1994 its sales were then £8.6 billion (Grundy, 1995) and profits £356 million, which is nearly an eighth of recent sales. Around that time Tesco had only just overtaken Sainsbury as UK market leader, and was primarily a retail grocer. In that period a number of breakthroughs crystallized – and I was very fortunate to be involved in some of these as a facilitator. These included:

- Breakthroughs: phase 1
  - non-food – embryonic;
  - financial services;
  - new formats: the smaller Express (now replicated worldwide) and Metro;
- and subsequent ones (phase 2) like
  - brand development;
  - Tesco Direct;
  - own label/sub-brands;
- and of course:
  - international.

And over that period it could be discerned that Tesco mobilized a maximum of only three at a time (although, as time advanced, new ones were given more focus as the existing ones were still in roll-out).

If we contrasted this tightness of focus with most organizations, we would find that the latter are typically overwhelmed by too many objectives and priorities. This dilutes the focus of the strategy and also one lacks real concentration of resources (see point coming soon). This clutter is one of the main reasons, in my view, why strategy is so often poorly implemented.

Probably the main reason for this clutter is that managers see the strategic plan as being the dumping ground for 'this is all the big things that we need to do'. They become anxious, therefore, if not everything goes in there. Also, as managers are often not particularly good at strategic prioritization (a kind way of saying that they don't know how to do it), they don't give more weight to some things and less weight to others. Nor can they seem to choose, as they should do, what they are *not* going to do, or do later. All strategic plans must contain a list of things that we have chosen not to do – an important point.

But there are two very good reasons why the number of breakthroughs should be limited to a small number: first because of the dilution effect that this has. As was said above, successful strategy depends on concentration of force sufficient to win real competitive advantage. In military theory the normal benchmark of superior force is two to one to win a battle. How many competitive battles are fought this way? (Obviously, with the cunning plan the concentration ratio might be less.)

Concentration of both point of attack (another military concept) and of resources can be best illustrated by the following quote from Sun Tzu's *The Art of War*:

> When the front is prepared, the rear is lacking. When the rear is prepared, the front is lacking. Preparedness on the left means a lack of preparedness on the right. Preparedness on the right means a lack of preparedness on the left. Preparedness everywhere means a lack, everywhere.

So if one devotes similar attention to everything, one will not have really made strategic choices, nor gained real competitive advantage.

The second reason for narrowing down to such a small number of breakthroughs is that this is cognitively simpler and much more within the cognitive constraints of organizations. Here we need to introduce the not-so-well-known rule of cognitive psychology called 'Miller's Law', or the rule of five plus or minus two, which says that:

- an average person can hold five things in their attention at any one time;
- a genius can hold up to seven;
- a not-so-bright person can hold up to three.

So if we assume that the average organization functions as a collective in a not-so-very-bright way, it seems reasonable to conclude that such organizations can only deal with up to three complex and challenging breakthroughs at a particular time.

STRATEGIC EXERCISE 2.4 Identifying breakthroughs –
10 minutes

- What have been the breakthroughs in your organization that have founded its current competitive position?

- Were these deliberate and planned, largely accidental, or somewhere in between?

- What do you think the merits of having a more deliberate process might be?

- What future breakthroughs – in your imagination – might take your organization to another level?

- How might you set about developing these embryonic ideas in an imaginative way?

Competitive strategy

Coined by Michael Porter as long ago as 1980, the term competitive strategy is a framework for thinking about how companies compete in their changing and dynamic environments. In two landmark books (*Competitive Strategy*, 1980 and *Competitive Advantage*, 1985), Porter offered a relatively complete framework for understanding the basic rules of competing and suggestions for the kinds of strategic choices that need to be made, for example:

- which markets to compete in: depending on their changing competitive pressure (or as Porter would call it, his 'five competitive forces' – coming later in Chapter 4);

- the broad menu of strategies that can be adopted: differentiation (value and price premium), cost leadership (lowest unit costs of meeting demand), and focus: narrowing the target market to one or more niches;

- the specific configuration of value-creating activities within a business to support a particular strategy, or the 'value chain'.

This is certainly a good framework for thinking and certainly has been found to be very resilient over time. My MBA students at Henley, for example, use this framework as the core structure in managing their strategy project.

So, briefly, what might be missing or underemphasized in this framework? In my view, if there are deficiencies, these are as follows:

- Too much emphasis is given to a particular concept – Porter's five competitive forces in determining market attractiveness: this doesn't reflect the wider factors in the environment (the political, economic, social, and technological (PEST) factors – we are coming to those later), nor the factors in the market which are driving its growth, so this is quite a partial picture.

- You can easily go through all of this process and still not have a cunning plan but an average plan: it is analytical at the expense of being inventive.

- It presents the menu of strategies in a very black and white way, for example you have to choose between either a differentiation or cost leadership strategy, whereas there can be a case for some blending of these elements together.

- The value chain is a relatively static and set-piece framework typically used to map the more obvious internal activities. Reconfiguring value-creating activities, resources and competences can provide a fertile ground for inventing creative strategies.

- Also, as the resource-based theory (which we are coming to in this section) of competitive advantage says, real competitive advantage is often to be discovered in the uniqueness of particular skills and resources that leverage customer value and are hard to imitate. So unless there is sufficient emphasis on these strategic assets, the emerging strategy can be not very effective or resilient. To discover these strategic assets involves real strategic thinking and not just analysis, as these are often found intuitively.

Nevertheless, the three key ingredients of competitive strategy above, suitably modified and complemented, are a helpful framework, particularly for extending our thinking beyond things such as simplistic SWOT and gap analyses.

Resource-based theory of competitive advantage

The resource-based theory of competitive advantage, or RBT, is a theory which suggests that a critical factor in organizational success is more likely to be whether it has distinctive skills or assets (resources) than how inherently attractive the environment is. So managers need to be very clear what these unique resources are. Also, they should be aware of how competitors might imitate what they do or how they do it. RBT stresses the importance of finding factors that are 'inimitable' or, as I would prefer to put it, 'not easily copy-able'. I believe that the latter will strike an easier chord with most senior managers than something like 'inimitable' which sounds very much like academic jargon.

Indeed, the language of RBT is highly economic and conceptual, which is a real pity, and one is perhaps best advised to avoid terms like 'competences and resources' which sound a bit like a mining company.

An excellent example of RBT is the British comedian John Cleese who was famous for *Monty Python* and *Fawlty Towers* and films like *A Fish Called Wanda*. In the heyday of management education he set up a company making management videos depicting him being a deliberately bad and stupid manager so that managers would learn never to behave like that, for example in meetings. The videos were very rich in learning and absolutely hilarious and became a 'must show–must buy'. I remember seeing the accounts of his company, Video Arts, and the turnover back then was £4 million and the net profit was £2 million: a fabulous return on sales of 50 per cent.

The obvious point here is that he was a monopoly because of his uniqueness and the difficulty of imitating him. He was also, as the economists would say, 'rare', another test of a strategic asset.

We deal with RBT extensively in Chapter 4 on economic analysis (Barney and Hesterly, 2002; Rumelt, 1991).

Project management

A project can be defined as being 'a complex set of interrelated activities that are intended to achieve a specific result in a certain time and cost'.

Projects have the element of at least some complexity and have three main variables with which there is a trade-off. For the more you attempt to pin down any single one of the result, time and cost, the more difficult it usually becomes to achieve the other two.

A strategic project is one which has a major role in terms of achieving the strategy at a particular level, and has to be managed within its environment. It is a project that will have a big impact on either competitive edge, on financial performance, on capability, or two or all three of these.

It has its own environment within the organization in that it will be affected by changing organizational conditions and influences, and also competes for attention and resources with other projects.

Project management might seem to be a less than obvious framework relevant to strategy. This is perhaps because it is usually considered as being operational. However, not only does strategy invariably entail some change in the business but it also requires implementation of new strategic options and, thus, projects. As these need to be broken down into action plans, they require detailed project management.

Also, the very process of developing the strategy and mobilizing it is also one which occurs over time, is complex and has predefined results, so that too is a project.

Finally, a third reason for considering project management as a core strategic framework is that the strategic breakthroughs often break down themselves into large and complex projects. These projects are of a strategic nature and have their own strategic goals, complex environments, implementation needs and stakeholders. So where an organization is very comfortable with project managing its main strategies, the resulting strategy is often as much a product of this project process as the planning process itself.

For the latter to be effective, though, project management must be a sophisticated process that not only uses traditional ideas like activity analysis, critical paths etc but also many of the tools that we will see later in this book, such as the strategic option grid, difficulty-over-time curves and stakeholder analysis. Microsoft project manager software or a 'Prince 2' qualification on project management won't do that for you alone, sorry.

Project management is a useful process which helps to structure the strategy implementation phase and particularly the management of change and any specific projects. This process takes us through the stages of:

- diagnosis of the project's scope and key objectives, and rationale;
- creation of strategic options for the project, and their evaluation;

- detailed planning of activities and resources, timings and deliverables;
- project mobilization;
- control and learning.

Doing a business or economic case is often a product of both the second phase, evaluation of options, and the third, detailed planning.

Another important point here is that project management is also relevant to the strategic planning process itself. It is essential that before launching into the strategy process, one should develop a 'plan for the plan'. This might, for example, contain:

- key issues and goals;
- key activities and their outputs and their interdependencies;
- tools and processes;
- data needs and sources;
- who is going to be involved, when and how.

It is frequently useful to do a short workshop to explore this, not only to get a better plan for the plan, but also to get a shared understanding of the issues and needs and also buy-in by stakeholders.

How much use of project management has been made in your organization in terms of developing and implementing the strategy, and could this be more/different?

Strategic cost management

Costs are frequently an issue, whether cost leadership is on your agenda or not. Costs are invariably a very big issue in a turnaround situation.

Costs are typically managed in a rather tactical way – with a short-term and internal focus, and also in an incremental way. In strategic cost management there are a number of fundamental differences which make it quite a different animal:

- Costs must be managed in alignment with strategic objectives.
- They must not undermine these objectives.
- They need to look at different time horizons: short, medium and long.
- This requires that costs must never be looked at in isolation from their value added.
- The output from the process is a combination of cost breakthroughs and continuous improvements.

It is crucial that we do as much strategic thinking about costs as we do for external strategic options.

Cost management is such a central feature, especially in mature markets, and is quite complex, so again – like projects – it warrants its own process. This is rather parallel to the strategic project management process. The suggested five stages here are closely parallel to those of strategic project management which we saw earlier:

- diagnosis of why costs need to be lower/add more value;
- creation of strategic options for cost breakthroughs, and their evaluation;
- project planning;
- implementation;
- control and learning.

This process makes use of a variety of strategic tools shared with many of the other processes, such as value-based management (value and cost drivers), tools for prioritization (possibly the strategic option grid) and stakeholder analysis for implementation. Gap analysis warrants a special mention here, as this is just as pertinent to internal resource planning as it is to externally faced strategies. This can take several different forms:

- the present gap in unit cost levels between the company and others offering similar customer value added: the current gap;
- the future gap between these levels and the level that competitors will be driving their costs down to at some future date, given current company plans/cost trends: the future gap;
- the future gap between these levels and the level that competitors will be driving their costs down to at some future date, given current company plans/cost trends and any possible cost breakthroughs: the revised future gap.

What areas of costs in your business do you suspect are out of line with many of your comparable competitors? How is this changing and, on current plans, is the cost gap likely to get worse, and what potential impact will that have?

Strategic cost management makes use of many of the strategic thinking tools, including particularly value and cost driver analysis (Chapter 6 on strategic options), and fishbone analysis and other implementation tools from Chapter 7 on implementation.

Change management

Change management comes into strategy in a number of ways. For instance, there are organizational-level changes that may need to be made (structure, skills, processes, values and mindsets) in supporting any repositioning in the marketplace, in business scope and general capability. If these require a lot of adjustment and they are quite complex, we are facing strategic change. Strategic change is so labelled not because it is the end of the world but to cover situations where a different organizational model is required. In this case we need to manage the complex dynamics of any transition.

I prefer the term 'transition' here to the somewhat trendier one of 'transformation', as the latter sounds rather grandiose and makes it sound like it is the hunting ground of the big consultancies.

Our five-stage model in this situation is again relatively similar to the other processes such as strategic project management and change management, as follows:

- diagnosis of, and scoping, the change;
- creating of strategic options for the change, and their evaluation;
- detailed planning of activities and resources, timings and deliverables;
- communication and implementation;
- control and learning.

Change management also shares a lot of the tools of project management and strategic planning (see below) generally, such as the difficulty-over-time curve, and stakeholder analysis as well. In terms of the dynamics of change it can be fruitful as well to use scenario storytelling – as we illustrated in our introductory chapter – to bring these dynamics to life.

In terms of those dynamics, models often seem to be based on more psychotherapeutic ideas which imply that change, particularly cultural in nature, involves a sequence of shifts at different levels of the corporate psyche (sometimes represented as a 'transition curve' – Carnall, 1990). For instance, the organization may go through phases such as:

- recognition and understanding of the change;
- discarding the old ways/resistance;
- surface adjustments: in new behaviours;
- deeper adjustments: in new beliefs and mindsets, attitudes, feelings and possibly values;
- settling in, commitment, and new levels of performance.

Here we see an easing-in to the change through recognition and understanding, followed by the 'unfreezing' and letting go of the old, or of resistance being manifest or slumbering in a passive form. Then there follows two overlapping phases of assimilation followed finally by the establishment of a new level of performance, or the 'refreezing' process. Here terms like 'unfreezing' and 'refreezing' are helpful in conceptualizing but sound far too HR-ish to be used at any everyday management meeting. They might well be used by consultants, but at some risk.

These phases are not necessarily sequential – two or more could be going on to a lesser or greater extent simultaneously. Also, there is no necessary reason why the performance after the change will be any better than previously – it could indeed be worse than the previous situation.

The implications of this transition process are that:

- the transition can take a long time and longer than expected;
- its end result and the dynamics can be very unpredictable;
- it is normally complex;
- change can be very uneven and adjustment will be made at different speeds;
- the quality of the change process, communication, and the leadership style itself will play a very big role in the outcomes.

An excellent example of the change management process is that of Legal Complaints, with the CEO's reflections on that, in Chapter 9. The main tools for this are found in Chapter 7 on implementation, plus stakeholder analysis from Chapter 2.

Strategic planning

This is our final process, which looks at how the strategy should be evolved. It is important here to flag up that there are many different possible ways of designing the strategic planning process. The choice is dependent upon the organizational context, the complexity of the business and the key issues and possible ideas for breakthroughs.

But it is also a function of the skills and style of senior management and the extent to which, cognitively and behaviourally, they can deal with the dilemmas and the political challenges that a particular process entails. For example, if these are limited in some key ways then a highly participative, bottom-up approach may not be the best way forward.

Where there are a large number of very big issues and the current strategic and/or financial position is weak and weakening, then almost certainly we have a strategic turnaround on our hands. In that situation we would need to phase the options phase into two: short term (for survival) and longer term, which would adjust the process. We might also need a refinancing phase as well in a turnaround.

Typically a model of a process for strategic planning would be the following (see Figure 2.1):

- defining the present position: external and internal;
- creation and evaluation of strategic options;
- identification and planning of strategic breakthroughs – the bigger wins;
- implementation;
- control and learning.

FIGURE 2.1 Strategic planning process

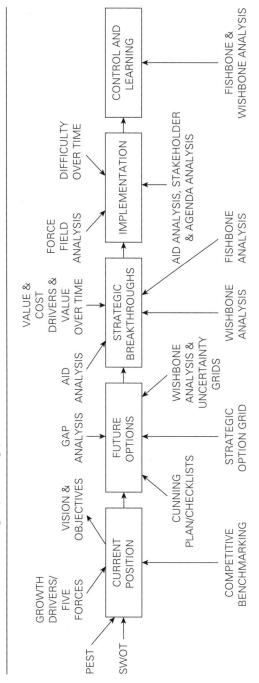

We deal with the various tools that are included in the picture at different stages of the book:

- SWOT: Chapter 1 – introduction;
- Competitive benchmarking: Chapters 4 and 5 on dynamic competitive positioning;
- Porter's five forces: Chapter 4 on economic analysis;
- PEST factors and growth drivers: Chapter 8 on the strategy process;
- Vision and objectives: Chapter 2 on the conceptual perspective;
- Strategic option grid: Chapter 6 on strategic options;
- Gap analysis: Chapter 3;
- Wishbone analysis: Chapter 7 on implementation;
- Uncertainty grid: Chapter 6 on options and Chapter 8 on the strategy process;
- Value and cost drivers (Chapter 3) and the value-over-time curve (Chapter 6);
- Attractiveness and implementation difficulty (AID) analysis, fishbone and wishbone analysis, force field and difficulty-over-time curve, and FT analysis – Chapter 7 on implementation;
- Stakeholder analysis: Chapter 3 on the influencing and political perspectives, and Chapter 7 on implementation;
- Stakeholder agenda analysis: Chapter 7 on implementation.

Notice that we haven't started off with 'defining goals' or that idea combined with 'vision' or 'mission' etc. I take the view that this can prejudice the direction that the organization will take and the options that appear to be attractive. I think it is usually far better either to park these to one side, maybe in the back of one's mind, or to address these once some robust strategic analysis and evaluation have been done.

Where there are major uncertainties in the future it might be useful to adapt some scenario development within the strategic planning process. This could be relevant, for example, with a start-up or some area of new product, market or geographic expansion. Here the phases of the process would be different. For example, the first phase might be to understand the future market and competitive dynamics, rather than to begin with defining the present strategic position.

STRATEGIC EXERCISE 2.5 Applying the various perspectives
– 10 minutes

For each of the frameworks that we have covered I want you now to think which of these would be of most relevance to your business and its strategy:

Strategic framework: Relevance:

	Very high 5	High 4	Moderate 3	Lower 2	Low 1
Breakthrough thinking:					
Competitive strategy:					
Project management:					
Strategic cost management:					
Change management:					
Resource-based theory of competitive advantage:					
Strategic planning:					

Given the analysis above, what are the top three things and to what extent do you think that implementing improvements in all three together would enable them to be more effective together?

Summary of key insights

This section was relatively long and it is now timely to summarize some of the key insights coming out of it as follows:

- The idea of market attractiveness isn't about how attractive the market seems to be, it is about its objective qualities.
- Strengths are far more than things we can do OK – they are distinctive strengths.

- Key concepts need to be defined – otherwise they are almost certainly going to cause confusions.

- It is a good idea to narrow down the range of more challenging strategies that you are contemplating so that there are just a few to really give sufficient focus to: ideally no more than three breakthroughs in a particular phase.

- It is also very healthy to have some 'strategic don'ts' that you are *not* going to do.

- Competitive analysis has a central role to play in strategy development.

- RBT adds the reinforcing message to minimize the exposure to being copied.

- Strategies in their implementation usually break down into complex projects and this means that we need to use project management.

- Costs need to be managed more strategically and in such a way that never neglects economic value – they entail strategic thinking.

- Costs must be managed using gap analysis.

- Change is often complex and requires many of the tools and processes common to strategic planning.

- Strategic planning processes need to be designed in a bespoke way, depending on the issues and the context, and the mindset and skills.

- Change requires making a plan for the plan.

The cognitive perspective

The cognitive perspective looks at the mindsets and the thought styles that can shape and predetermine the thought process. These are always very powerful determinants of the outcomes of strategic thinking and we need to be aware of them and their influence and manage them.

Mindsets: these are the perceptions, expectations and assumptions about your industry and your position and prospects in this. 'Perceptions', here, include ones about the level of the market's attractiveness and of the relative perceived strength of the different players, including yourself, and the rules of the game. 'Expectations' are how you see these as being similar or changing, in the future. 'Assumptions' are more specific parameters in the future that will hold. These will also have some perceptions of the level of their certainty.

Sometimes the idea of 'frames of reference' is used as a very similar term. In my view, it is very difficult to define this term in any way other than to mean anything other than mindsets. In the spirit of demystification, the term 'mindset' is probably easier to resonate with – and is therefore preferred.

Mindsets will be used by people to interpret the strategic world around them and how attractive various strategies will be. If they are significantly out of alignment with reality, they can misdirect strategic decisions.

Mindsets can be identified at a number of levels: the industry level, the company level, the function or team level – and at the individual level.

One possible exercise, therefore, is to do a collective brain dump of what these mindsets are, so that they can be challenged if needed, or simply put into suspense. Owing to the fact that mindsets can be discovered at a number of levels and may not be shared equally by different individuals, this invites either individual work and pooling of the results, or work in a group surfacing them collectively – an interesting process.

STRATEGIC EXERCISE 2.6 Identifying mindsets – 10 minutes

For the main ingredients of your strategic mindsets, map out the following:

Mindsets:	What these are?	What positive aspects?	What negative aspects?
Perceptions			
Expectations			
Assumptions			

Mindsets profoundly shape the way in which a company looks at its own strategy and also frames its strategic intent (or what it is trying to do strategically). One fruitful concept is to be found in the strategy-style categories of Miles and Snow (1978), who characterize the most proactive mindset as being 'prospector' and the least as a 'reactor' (which can't seem to take external strategic changes on board and reacts tactically).

A prospector has an aggressive mindset, versus a defender mindset, at the other end of the spectrum. Miles and Snow also list an 'analyzer' as midway between prospector and defender. 'Shifts in mindset style are likely to be caused by things like: the company and market life cycle, industry and company – specific shocks, leadership and attitude, corporate inventive schemes etc.'

It is a useful exercise here to consider whether you have slipped from being a prospector to a defender and, if so, how and why this happened. What could you do to adopt a prospector mindset again? Which stakeholders might be most receptive to that concept, and what potential breakthrough ideas could spark off a new and imaginative momentum?

Having looked at mindsets, let us move on to the related issue of thought styles. Thought styles are the different ways of thinking that we have regarding strategic ideas – the mental processes that are used to model strategic issues. These are complex, as the following list from my experience and research over the years tells me. Here is a list of just 20. Can you add any more?

STRATEGIC EXERCISE 2.7 Analysing your strategic thinking style – 15 minutes

As a diagnostic you might find it helpful to rate the extent to which you do these a lot or not so much in your team:

	Do most of the time 5	Do a lot 4	Do moderately 3	Do not much 2	Do rarely 1
Analysing:					
Arguing and disagreeing:					
Categorizing:					
Challenging:					
Criticizing:					
Describing and explaining:					
Developing ideas:					
Devil's advocate:					
Diagnosing:					

	Do most of the time 5	Do a lot 4	Do moderately 3	Do not much 2	Do rarely 1
Dismissing:					
Doing nothing and keeping quiet:					
Drawing out insights:					
Evaluating:					
Hypothesizing (what ifs?):					
Identifying patterns:					
Imagining and visionary:					
Interpretation/sense making:					
Mediating/reconciling:					
Summarizing and synthesizing:					
Testing:					

Most of these thinking behaviours are normally positive, unless they are overdone. For example, arguing and disagreeing can be a healthy thing, but if done in excess it will drag the thought dynamic down, as would a lot of criticizing. If many of these are not evident, this is suggestive of a somewhat dull team environment. If describing and explaining behaviours and/or analysing predominate, and not really much else, that is almost certainly going to be dull and is probably too detailed a management style.

Of course, there are different individuals in any team and they have different default cognitive styles. So while there may be quite a lot of certain thought behaviours such as challenging and testing, these might emanate from just one or a couple of people in the team. It is a good idea to monitor some of these group thought patterns in real time and to see which typically lead to more inventive versus limited thinking. A good place to start is with oneself, for example by scoring one's own thinking behaviour at a recent strategic meeting, using Strategic Exercise 2.7 above.

Another useful strand of thinking comes from the idea of 'sensing' or of intuition in strategic thinking. There is a focus on this aspect in the literature on scenarios and on uncertainty, where 'weak 2' environmental signals are sensed and uncertain assumptions are systematically surfaced (see the uncertainty grid in Chapter 6 and scenarios in Chapter 8).

The notion of sensing also has relevance to the idea of emergent strategy, where decisions are made more intuitively and are frequently based on tacit thinking. Strategy is very much based on judgement and even softer intuition, and we need to remember that it is always at work within a formal process and with formal tools. Indeed, there is always the risk that this can be crowded out or be an overly structured and bureaucratic process, especially when driven by top-down objectives and goals. A very useful and succinct account of sensing and intuition is given in Tovstiga (2010).

Overall, in looking at the cognitive perspective there are a number of things that we need to watch out for, otherwise we can get easily carried along by strategic delusions about where we are, where we want to be, how we need to get there etc.

Summary of key insights

Summarizing this section, we see that:

- Mindsets play a very big role in shaping strategic decisions.
- They have an influence at industry, corporate, function, team and individual levels.
- They can be positive or negative, and this often depends on the situation.
- We normally need a rich variety of these thought styles to be strategically inventive and agile.

Too much emphasis on describing and explaining, and analysing, can greatly impede the more inventive group thinking processes that we are really looking for.

The emotional perspective

The emotional perspective is a third and very important means of understanding strategy. It almost goes unmentioned in the strategy literature, which is dominated by the conceptual dimension. We saw this perspective earlier in the context of buying a wedding dress and a wedding cake (see Chapter 4) – in terms of lowering buyer power and increasing margins.

I first became interested in this more behavioural element when doing some very interesting research in a strategy team at BT some years ago, when I decided to explore how their strategic behaviours shaped strategic thinking (Grundy, 1998a).

The discovery of strategic behaviour

Strategic behaviour can be defined as 'the patterns and style of interaction at a cognitive, emotional and political level which influence the strategic thinking of a team'.

What I found particularly interesting about this study was that looking at a team as the 'unit of analysis' emphasized the extent to which strategic thinking is very much a group process in many cases, rather than something that primarily the individual does – solo. For the BT team, while being intensely individualistic and with strong views of their own, nevertheless felt that they should swim along in the soup – and it was a soup – of the strategic debate of the team as a whole. So the behavioural constraints of the entire team shaped the debate profoundly, thus posing limits on the strategic thinking of the individuals themselves.

Do you recognize any of this in your own team? What do you think is really going on?

This was a fascinating study and yielded many insights, many of which were emotionally very relevant, on what really drives strategic thinking. Emotions were creeping in all over the place, despite the fact that the topic was that of 'What global technical strategies should BT be looking at and why?' – which might seem rather dry, but it wasn't at BT. To the contrary, emotions ran hot on should we go this or that way... people were most passionate – and this was very much a mixed blessing.

Emotions ran deep in that team not only about strategic issues in content terms, but also around personal status and vulnerability. For not only are strategic issues highly uncertain and ambiguous at times, which caused much anxiety, but also people's roles in their team and the judged quality of their ideas. They felt that they were potentially being judged through everything they said, and how they said it.

Now, not all managers are intensely aware of their emotions and how they show them, handle them and communicate them – they don't all have very high emotional IQs, as the reader will appreciate! So if we thrust managers into strategic debate with muddled mindsets, no effective strategic tools and process, and make them highly anxious and worried, we will quite often get... a resulting soup.

A further case was in one of Microsoft's big operating divisions in Europe. I was asked to help their top team to see if it could develop its capability and add more value. It met once a week for several hours and was comprised of functional heads reporting through a global matrix structure to HQ in Seattle. So, locally it had no clear role or leadership.

In a two-day offsite workshop I was able to get them to have a meeting as if they were holding it for real and I observed their behaviours and how these interacted as a system (or their 'system of strategic behaviour' – Grundy, 1998a). This identified things such as having a clear strategic agenda and targeted outputs, the team mix and default styles, the processes, concepts and tools, meta-behaviour (the active role of summarizing and team direction – setting, and maintaining, a 'helicopter level' to the debate – inter alia, determined the quality of its behaviours).

The patterns and the root causes of dysfunctions were then analysed in real time, and fed back to them. We then worked together to look at what options were available to make a set of coherent changes that would provide them with a new model. This involved setting the criteria for choosing a leader. These were then prioritized and planned in detail, and included:

- arrangements for team leadership – they hadn't had one previously – and leadership rotation;
- who would add most value to the team and a slimmed-down representation from the functions;
- definition of its value-creating activities and what it wasn't there to do;
- an agreed agenda of issues, including embryonic plans for a small number of cross-functional breakthroughs;
- better processes and tools for decision making.

In effect there was an entire re-engineering of the team, which went very smoothly and successfully: an interesting model.

Moving on now, I would like to drill down a little more into the core of the emotional perspective.

On the nature of emotions in management

Everything, as we said, should be defined, so here we go: 'Emotions are the feelings that we have when sensing situations, events, people and their actions and intentions, in a very direct way, rather than through the lens primarily of cognition.'

Here the ingredients are:

- Feelings: so they are analogous to physical feelings – they can be about pain or discomfort or pleasure. But emotions have a greater variety of flavours: for example, approval, excitement, ambivalence, worry, feeling threatened, disrespected etc.
- They can be generated by a whole variety of things, such as a sequence of conversations, some strategic data, analyses, evaluations or interpretations.

STRATEGIC EXERCISE 2.8 Exploring your strategic emotions
– 10 minutes

In this next exercise we encourage you to explore some of the emotions that you have had, either generally in strategic meetings or within a particular one.

To what extent have you had the following emotions? These have been structured along a continuum, with the lightest and most positive first. 'Boredom' was felt to be as much of an emotional state as a cognitive state, and because it might well be experienced reasonably frequently it was included. Also, I added 'fun' to the shopping list as I felt that a lot of the successful strategic meetings had had a certain fun or lighter element – even if the issues had been rather serious. Fun doesn't mean being frivolous.

Clearly no state is inherently good or bad, except perhaps anger, at the end of the spectrum, which isn't generally a positive feeling and shows itself very easily, as we see in the table below.

Please complete the table as an exercise:

	Experienced: Very frequently indeed 5	Very frequently 4	Moderately frequently 3	From time to time 2	Rarely 1
Exhilaration:					
Excitement:					
Delight:					
Fun:					
Pleasure:					
Surprise:					
Doubt:					
Boredom:					
Anxiety (general):					
Worry (specific):					

	Experienced: Very frequently indeed 5	Very frequently 4	Moderately frequently 3	From time to time 2	Rarely 1
Insecurity:					
Regret:					
Disappointment:					
Embarrassment:					
Frustration:					
Anger:					
Panic:					

I now briefly reflect on a team of which I was an integral member for a couple of years. Over time, the team had to deal with a number of strategic issues. I would say that there were only very rare moments when the top seven emotions occurred – other than fun which was a brighter element. There was certainly an element of boredom and there was quite an element of routine in the way the team tended to work. My sense was that there was some insecurity and anxiety around certain topics. Generally the team did tackle the really key issues but there were still potential improvements available within their processes and dynamic behaviours.

So what might have been done to inject more vitality into a team like this and to inspire their discussions to a higher level?

- They might have used some strategy tools to enlighten selective issues – and certainly got themselves a whiteboard.
- The format, which was quite set piece, could have been varied, for example to include some visits to sample competitors' offerings first.
- They could have set aside some time dedicated to more free and creative thinking, even if the focus was quite operational.
- They could have cut back time spent reading through a report that we had all read, and spent this additional time at a more helicopter level on, for example, what we might do that we weren't doing strategically, and on the evaluation of the options coming out, rather than to go mechanically from problem to solution.

Again, this sort of process makes one far more reflective as to what is really going on when managers are ostensibly trying to develop strategies: probably half of the strategic consciousness is absorbed in the emotional – as opposed to the cognitive.

When someone is experiencing strategic emotions these are often a give-away, not just through verbal communication, but also through non-verbal communication. Non-verbal communication is a very important medium of transmission of feelings. For example, examine the experience described in the next subsection.

Observing non-verbal communication

Working with a division of HSBC, there were no fewer than 13 strategies and it was quickly realized that 13 were too many – a bridge too far. So the team set about prioritizing these, and car leasing seemed to be not parti-cularly attractive at all, as it was a commodity business with few real competitive advantages. So the team agreed to exit this business. While the director responsible for this business agreed that they should exit it, there was some ambiguity – which was left open – as to the timing and mode of the exit.

Worse, I observed some very negative body language from that director. His body was very tense, there was a definite tightness in his facial expres-sion and tension throughout his body – his limbs seemed coiled around himself, crossed legs and arms too. In fact he almost looked as if he was try-ing to do one of my favourite (hot) Bikram yoga postures: the eagle posture, except that he wasn't doing it standing on just one leg!

I thought at the time that there was absolutely no way that he was really going to preside over such an exit, at least not without a lot of passive resist-ance. Two months later, after there had been no real movement, the issue came up at another meeting and he then made up lots of excuses for in-action: he was confused; he thought that they had just agreed to look at the options; and also, actually, he still felt that they should stay in that game. Eventually the CEO kicked the ball into the net that I kept crossing to him ('What, me? Centre forward, Shoot?', he seemed to be thinking), and the team decisively agreed the exit details.

I had a quiet conversation with the CEO afterwards: he hadn't honestly thought that there was going to be all that resistance, even though the non-verbal signals were so strong. He hadn't picked them up at all.

When cognition and emotions interact... and organizational energies

Our final point on the emotional perspective is on the way in which the cognitive and the emotional interact. It may seem obvious that the emotional will shape the cognitive, as we all tend to think along lines that are especially fitting with our emotions at the time, unless we have well-developed mindfulness skills (which doesn't mean that we need to be Zen Buddhists, although that might be of some help). But less obvious is the surprise that cognition has a major influence on how we instinctively react at the emotional level.

I discovered this very clearly during my study of strategic behaviour at BT when, after observing the behavioural soup of the team's interactions (which they were very aware of), I staged an interesting experiment. I took a couple of the strategic tools (which we will see later) for prioritization and facilitated a session where they worked using these few tools on some of their issues. I was very surprised to find that when they started to do this (and it was all recorded), they calmed down, got on with it in a focused way, and appeared to be able to set aside some of their excessive passion. The result was a good and creative attempt at problem solving and also they found it a much easier and less stressful experience.

What I had witnessed was the emotionally driven behaviours of a group being harnessed through a cognitive intervention! So it cuts both ways: the emotional shapes the cognitive but the cognitive can be used to channel the emotional (see Grundy, 1998a).

This was over 15 years ago, and if it happened today I would be far less surprised. Since then, the framework of cognitive behavioural therapy (CBT) has become much more developed, well known and understood. A central tenet of CBT is that emotional and dysfunctional states such as depression can be mitigated by mindful and structured reflection. Much of this involves uncovering the system of beliefs that people have about themselves, and examining and challenging those beliefs. This is not unlike the role of mindsets, which we looked at earlier in this chapter.

The rather big 'so what' to share with you here is that really thinking strategically demands not just conceptual skill and instinctive creativity, but also a high level of self-control over one's thought and emotional processes. This isn't the central issue on the management development agenda, but perhaps it should be. Indeed, if one can cultivate a meditative state then strategic thinking will come about more easily, once you have turned down the 'monkey mind' that wants to think about everything all at once.

Coincidentally, I took up meditation about 15 years ago as well, and I have found it much easier to focus my thoughts and to get inspiration than before, and am less inclined to react under pressure to emotionally turbulent states. Maybe some readers might try that....

Something worth touching on briefly is that cognitive and emotional states are underpinned by individual and pooled human energies. So these energies will shape those behaviours and thoughts. There is plenty of evidence that such energies exist; for example, many people can sense that they are being looked at if someone just observes them from the back.

I take a small risk in mentioning it here because I feel that these energies are very influential in shaping organizational interactions and it is as well to cultivate an awareness of these and their shifts. We probably know these as 'climate' but this is something that isn't an abstraction – it can be sensed.

You have probably had something like the experience of going into a room where there has been a meeting and feeling either a good or bad feeling about what has been going on there: that is a stage in sensing energies. There are things you can do to enhance such an awareness, as exemplified by mindfulness: mine has mainly been developed through certain advanced meditative techniques which allow this sensing to happen quickly, easily and with a high level of reliability. As a facilitator, this has proved invaluable over the past 15 years on a number of occasions, even down to spotting someone likely to cause difficulties before even meeting them.

I have worked with these energies in some quite major corporations, such as Prudential and Direct Line, and it has been truly surprising that some managers are naturals at it and one can pass over skills quite quickly. (Ask me direct after finishing the book if you want to know more!)

A somewhat amusing example of this was when my new wife, who is a psychologist, moved office after some staff changes and took some sage into work, set it alight so that it smouldered and used it to clear away the old energies. People were puzzled at first but when she explained what she was doing – clearing the energies – everyone said 'what a good idea'. Imagine doing that during a boardroom discussion at plc level!

You can see that an eclectic approach to strategy sees it in its total context to find out what is going on at all levels.

Summary of key insights

Key insights from the emotional perspective are:

- Strategy discussions often generate a lot of anxiety, which affects behaviours and the process.
- Strategy is also a very emotional thing generally, and these emotions are complex, diverse and will be experienced by different team members in different ways.
- Non-verbal communication is very influential and can shape the outcomes of interactive behaviour greatly.
- Cognitive interventions are sometimes very useful in stabilizing a team behaviourally and politically.
- Emotional and cognitive states are conditioned by the energies of an individual or group or their climate, and you can be mindful and intuitive in sensing and recognizing these.

Key insights from the chapter

- The idea of market attractiveness isn't about how attractive the market seems to be, it is about its objective qualities.
- Strengths are far more than things we can do OK – they are distinctive strengths.
- Key concepts need to be defined – otherwise they are almost certainly going to cause confusion.
- It is a good idea to narrow down the range of more challenging strategies that you are contemplating so that there are just a few to really give sufficient focus to: ideally no more than three breakthroughs in a particular phase.
- It is also very healthy to have some 'strategic don'ts' that you are *not* going to do.
- Competitive analysis has a central role to play in strategy development.
- RBT adds the reinforcing message to minimize the exposure to being copied.
- Strategies in their implementation usually break down into complex projects and this means that we need to use project management.
- Costs need to be managed more strategically and in a way that never neglects economic value.
- Costs must be managed using gap analysis.
- Change is often complex and requires many of the tools and processes common to strategic planning.
- Strategic planning processes need to be designed in a bespoke way, depending on the issues and the context, and the mindset.
- We normally need a rich variety of thought styles to be strategically inventive and require an agile mindset and skills.
- Change requires making a plan for the plan.
- Mindsets play a very big role in shaping strategic decisions.
- They have an influence at industry, corporate, function, team and individual levels.
- They can be positive or negative, and this often depends on the situation.
- Strategy discussions often generate a lot of anxiety, which affects behaviours and the process.
- Strategy is also a very emotional thing generally, and these emotions are complex, diverse and will be experienced by different team members in different ways.

- Non-verbal communication is very influential and can shape the outcomes of interactive behaviour greatly.
- Cognitive interventions are sometimes very useful in stabilizing a team behaviourally and politically.
- Emotional and cognitive states are conditioned by the energies of an individual or group or their climate, and you can be mindful and intuitive in sensing and recognizing these.

In conclusion, the conceptual and the cognitive are closely related perspectives, but surprisingly the cognitive and the emotional are also more closely interdependent than you might previously have thought.

Embracing the strategic world – part 2

Introduction

In this chapter we take a look at three other perspectives:

- the influencing and the political: how these twin processes can be managed to channel strategic decisions and the urge to make and to implement these;
- processes: the way in which the management process is supported and coordinated and made inventive rather than run of the mill;
- implementation: for example through projects, change management and other interventions and processes.

These three perspectives are grouped together as they are concerned more with process issues than with the cognitive and emotional perspectives which we saw in the previous chapter.

Reviewing this chapter, I would say to the reader to expect, as in Chapter 2, a lot of meat and richness and to realize that some rereading of the material, say after a week or two, even if selectively, would pay dividends. You may be advised to read just one of the perspectives at a particular sitting.

The influencing and political perspective

Strategic influencing is the handmaiden of strategic thinking. While strategic thinking can be quite a challenge, an even greater challenge, typically, is to be able to cope with the subtleties of mobilizing strategic thinking within the organization, through influencing. Strategic influencing can be defined as 'the process of understanding the positions and agendas of stake-holders and of getting them on board with ideas, options, decisions, plans and changes'.

Who are stakeholders?

The above definition thus puts stakeholders in a central position. We define a stakeholder as 'anyone who has an influence over a decision, or who may be involved in its implementation, or who may be affected by it'.

Each stakeholder will have a position in terms of his or her influence level, both generally and on this specific issue. In terms of stakeholder analysis (which we will see soon), usually we focus on that stakeholder's influence on that specific issue.

Stakeholders can be either grouped together or positioned individually – it depends on how complex the situation is and how detailed we need to go, especially where they are not homogeneous.

Their positions will also depend on their attitude as well as their influence, which could be:

- for;
- neutral;
- against.

Stakeholders exist at a variety of stages of the decision-making process: the ideas stage, the options, decisions, plans and changes. As these decisions crystallize within the management process, stakeholders may take on clearer positions or shift them and change in their influence levels. This is a highly dynamic situation.

Stakeholder analysis is one of the most powerful and insightful tools of strategy. Different formulations exist, including a popular one in the form of influence and interest on a two-by-two matrix. My strong personal preference is for Nigel Piercy's (1989) version of attitude against influence (see Figure 3.1). This uses the vertical axis for rating stakeholders as for, neutral, against. The horizontal axis rates them along that dimension as high, medium and low influence.

Looking at Figure 3.1, we also see some generic influencing strategies that might be deployed to influence stakeholders:

- coalition building: taking two or more stakeholders who have lower influence and encouraging them to align and collaborate;
- leave alone: there isn't much point in focusing on negative stakeholders with low interest;
- turning negative and high influence stakeholders around.

In order to get a sense of where a stakeholder is, you need to look at them from their own perspective: I frequently call this having the 'out-of-body experience'. This means understanding their deeper agendas and the emotions that they have (see 'The emotional perspective' in Chapter 2).

FIGURE 3.1   Stakeholder analysis

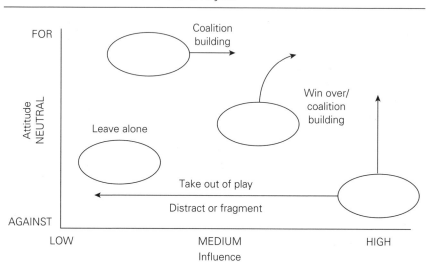

This tool is based on earlier versions by Piercy (1989)

In terms of interpreting the results:

- Where there is a preponderance of stakeholders who are towards the top and few anywhere else, this particular strategy ought not to be problematic.
- Where there is a more scattered profile, you need to attend to those who are of more influence and in neutral or against.
- Where there is a weighting towards the bottom, there is a very real challenge.
- Where there are simply a very large number of stakeholders, the situation is complex and you might be advised to reformulate the strategy to be simpler and involve fewer players, even if this involves you starting again.

STRATEGIC EXERCISE 3.1   Doing your own stakeholder
analysis – 15–20 minutes

Taking a strategic option of your choice, consider, preferably using Post-its on a flip chart or whiteboard (so you can move them around):

- Who are the stakeholders?

- Who is the 'one big stakeholder' that you have still forgotten?

- What is their level of influence? High, medium or low?

- What is their attitude? For, neutral, against?

- What, given these ratings, is their likely position on the grid?

- What pattern emerges?

- What influencing strategies can you come up with?

- What new positions are likely to emerge?

- How might their positions shift over time as the options move through the decision-making and implementation processes?

- How will you manage these issues and the stakeholders' agendas through further influencing strategies?

As can be seen above, this is a very thoughtful and possibly detailed process. But it is one that is very rich in insights. What did you learn from the above exercise? What other things should you apply this kind of thinking to in future?

Stakeholder analysis can be applied either secretly or quite explicitly by using it as a tool with the stakeholders themselves to uncover their own positions and to reflect on their reasons: are these grounded in real business concerns or are they wound up in their emotions and political agendas? If the latter, does this process encourage them to soften or even abandon that stance?

A further use of the technique is that it can be used at an informal level to sense where someone is coming from – and thus collect data.

I haven't said it yet, but you will definitely get value out of plotting yourself on the matrix. For example, if you are project managing this strategy personally, and you are in both a lower influence and a neutral position, you really do have problems! Here you will need to do three things:

a) Decide where you stand on this.

b) Find some strategies for increasing your influence.

c) Think about whether the organization should be doing this anyway.

Stakeholder positions are likely to change a lot over time, in terms of both their attitude and influence. They need to be tracked and a new map of where you see them periodically drawn up. These positions may even change during a single strategic meeting and need to be tracked accordingly.

Influencing strategies also need to have a cunning plan: all too often they entail just going to talk to someone and to put the case. A more cunning approach might be, for example, to encourage others to see this as a natural and attractive strategy through their own volition. This means that one should always approach influencing through strategic thinking.

Stakeholder analysis can be beneficial:

- at the start of a strategic process, eg when doing the plan for the plan;
- at the strategic options phase;
- when doing the detail of the strategic plan, eg in project planning;
- when planning the detail of implementation;
- during each key phase of live implementation;
- as part of change management;
- as part of a review of the strategy's success: to draw the learnings out;
- as a core part of the communication process: to target who will be told what, how and when.

Key benefits of stakeholder analysis are that it enables you to:

- deal with the political dynamics more smoothly;
- see the issues from the changing perspectives of a variety of stakeholders;
- challenge the basis of the assumptions that stakeholders are making that will be influencing their attitudes;
- use it as input to the stakeholder acceptability criterion of the strategic option grid, as part of the evaluation process;
- facilitate team building.

As a final comment, stakeholder analysis may need to be done separately not only for different strategic options for what to do but also for different ways of implementing them. Also, it may need to be done for the different strategic issues which are under scrutiny in the first place.

Stakeholder analysis is thus a key ingredient of the influencing process but there are other elements, too. Influencing needs to take into account the dynamics of the decision-making process. This entails thinking through the buying process within the organization and also the different influencing skills that are called for, stage by stage. This requires looking at two further frameworks which are normally very helpful.

The buying cycle

In terms of Figure 3.2, we can see that there is at least a five-stage process of moving through the buying-in cycle:

- issue recognized;
- desire for action;
- agendas influenced;
- decision;
- action.

FIGURE 3.2   The buying cycle – stakeholders

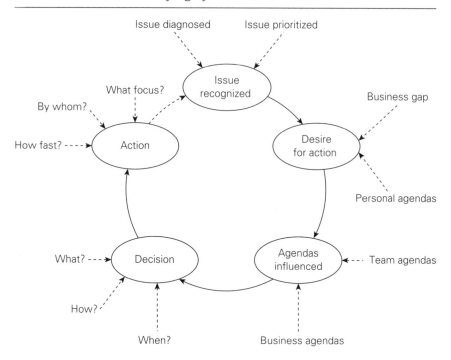

In terms of issue recognition, organizations vary greatly in the speed at which they recognize an issue: for example, increased competitive threat, regulatory change, major cost reduction, the need for a big restructuring, a business entering a 'turnaround' phase etc. Here the issue has to be both recognized in the first place and given some priority, too.

Next, there needs to be some degree of desire for action. This will be greater if there is a clear gap analysis and dealing with this issue will address that. At this point the personal agendas of the different stakeholders will play an increasing part.

Agendas will then need a conscious influencing process. These will be the pooled agendas of the team: the 'strategic soup', and also the particular issue will have to be nested in the context of the wider agendas for the business: what other problems and goals does it address or what other initiatives does it compete with for attention or cut against?

The decision here breaks down into a number of key elements:

- the 'what' of the decision;
- its 'how?';
- its 'when' – its timing.

Finally, action requires another level of thinking about how fast implementation should proceed, who should be doing it, and what focus the implementation should actually have.

To illustrate how this process can be most informative in practice, let's take an experience I had with a very large Scottish insurance company. I was invited to meet the group finance director and the finance director of the life business to get their views on value-based management (or VBM) as an organizational project (Grundy, 2002c). HR already thought that this would be a good idea and were behind it, but wanted me to meet the top finance people before I finalized my proposals for some workshops on VBM to support this possible project.

When I went into the meeting, which was at a small table in a very big room with some delicacies such as smoked salmon, I felt straight away that they were both quite apprehensive, judging from their body language. I hadn't expected that. I figured that while these guys had top positions, they might be unnerved by the fact that part of my PhD was partly on VBM and I had written books etc on the topic.

I had assumed that the issue was some way around the buying cycle, and so my main challenge was to put the ball in the net! Not so! As I began to get some very stiff cross-questioning on 'what is the value of VBM?', to which I had a lot of answers, and 'isn't this the same as "lean management", and if so, why bother?', it became apparent that this provocative and challenging response was a very long way from being a decision. With the buying cycle in my mind I figured that my two possible clients here within the finance community were only at the 'issue recognition' phase – at the very top of the buying cycle, so that I should definitely stay with them in that zone, rather than persist in taking this as a 'how?' issue rather than a 'whether' one.

That realization helped me a lot in reframing the conversation because they also became aware that that was where they were, too, which was a little embarrassing, but I was sympathetic and flexible and indicated that fact. Although the goal was never scored, it became a more productive encounter and if the hidden stakes against VBM hadn't been there already, there would have been a fair chance of moving forward on this.

As can be appreciated, there is a fair amount of complexity surrounding stakeholder positioning, which needs unravelling. Also, as the issues will need a lot of working through and they will have to compete for attention with other priorities, this could take quite some time to do. Indeed, it has been said in the literature on the strategy process (for example, Mintzberg, 1994) that often decisions can seem to take a very long time to crystallize: months if not years. This means that the successful strategic influencer mustn't be like a bull in a china shop but must cultivate a high level of patience.

This is captured well in the words of a previous client of mine. This was the HR director of a major water company which was then undergoing an equally major downsizing. His comment was made in relation to the likelihood of eventual changes that he foresaw at the top, when addressing the middle managers: 'I want you all to be like the Vietcong: if need be, tunnel underground and wait for the right moment to resurface!' This neatly underlines the need for patience and also favourable timing in the way one should set about managing and influencing stakeholders.

Turning next to Figure 3.3, this has the same stages as we saw in Figure 3.2, except that here the story is told from the point of view of the influencer.

FIGURE 3.3 The influencing cycle – advisers

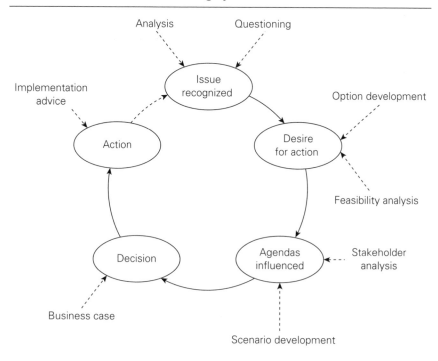

Here the key skills needed in issue recognition are those of analysis and questioning. Analysis here looks at both making sense of the data and diagnosing any problems. Desire for action requires skills in option generation and feasibility testing, no doubt using the strategic option grid (which we will be going into later) to put some structure on that.

At the agendas influenced phase, this calls for a good deal of stakeholder analysis to position these, to understand what is going on beneath the political surface and also to develop some powerful and naturally appealing influencing strategies. In the course of this work it might also be an idea to do some scenario storytelling on how the political environment may shift, and also what specific stakeholders might say – or do – that might influence events. Indeed, this can extend to actual role playing.

There is also a strong influencing role to be had for developing a business case to support the economic case for the decision. This can be extremely useful in dissolving away any residual personal and political agendas that might be in the way of moving forward.

The action phase may require assistance in implementation planning, for example through project management and change management.

So there are a lot of different skills to develop in order to be a successful strategic influencer. These skills are also diverse and embrace those across the spectrum of 'hard' and 'softer' elements.

STRATEGIC EXERCISE 3.2 Analysing the buying cycle –
5 minutes

For one issue or decision that is currently being processed by the organization (preferably something that has an impact on you or that you can influence, or both):

- Where is the issue currently, within the buying cycle?

- What influencing has been done to date?

- Has this been effective or not, and if not, why?

- What could now be done to move it forward?

Deploying the 'P' behaviours

Turning now to the political perspective more centrally, not only can we deploy stakeholder analysis and the buying cycle, but there are a number of recipes that can come in handy. These include the 'P' behaviours.

This was created in a joint exercise with Dave King, the then business development director of Dowty Case Communications, an international telecoms business. Dave and I were working on a strategic review and we were planning a two-day strategic decisions workshop for the board. Dave was getting increasingly anxious as this drew closer and, in a pub in Watford (after a few lunchtime pints), at his suggestion we began to brainstorm all the words that were negative behaviours for things we wanted to avoid, and which began with a 'P'. The 'P's tool was thus born and has since been used hundreds of times.

In practical terms, here one gets a team, which is about to embark on a strategy session, to define all the behaviours that they agree collectively they don't really want to engage in. It is, as was found at Dowty Group, who were in aerospace and telecoms, punchy to use only words that start with the letter 'P', and there are lots of behaviours that do. A good list – and any facilitator can prompt them if people can't think of them – is:

- political;
- pedantic;
- procrastinating;
- picky;
- prickly;
- personal;
- pessimistic;
- parochial.

You can add more... maybe some 'fun' ones such as 'paralyzed' or even 'psychotic'.

Typically this provides a brake on the political influences. If anyone starts to behave even a little bit along those lines, they can be challenged, and by anyone – that is the rule. This gets managers to be far more mindful of any behaviours which do have a political undercurrent. In my experience, this method, which takes only around five minutes or so, will frequently give a clear political climate for some time, and any infringement of the rule is exceptional.

What happens if you don't invest the five minutes? Well, I can tell you: as a team leader or facilitator you are running big risks. Once the show has started to go off the road due to a political dynamic, it is very hard to recover. Imagine trying to set these rules in place after some quite major argument/difference of view. This once happened to me.

I was working with a charity's team. I had met the key players before and they all seemed such nice people. I felt that I could do without using the 'P's. We had done some option generation which had been extremely productive, but when we started to consider the evaluation a major rift became apparent between two of the directors, which crystallized over a deep disagreement on a particular option. I would stress that using the strategic option grid, as we were, this was very unusual. Anyway, suffice it to say that this became quite acrimonious. I had to call a break so that we could all cool off, and then attempted to put the pros and cons of the two different sides that had been discussed and suggested we move on to other issues.

I am quite convinced that if I had already put the 'P's in place, this conflict would have been a fifth as bad. So that's a warning to you not to do short cuts!

Another similar method is just to get the team leader to announce, for example, that 'the next two hours will be a politics-free zone'. This needs some positioning, otherwise people might feel gagged. For example, if you are embarking on a major restructuring, downsizing or cost reduction, the rationale might be that you really cannot afford delay or dilution of decision making. Also, you can easily say that this will make it a much easier process because no one will be torn between making decisions in the corporate interest and in parochial interests.

I taught this technique to the MD of the same water company where middle managers were invited to become 'like the Vietcong'. The MD needed to cut through some difficult politics that were impeding the restructuring. So he got some of the directors together and asked them to work through the key choices on that same politics-free basis. When I saw him the next time and asked him how it went, he was positively beaming!

Generally my one-time aversion to having to deal with politics has gone down a lot over the years and my fascination with it has increased. What I have discovered is the richness of this perspective, just as a biologist could find the insect world so fascinating that it becomes irresistible to look under stones to see what wriggly insects are to be found hidden underneath: the analogy is a deliberate one.

As a part of your own development path to becoming a director, CEO or whatever, the art of influencing, especially strategic influencing, is on the critical path of personal development.

Key insights into the influencing and political perspective

To recap on the influencing and political perspective:

- Stakeholder analysis is a very powerful and essential strategic tool which needs continual use.
- It is particularly effective when you actually imagine that you are the other stakeholder – through the out-of-body experience.
- It should be applied to different strategic issues and also to both the 'what' of a strategy and the 'how'.
- Stakeholders may change positions over time and this needs tracking.
- Influencing strategies should not be average but cunning.
- The buying-in process in organizations is complex and can be long and tortuous.
- Patience is therefore a virtue.
- Business and personal agendas often get mixed up together and need untangling.
- Lots of very different skills are needed at different stages of the cycle – and range from those at the 'harder' end to the 'softer' end.
- The P's is a very effective way of channelling the politics.
- As is declaring, or suggesting, a 'politics-free zone'.

The process perspective

The process perspective entails looking at the way strategies are formed into being. It is very closely linked to the influencing perspective and that's why we take it next. Strategy at business schools is normally taught with some account of that perspective, which is a very good thing. In terms of process, there are a number of ways of looking at this:

- the forms that strategy takes;
- the forces shaping the process;
- the sequence of stages and tools that might be used;
- vertical versus horizontal strategy development;
- the fit within the management process(es).

Without sufficient strategic processes, strategic thinking will struggle to gain traction and get off the ground.

The forms that strategy takes

Strategy can take at least two key forms: deliberate or emergent (Mintzberg, 1994).

A deliberate strategy can be defined as being 'one which has a clear logic, is based on the position and prospects of a company and has a clear set of strategic decisions'.

Deliberate strategy is the mindset that most managers have. However, it is often elusive in reality as the planning process is frequently not really good enough to deliver this.

An emergent strategy is a pattern in a stream of decisions or actions. It is thus often observed only after that pattern has materialized.

Mintzberg describes the ideal model of the strategy process as rather like walking: you use both feet equally; if the right foot is 'deliberate' then the left is 'emergent', and you should use both equally to walk in a straight line. Unfortunately, it seems that the emergent strategy is often the dominant force. I often illustrate this with managers by asking them, 'How am I going to walk if the emergent foot dominates the deliberate foot?' When they have told me, I then demonstrate by walking round in one dominant direction in circles!

Figure 3.4 is a good illustration of deliberate versus emergent strategies. It shows the neat alignment of emergent strategies as smaller arrows. I contend that this model is not too realistic in the majority of cases, as in most organizations there is too much complexity and politics for that to happen *au naturel*. Where an emergent form of strategy is likely to be most effective is:

- when there are conditions of strong and clear leadership, eg in an entrepreneurial context;
- where the emergent strategy becomes quickly tested and deliberate;
- where the environment is changing and very fluid, and flexibility and agility are key.

FIGURE 3.4 Deliberate and emergent strategies

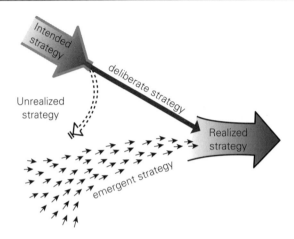

When explaining this picture I frequently make reference by analogy to an experiment in physics where you put some iron filings on a piece of paper randomly, and then observe what happens when you place a magnet underneath: the iron filings all line up in a pattern. In theory, emergent strategies line up in a similar way through the results of leadership and management processes. But in reality, if these alignment forces are inadequate or not really there at all, a true pattern won't really be formed. And often that influence in a consistent direction is lacking on the organizational level.

Besides these two basic forms of deliberate and emergent strategy, I believe that it is helpful to look at some other forms as well (see Figure 3.5):

- submergent strategy: where the strategy isn't really working but it is still being pursued;
- emergency strategy: where the strategy clearly isn't working but there is no new strategy in place;
- detergent strategy: where strategy to sort the mess out is under way.

These strategies tend to move round the cycle in Figure 3.5. Strategies that begin as deliberate often lose their form, and the pattern even of an emergent strategy disintegrates. Management then still pursue these strategies owing to recognition lags and because they are too recently communicated for any reversal to be other than very embarrassing. Once they fall apart ('emergency strategy'), sorting out has to begin ('detergent strategy').

FIGURE 3.5   The strategy mix

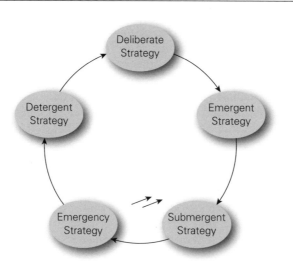

The strategy mix has advantages in that one can use it to diagnose which forms of strategy are ascendant at a particular time. This can vary at the corporate and business levels: often strategy at the corporate level, for example, is more emergent. Also, it is a very good way of understanding past patterns of strategy development in a company, especially ones associated with a lot of change, or anticipating the future dynamics.

STRATEGIC EXERCISE 3.3   Analysing the strategy mix –
10 minutes

Using the strategy mix for your organization:

- Where are the strategies on that cycle?

- What has their trajectory been to date?

- Where do you think they might be going in future?

- What, if anything, should be done to influence that?

In terms of strategic thinking generally, it is quite possible to have – even in the situation of an emergent strategy – the application of deliberate strategic thinking. Indeed, in that more fluid context, arguably, one might have even more call for some more structured thinking – at a deliberate level – to help cope with that uncertainty and ambiguity. So it is no excuse, in terms of not doing much systematic strategic thinking, that the strategy is highly emergent and that this is unlikely to change much.

A final refinement of the model is to look at another possible form: contingent strategy. A contingent strategy 'is one which one might do in the future if the conditions for its success are all lined up'. A contingent strategy is likely to be particularly helpful for situations where a strategic context is highly uncertain. In that situation, which is very common, it would be foolish to set a deliberate strategy. Also, an emergent strategy would be too loose.

So a contingent strategy is one which is more flexible, and is potentially more resilient. The drawback is that this doesn't necessarily sit well with a structured planning, budgeting and communication process that can't easily accommodate contingent decisions. In that case, my view is that those systems should become more adaptive rather than preventing that kind of strategy being adopted, if that's best. Contingent strategy (as an idea) is unique to this book.

Can you identify any contingent strategy that was being considered by your business sometime in the past (eg an alliance, a new product, an acquisition)? What were the conditions for its success, how completely identified were these and what was the eventual outcome?

We will be covering contingent strategy in more depth in Chapter 9. Contingent strategy has major implications for strategic thinking – taking it into the land of positing quite contingent conditions – and thus requires the suspension of commitment.

The forces that shape the process

There are a number of forces that shape the strategy process. To begin with, strategies tend to evolve incrementally in organizations over time. So a decision to launch a new product may be followed up later on by a decision to take it to a new market. These decisions might have been isolated and yet make sense, increment by increment.

This process of bolting on one decision to another introduces increasing complexity over time, which can dilute competitive advantage and shareholder value alike. It can result ultimately in a mess. This isn't unexpected as it is rather like playing chess by thinking only one or at best two moves ahead – it isn't a very good way of doing things.

Even where there is a strategic vision, this could be too broad to be truly effective in screening new strategies, and a lot of strategic rubble can still be force-fitted into the strategy.

This phenomenon has sometimes been called 'logical incrementalism' (Quinn, 1980), but there is quite a case for dropping the 'logical' part as it is so rarely that rational! A more honest description has been that it is 'muddling through'. Arguably, in incremental strategy, strategic thinking is very limited and constrained.

Logical incrementalism (something of a mouthful) also highlights the fact that many strategies are interdependent. This means that quite often their economic value needs to be assessed in some particular combination and not in isolation. Also, these interdependencies need to be actively managed.

Other forces can be:

- leadership;
- stakeholder forces (which we have already covered);
- politics (ditto);
- ownership changes;
- mindsets.

Figure 3.6 shows this as a system.

FIGURE 3.6   Forces in the strategy process

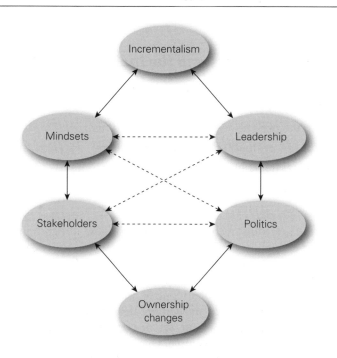

Leadership is such an important ingredient in the dynamics. Over the past 24 years I have been asked to facilitate strategy for teams which have been somewhat rudderless in that department. In such situations, however good the process and the strategy output, invariably the strategy doesn't move forward successfully. Leadership is often the weakest link that needs to be in place. So there are some complex forces that determine the strategy process in everyday reality, and if these aren't all, more or less, lined up, you are very likely to have problems.

As an everyday example of incremental thinking, my wife and I had a mini strategic project to sort out how to store all of our shoes in our new house. I can call this a strategic project as it was complex, also severely resource constrained (space) and had stakeholder and behavioural implications for our overall family set-up. So we had a chat about it – having measured it all up under the stairs – and had decided, looking just at that storage as an issue, what the shoe-rack solutions were. My wife was tired and didn't want to go back downstairs and look again at the problem, and when I did persuade her we saw, obviously, that our feasible decision would mess up other goals that we had.

Number one: where were we going to store the Dyson carpet cleaner, and be able to get at it without wrecking the rest of what was stored underneath the stairs? Number two: where were we going to put the kids' bags, which weren't there at the time, when they came home from school? So we had, through looking at the problem incrementally, not seen the bigger, and more strategic, picture!

The sequence of stages and the tools that can be used

There are some basic steps or stages, covered earlier in Chapter 2, for structuring the strategic process, and these are worth recapping briefly:

- defining the present position: external and internal;
- creation and evaluation of strategic options;
- planning strategic breakthroughs;
- implementation;
- control and learning.

In terms of the key tools, we will be going into these in depth in the rest of the book and especially in Chapters 4–7. Here some tools can be used a number of times, for example fishbone analysis for definition of the present position and for diagnosing implementation difficulties, and also for analysing problems in delivering results (control and learning). Also, stakeholder analysis can be used at a successively more detailed level for every stage.

Where a company has a unique set of constraints, this may affect the ordering in the sequence. For example, where a company has major internal capability issues, it may not be best to start off with analysing the external opportunities and position, as this might frame too ambitious a set of strategic goals. One may need to do an assessment of how capability can be improved first, and only then go on to do the external analysis.

Another example is where a company has only just begun to address a (relatively) uncertain market opportunity and the main issue isn't current position but the future potential of that market. In this case, one might cut back the current positioning, or even not start with that at all, and instead focus on storytelling the future.

Vertical versus horizontal planning

Vertical planning exists where plans are formulated within a hierarchy. This can take two forms: top-down planning and bottom-up planning. Top-down planning is a process where the top level in the organization (corporate or at the business level) decides the strategic objectives of the organization, and levels beneath are tasked to come up with their goals and their strategies which will deliver them. Bottom-up planning is where all the units come up with their plans and these are aggregated to arrive at the company strategy.

While top-down strategy is clear and relatively straightforward, as a process it suffers from being unrealistically stretching and unsophisticated. Bottom-up strategy can be more effective as it encourages much more focus on what is feasible.

A better process is one that combines top-down and bottom-up processes. The trick here is to get the balance and timing of communication flows between the various levels so that:

- there is sufficient context around any top-down goals: how do these sit in terms of background assumptions about the general economic environment, and also market growth rates etc?

- there is sufficient coaching of the lower levels so that their work is treated in a constructive dialogue and not one of excessive challenge;

- the process is kept as free from political gaming as is possible.

Finally there is also the dimension of horizontal planning, which entails two-way dialogue across the organization about the optimal strategies. Clearly there ought to be some discussion between business and support units as to how the value of internal services can be optimized relative to the cost. But true horizontal strategy is a lot more: where different outward-facing business units discuss joint opportunities together in order to optimize these. Where top-down and bottom-up processes merge with the horizontal, one might find a true, strategic planning utopia.

STRATEGIC EXERCISE 3.4 Developing our planning process
                                  – 10 minutes

Thinking about your planning process:

- To what extent is it top-down and what are the pros and cons of this?

- To what extent is it bottom-up and what are the pros and cons of this?

- To what extent is it horizontal and what are the pros and cons of this?

- What improvements can you see out of this for your planning process?

- How attractive/difficult to implement are these improvements?

The fit with the management process(es)

Strategic planning doesn't sit on its own but should be nested within other key management processes. These include no fewer than 12 things potentially:

- project management;
- business cases;
- value-based management/cost management;
- budgeting;
- financial reporting;
- rewards and recognition;
- business process re-engineering/lean management;
- balanced score card;
- key performance indicators (KPIs);
- change management;
- culture change;
- governance.

We can see from this list that there are many management processes that need aligning. So, where a new form of strategic planning is implemented, this will require a lot of adjustments elsewhere. Also, where there are developments in the other processes, this may lead to changed needs and other opportunities in strategic planning.

For example, if improved project planning and business cases are put in, this may be an opportunity to make strategic projects the building blocks of the strategy. Or, if VBM is implemented, this means that strategy evaluation should be done primarily through economic analysis rather than in terms of accounting profit/returns.

We will now take each of these processes in turn.

Project management

As we saw earlier, project management should be used in framing the overall project of doing the strategy, beginning with the plan for the plan. It should also be deployed for managing the strategic breakthroughs that are at the core of the new strategy. Also, it should be used for more specific interventions such as change management, VBM, business process re-engineering etc. We go into this in real depth in Chapter 8 on managing the strategy process.

Business cases

These are the economic justifications of specific breakthroughs/strategic projects. Here we are doing an assessment of the value and cost drivers that underpin the strategy.

A value driver is defined as 'anything either inside or outside the business that has either a direct or indirect influence over the future positive cash flows of the business, both now and in the future'. A cost driver is defined as 'anything either inside or outside the business that has either a direct or indirect influence over the future negative cash flows of the business, both now and in the future'.

These value and cost drivers can be represented visually as tree pictures. Figures 3.7 and 3.8 are examples – drawn to represent these drivers for the economic analysis of a new high-tech supermarket that goes in a straight line. This might add value both to customers (which could be captured by the company in the form of switching of customers avoided and also new customers won). It would also have different cost drivers over the life cycle, especially the upfront and the ongoing costs. These pictures are essential preparation for doing the economic case for the project.

FIGURE 3.7   Value drivers

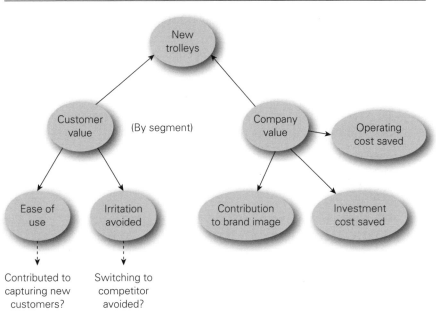

By kind permission of Tesco Stores Ltd

FIGURE 3.8   Cost drivers

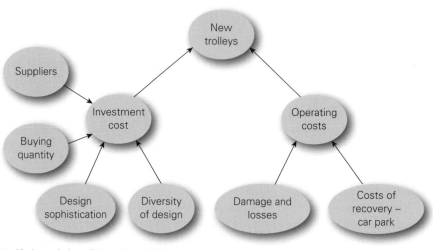

By kind permission of Tesco Stores Ltd

This means that the value and cost drivers will cover both the more tangible and the less tangible effects on cash flow. These value and cost drivers will be both internal and external. For example, competitive rivalry is a negative value driver. Competitive advantage gained through premium customer value is a positive value driver. Examples of cost drivers include business complexity, process efficiency, economies of scale, organizational hierarchy, organizational speed, cost consciousness etc.

Having defined our list of value and cost drivers and assessed the impact that the breakthrough has on it, we will then make some specific assumptions – quantitatively – as to how these will operate in the future environment. These will incorporate assumptions for things such as sales growth, margins, volumes, prices, marketing support, costs etc.

Finally these need to be financially modelled and then risk-assessed. Once the risks have been identified and prioritized, the appropriate sensitivity factors can be used as a test. As a guide we can use:

- low risk: 5%;
- moderate risk: 10%;
- high risk: 15%;
- very high risk: 20%;

rather than the more usual 10 per cent that is so often applied. All that a broad 10 per cent test really tells you is which variables, when they do go adverse by 10 per cent, have the most impact on economic value added. I recommend that you don't use this, but the above parameters instead.

As the above financial assessments are based on an economic assessment, they are cash flow based and are thus free of the distortions of conventional accounting profit and accounting assumptions. While the impact on accounting profit is relevant in the management process, as management sets a lot of store on achieving short-term numbers, it should not dominate thinking and decision making.

We will say a little more on doing a business case in Chapter 8 on managing the strategy process.

Value-based management

VBM, as we have said above, is not just about a change in performance metrics but also uses new concepts that are designed to get as close as possible to cash flow. VBM means understanding the following key variables – and the sub-variables that go behind them to arrive at future cash flow (see Grundy, 2002c):

- sales growth rate: this is determined by market growth, relative competitive advantage and improvement, competitor moves, discounting, premium pricing, price deflation etc;
- profit margin: sales less operating costs as a percentage of sales; this is determined by relative competitive advantage and improvement, competitor moves, price deflation, cost reductions etc;
- investment needed to maintain the business (fixed and working capital);
- investment needed to grow the business (fixed);
- competitive advantage period (or CAP);
- corporate tax rate;

making six in all. (Usually the maintenance fixed capital and the maintenance working capital are split from each other, giving seven value drivers.)

These value drivers are estimated and the results are worked backwards using a discounting formula to get to the present value (or the 'net present value' – after deducting the upfront investment cost). The cost of capital is thus the seventh value driver.

It is important that this doesn't become a numbers game and that the underlying and specific value and cost drivers that underpin a specific decision are thought through before making global assumptions, especially to avoid simplistic extrapolations of past trends. In particular, the variable of the 'competitive advantage period' needs probing as it is frequently assumed that competitive advantage will continue over the planning period. This may or may not be the case. Indeed, a more realistic assumption might be that after three years, say (depending), it begins to decline, so that sales growth rate (SGR) and operating profit margin (OPM) reduce, too. We will see how competitive advantage is very much a dynamic thing in Chapter 5.

Regarding cost management, we discussed strategic cost management earlier; the important thing to note here is that this relies on the identical language of value and cost drivers.

Budgeting

Budgeting is a core process that has a big influence over short-term allocation of resources. Budgets need to be aligned with, and sufficient to support, the strategy. Otherwise there will already be a gap created between strategic objectives and the likely out-turn, and you are likely to have an unrealized strategy, or at best diluted results.

The strategic planning process should therefore take place before the detailed budgetary process, so that the budgetary process is informed by the strategy. But the probable effects of the strategies being considered on both financial spend and headcount resources do need to be anticipated at the strategic planning stage – at least in broad terms.

Generally, budgetary rigidity and target setting is one of the root causes of weak implementation as resources are spread too thinly or inappropriately and there is insufficient investment in breakthrough strategies. Also, revenue expenditure with longer-term benefits still gets written off in the profit and loss account, so if that is the predominant financial target or metric, as opposed to economic profit, it will tend to choke off spending which won't fully pay off in the year that it is spent and expensed. More flexible budgeting and change management, and more fluid organizational structures, can also help this.

Financial reporting

Such systems seem to live a life of their own. As a one-time accountant (escaped) myself, I remember not giving too much thought at all to the reporting structure and emphasis in relation to the longer-term strategy: that is, of course, until I did an MBA. For in an ideal world, the financial reports should be looking particularly (and on a quarterly basis) at the attainment of strategic goals, for example margin improvement, cost reduction, breakthrough projects etc. Financial reporting should nest within a bigger process of strategic management reporting where the financials provide the backbone but the flesh is the business context: so in looking at the numbers one must always be asking: 'How are the key value and cost drivers behaving? What is going on in the marketplace? What are the key issues that might impact on future business performance?'

Rewards and recognition

Rewards and recognition systems also play a key role in influencing management behaviour, not only during the planning process but also during implementation. If rewards are based very much on the size of your department, no one is going to be very interested – other than the CEO/FD/HR director – in cutting numbers back (and the FD/HR director similarly for their own areas). Also, where the strategy is influenced by very specific goals, such as it was at Shell in the early 2000s by '15 per cent growth' in sales – they will be driven far too much towards delivering that mantra. This can actually destroy shareholder value, as it did at Shell through inappropriate booking of oil reserves – which implied that future growth goals were attainable.

Alignment of rewards and recognition systems is possibly one of the trickiest of challenges to be overcome when upgrading one's strategic planning process. If this gets left until after the plan has been done and dusted, that is far too late and you are most certainly going to run into problems on this.

Business process re-engineering/lean management

Business process re-engineering (or BPR) is 'the re-examination of key business processes as if they were ones in perfect alignment with either value model of the business and in the simplest and most astute way possible'.

BPR is thus a way of visiting business processes in a fresh way: almost as if they had been forgotten through corporate amnesia, and were there to be designed from scratch. Sometimes this is called 'zero-based thinking', which is very powerful. BPR is a subject in its own right and we will not go off on a tangent on that here: it is a potentially mixed blessing and, if not well orchestrated as not merely process change but also behavioural change, it often meets very mixed success.

BPR can play a key role in helping deliver major cost breakthroughs – along with any other organizational changes needed. Besides its use in the wider business context, BPR can be used to redesign the planning process itself.

Lean management can be defined as 'a management philosophy whose assumptions are that resources and processes are subject to a rigorous test of strict minimalism, ie what are the truly essential things that need to be done to add value to the customers, whether directly or indirectly'.

Defining it in this way reveals that it is not very far removed at all from things like BPR and strategic cost management. Indeed, these are very much variants of the same thing, rather like Catholicism, Protestantism, Methodism being variants of the Christian religion. This is not a flippant analogy at all, as different varieties of religion differentiate themselves through somewhat different prescriptive emphasis and beliefs and also in the way they convey them – with varying fervour and style.

BPR/lean management should not cut across strategy at all, and are vehicles for organizational transformation, which is a positive thing. As long as their rather detailed, linear and operational thought styles don't cut across the more fluid processes of strategic thinking, they are a good thing to have around. They should increase management sophistication, for example in problem solving, as many of the thought processes are quite similar to planning generally.

By the latter period of this book's lifetime (10 years) no doubt these will be rebadged one more time as something *new*, and *even better than before*. All it needs is something catchy like TIP or totally integrated planning, which embraces BPR with lean management and Six Sigma (quality management), the balanced score card (see below)/KPIs, project management/Prince and strategic thinking. Who knows, I could be its guru – unless one of my readers gets there first!

The point here is for the need for you to exercise real discernment in cherry picking the useful things from such frameworks – you have to remember that they are a product and sometimes there is a temptation to throw in ideas from everywhere to make it seem awesomely comprehensive. Sometimes a little less is a lot more.

The balanced score card (or BSC)

The balanced score card can be defined as 'a system of targeting, monitoring and controlling business performance where the financials don't dominate and there are other indicators that are attended to similarly in assessing this'.

The BSC is thus an attempt to broaden the key instruments that give management an awareness of how well the business is doing in the round. The conventional split of these metrics is grouped in four quadrants:

- financial (typically profitability or return);
- customer value added;
- efficiency;
- the fourth factor....

The fourth factor is the one that is the most commonly varied. In the early BSC models it was typically that of organizational morale/satisfaction: for me, that is typically too narrow and not important enough *vis-à-vis* most senior agendas to attract the attention that the others will get. Personally I believe that this fourth one should be reserved for the development of capability: otherwise there will be very little focus on this important area and on the future in particular.

The other area that is conspicuously absent from most BSCs is relative competitive positioning. Why should we incorporate the dimension of customer value/satisfaction and not relative competitive positioning, which is equally important? It doesn't make sense – especially if the BSC reporting is going to be of use as an input to the strategic planning process.

So a more enlightened list (as I once advised HSBC) is probably:

- financials;
- customer value added;
- relative competitive position;

- efficiency;
- capability development.

Key performance indicators

KPIs are now defined as 'the carefully chosen list of indicators and measures of business performance used for controlling and measuring it'. The focus on the words 'carefully chosen' in relation to indicators and measures is very deliberate as it is so easy to just keep adding to the list. These are some of the key variables that lead to superior business performance. So for a health club chain these might include:

- net joiners/leavers;
- member attrition percentages;
- marketing cost per member;
- sales per square foot;
- profit per square foot;
- net profit as a percentage of sales;
- increase/decrease year on year of sales;
- non-membership revenues as a percentage of total revenues;
- return on capital as a percentage;
- staff costs as a percentage of total costs;
- maintenance costs as a percentage of total costs;
- average revenues per member;
- complaints: number per month;
- customer satisfaction ratings;
- attrition rate of staff.

These amount to 15 in total, which isn't too bad. All of those listed look important and informative and don't look redundant. All cover three of the five potential key areas of the balanced score card, which is a good check. Not covered here, though, are the areas of relative competitor position and capability development. These might need to be tracked and included on a more qualitative basis to give a better overall picture.

So relative competitive position can be looked at via estimates of relative (local) market share – if one could find out the number of members of the club, for example by doing a tour as if one is a customer and asking how many members they have (if that could be trusted) or by finding out from leavers of competitors who have joined you etc.

In judging their effectiveness one could take a view as to what variation in performance is accounted for by these KPIs: if it is at least 85 per cent, that's pretty good.

STRATEGIC EXERCISE 3.5 KPIs in your business –
                                                    10 minutes

For one of your businesses:

- What are your KPIs re the customers?

- What are the key performance drivers re efficiency?

- What are the key performance drivers re financial performance?

- What are your key performance drivers re capability development?

- To what extent have these shifted over the last year (up or down) and what is this telling you?

Finally there is the question of whether CSFs (critical success factors) and KPIs are related or different. In my view, CSFs are certainly the general strategic recipes or reminders that one will have to be mindful of in tracking the strategy's translation into performance. They are a bridge between the strategy and operations and action. KPIs are generally more tactical, but in my view there should, as we saw in the above listing of possible KPIs, be things of some strategic impact too. KPIs are generally of a level of detail lower down than CSFs and are also more specific and generally measurable.

Change management

Trendily rebadged in the 2000s as 'organizational transformation' (can the gurus and the consultants charge more for bigger words and the more vague a concept is?), change management can be defined as 'a useful process for ensuring that change projects have a clear strategy which takes into account the internal context, and which anticipates and manages the dynamics of change proactively'.

Change management has its roots in the mid/late 1980s and was one of the first codifications of organizational process held out as being essential to be a high-performing organization. It has certainly played an influential role in helping make modern organizations more adaptive and responsive to external and internal change (Peters and Waterman, 1982). But it must have a strategic point to it. Many changes are instigated on a 'gut feel' basis and without proper diagnosis and research. So there needs to be a careful process of finding out what's behind the current position, what the strategic goals are, what gap exists and what the best implementation options are, so again we are back to the basics of strategic thinking in looking at how it is structured as a process.

Without sound change management, implementation is probably going to be something of a nightmare.

Culture change

Culture change can be defined as 'the process of shifting patterns of behaviours, attitudes, mindsets and beliefs, and values of an organization, whether through a deliberate or an emergent strategy'.

Culture change is thus about surface behaviour and deeper cognitive elements such as beliefs, both internal and external, and also more emotional things such as values that invoke feeling and a sense of identity and belonging that develops over time when with an organization. Culture change can be initiated deliberately through customer care programmes and through internal interventions that aim to encourage shifts in cultural patterns in the organization, such as leadership development and team building. Or it can be something that simply happens through organizational ageing or becoming a public company or by becoming more global, for example.

Where there is a culture that is very operational, risk averse, slow to make the necessary decisions – relative to competitors – or to implement these, the company is likely to begin to experience strategic drift. Strategic drift is a state where the external environment is changing faster than the company's internal change; a classic case of this was the British retailer Marks and Spencer in the period from 1995 to 2005, which saw it overtaken by other retailers in store ambiance and experience, the relative value for money of its products, the appeal of its brand, its cost base and its management capability and leadership. The result was a collapse in its profits from £1 billion a year (on sales around £8 billion) to around zero and a recovery over that period of just 60 per cent to around £600 million as a result of its strategic drift over a long period.

Culture is thus often a strategic issue in its own right and if not addressed will prove to be a major implementation constraint which will impede delivery or strategic goals and delay them.

Governance

Governance is 'the processes through which an organization regulates itself to pursue goals in the interests of all of its stakeholders, and to deliver an appropriate mix of return and risks that will satisfy its shareholders'.

Governance is a slightly newer kid on the block but can play an important influencing role in strategic planning, for example through:

- the influence of non-executive directors, for example in ensuring that any strategies have been properly tested and are robust;

- providing a check on the strategic decisions made by the board;
- getting shareholder (economic) value onto that decision-making agenda;
- making sure that risks are properly evaluated, implying some risk management processes;
- ensuring that board rewards are based on appropriate metrics and aren't excessively short term or skewed too narrowly, eg not to just growth.

Governance processes are more evident in public companies or government organizations where there is more emphasis on stakeholder management.

Phew, looking at the list we started with and have now covered, we become aware of just how many influences there are on decisions in modern organizations and how much work is needed to align strategic planning to these, and vice versa. This is something that most managers are dimly aware of. It is definitely good to have mapped this out.

Key insights from the process perspective

The main insights coming out of the process perspective are that:

- Strategy may take different forms over time: deliberate versus emergent etc.
- Too much emergent strategy is often a bad thing.
- Often the strategy seems to move around a cycle and go through more chaotic phases before being re-formed.
- When in a state of flux, contingent strategies can be helpful.
- There are many different management processes that strategy may need to interface with, which needs a lot of alignment.

The implementation perspective

Implementation is often viewed as being the graveyard of strategy. Even if you have the cleverest and the most cunning of strategies, there is little value added unless it is implemented effectively. So we need to think most carefully about its implementation, not just during the strategy formulation process but also in implementation planning itself. Strategic thinking in implementation doesn't get turned down – if anything, it should be turned up.

A crude strategy equation, beginning with resulting performance, which is useful to look at here is:

$$\text{Performance} = \text{(the quality of strategy)} \times \text{(the quality of implementation)} \times \text{(its timing)}$$

or,

$$P = Q(S) \times Q(I) \times T$$

So it is important too that the strategy is well timed in terms of environmental conditions and change, and also competitor moves.

The implementation perspective reminds us that we need to bring together things that we saw earlier in the 'process' section, such as:

- project management;
- change management;
- balanced score card/KPIs.

If we are going to introduce KPIs at the implementation stage, these must have some strategic focus; we must ask, for example, 'What are the longer-term target KPIs that we are reaching for?' And also: 'How do we ensure that these have a significant impact and represent a step change in the business?'

Besides stakeholder analysis, which is absolutely central in managing implementation issues, we should also deploy other tools such as:

- fishbone analysis: for diagnosing implementation issues;
- FT analysis for change gap analysis and for scoping change projects;
- AID analysis;
- force field analysis (for the enabling and constraining forces);
- difficulty-over-time curves (for understanding the dynamics of change).

We will be exploring these tools in more depth in Chapter 7.

Strategy implementation has a lot in common with change management, as much strategy implementation involves either doing old things in a new way or doing new things and thinking differently. So let's extract some of the central lessons from change management next.

For the present, we will concentrate on the macro aspects of change without getting too bogged down with prescriptive change theories, which remind me of baking a cake: here it is assumed that what tasted good in one particular case will work across the piece. The context and ingredients of change vary so much that it is very hard to come up with a single baking recipe. The change context will vary enormously, for example in terms of:

- whether the major driver for change is external or internal;
- whether it is largely voluntary or enforced by circumstances;
- whether it is proactively initiated, or reactively;
- the extent to which the organization is run in a more directive style, or in a more participative style;
- whether it is localized in scope, or has a much wider reach;

- whether its duration is short term, medium term or longer term;
- whether the organization is naturally highly adaptive or the opposite.

So there are probably too many variables to say, for example, that 'it must be led charismatically by top management'.

More resilient change theory, in my view, tends to come from some deeper understanding of the change process. If one were to distil from the best of such theory, one would probably come up with something like the following:

- gestation: the period during which the need to change and the realization of this need have been building;
- diagnosis: understanding where we are now;
- visioning: visualizing where we want to be in the future;
- option generation and evaluation;
- detailed planning and preparation;
- mobilization;
- consolidation of the change;
- control and learning.

We have an unusually large number of phases, but most readers will recognize the need to think about these separately. For example, the gestation period is an important one as it conditions the urgency of change and its earliest issue definition, which may be crude and potentially inaccurate. Also, the phase of visioning needs some separate attention before plunging into option generation and evaluation.

Besides planning, there is also an element of preparation, for example in signalling that some change is on the way – to diminish unnecessary shock and to also get senior management in the right mindset for how the organization is likely to respond, especially from those most vocal at middle levels. Finally, implementation breaks naturally into the earlier phases of mobilization and, later on, consolidation.

It is possible that some of these phases were not strictly linear and there is a degree of iteration: for example, during option generation and evaluation there may still be some diagnostic work going on. Also, there may be occasions when visioning is being revisited during or after the option evaluation phase.

An example of a set-piece change management process at a global level was the classic Project 1990 at BP where I had a role in assessing its economic value added. This project ran over several years' gestation: the period during which the need to change and the realization of this need have been building.

Here we can characterize the phases as follows:

- diagnosis: understanding the deficiencies in BP's existing culture;
- visioning: defining the ideal future culture for BP;

- option generation and evaluation: benchmarking culture change elsewhere, and exploring intervention possibilities;
- detailed planning and preparation: prioritization, scheduling interventions, planning central support, major organizational downsizing and simplification of BP HQ's decision making;
- mobilization: launch to the top managers of BP at Henley over a weekend, coverage simultaneously in *The Sunday Times* – as a pre-planned scoop;
- consolidation of the change: adaptation of rewards and recognition and other HR processes;
- control and learning: evaluation and valuation of the intervention(s).

While not without its drawbacks, this appeared to be a well-orchestrated change process.

STRATEGIC EXERCISE 3.6 Managing change – 10 minutes

For a change that has already happened in your organization:

- How did it go through the seven phases of change that we saw earlier?
- Which phases went well and how was this brought about?
- Which phases had the most difficulties and why?
- What was the overall result and to what extent was this affected by the way in which the process was managed?

Summary of key insights from the process perspective

In terms of the overall insights that we saw coming out of the implementation perspective, we see:

- Performance = (quality of strategy) × (quality of implementation) × (timing) is a useful equation.
- There isn't a simplistic recipe for change generally – it needs to be tailored to the context.
- Implementation has very much in common with change management.
- The change management process has many phases, including gestation, diagnosis, options, planning, mobilization, consolidation, control and learning.

Key insights from the chapter

- Stakeholder analysis is a very powerful and essential strategic tool which needs continual use.
- It is particularly effective when you actually imagine that you are the other stakeholder – through the out-of-body-experience.
- It should be applied to different strategic issues and also to both the 'what' of a strategy and the 'how'.
- Stakeholders may change positions over time and this needs tracking.
- Influencing strategies should not be average but cunning.
- The buying-in process in organizations is complex and can be long and tortuous.
- Patience is therefore a virtue.
- Business and personal agendas often get mixed up together and need untangling.
- Lots of very different skills are needed at different stages of the cycle – and range from those at the 'harder' end to the 'softer' end.
- The P's is a very effective way of channelling the politics.
- As is declaring, or suggesting, a 'politics-free zone'.
- Strategy may take different forms over time: deliberate versus emergent etc.
- Too much emergent strategy is often a bad thing.
- Often the strategy seems to move around a cycle and go through more chaotic phases before being re-formed.
- When in a state of flux, contingent strategies can be helpful.
- There are many different management processes that strategy may need to interface with – which needs a lot of alignment.
- Performance = (quality of strategy) × (quality of implementation) × (timing) is a useful equation.
- There isn't a simplistic recipe for change generally – it needs to be tailored to the context.
- Implementation has very much in common with change management.
- The change management process has many phases, including gestation, diagnosis, options, planning, mobilization, consolidation, control and learning.

In this chapter we have thus shown how strategy needs to be enlightened through a triad of perspectives of: influencing and politics, processes, and implementation, all of which are highly interdependent with one another.

In terms of the most important interdependencies between these six perspectives, we now have for any organization:

- The conceptual: this is the conceptual process that facilitates understanding the strategy and is about external and internal positioning, option generation and decisions, and planning. The battery of tools and frameworks here will help facilitate politics and influencing, calm the emotional, condition the cognitive understanding, offer opportunities for structuring the process, and the tools can be used during implementation itself.

- The cognitive: beliefs and mindsets may distort the use of concepts, will have a subtle role in shaping the emotional climate, will possibly fuel politics and inhibit influencing. They may also distort the process.

- The emotional: this will govern where the conceptual analysis and thinking influence the process and subsequent implementation, and reinforce mindsets etc. They will be the engine of the politics.

- The influencing and political: this will direct both the conceptual and the cognitive, possibly inhibit the process and implementation, or distort these, and its dynamics will cause emotional shifts and disturbances.

- The process: this will help to neutralize political and emotional agendas and help provide a vehicle for the conceptual and the cognitive, and for implementation (eg through change management and project management).

- The implementation: this will help to anchor more conceptual choices, shift the emotional by moving things on and equally the cognitive. It will help channel the political.

04 Analysing strategy economically

Introduction

Economic analysis provides much of the conceptual basis of strategy. It can be defined as 'the systematic analysis of the market and competitive forces and of the company's own position, its resources and competences that determines its prices and costs and thus the economic profit of that enterprise, past, present and future'.

The ingredients of this are therefore:

- systematic analysis: of the key variables and how they interact dynamically – as a game;
- market and competitive forces: the external environment;
- position, resources and capability: the quality of its strategic assets, their ease of imitation etc;
- prices and costs: with the price mechanism and factor costs;
- economic profit: the present value of future net cash flows;
- past, present and future: with changing views over time.

In the first three chapters we have paved a lot of the way for this, but now we are ready for the main course. In this chapter we will be looking at a number of case studies and inviting you to do another series of practical exercises.

Here we will:

- examine what the gurus say;
- assess the environment: the 'onion' model of strategic positioning;
- look beyond Porter's five forces;
- distil the 'so what's?'

This chapter will be somewhat shorter than Chapters 2 and 3.

What the gurus say

The main gurus that we will cover are:

- Michael Porter;
- Hamel and Prahalad;
- Rumelt;
- Blue ocean: Chan Kim and Mauborgne.

Michael Porter

Michael Porter is a Harvard professor whose background is one of economics. He managed to distil much of the essence of microeconomics to just five forces which we will see in depth in the next section:

- bargaining power of the buyers;
- competitive rivalry;
- entry barriers;
- substitutes;
- bargaining power of the suppliers.

See Figure 4.1.

Each of these forces can be analysed in terms, for example, of what they are, how they are changing and, most importantly, how attractive they make the market. They are very good predictors of the economic profit across a market, and also partial predictors of company economic profit as well.

The buyers are both the end customers and intermediaries.

The suppliers are the suppliers to you (and not you, yourself).

Competitive rivalry is largely the result of the other forces, but has an autonomous role too.

Entry barriers may be the ones at the boundary of the market, or geographic or other barriers. Thus even if market entry barriers are high, they may not be so high for a new entrant from a different geographic territory, for instance.

Substitutes should be looked at in the broader context of being substitute ways of meeting the same or similar needs to the ones you are addressing.

Porter's five forces (Porter, 1980) are depicted, from left to right, as an industry value chain, from suppliers through core competitors to buyers. This is often an oversimplification as there may be suppliers to the suppliers, and customers of the customers, so we may be slicing through many industries vertically. In addition, there may be different channels to the same/different customers downstream – so again it can be more complicated. Also, the forces of entrants and substitutes mark the industry boundaries the other way.

FIGURE 4.1 Porter's five forces

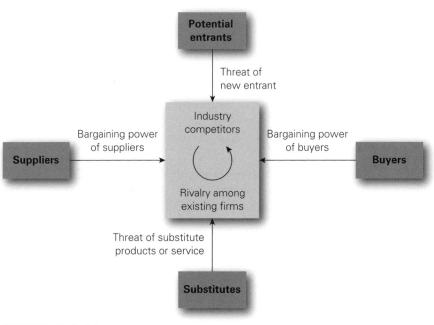

SOURCE: Porter (1980)

These industry boundaries have got a lot fuzzier since Porter's five forces were first developed, especially as the internet has opened them up and also many companies' brands have become more elastic. So one cannot necessarily see 'the industry' or 'the market' as self-contained. For example, retail and financial services have quite fluid boundaries, which means that retailers have encroached on the terrain of the retail networks of banks and insurance companies. Interestingly, almost all MBAs seem to be unaware of that, and their analyses, which appear good on the surface, are superficial. Strategic analysis shouldn't crowd out strategic thinking here.

So, in effect, we are thus implicitly mapping the industry with Porter's five forces, so the analyses might get a little more complicated. There will be 'contours' of strategic attractiveness. As we will see later, the forces will vary over different product/market geographic segments. We are in effect thus mapping the competitive landscape of an industry, and the industry attractiveness will be very variable. So to say 'this industry is attractive!' is somewhat akin to saying that 'France is an attractive country': for sure, Nice and the Dordogne are very attractive indeed, but, as with all countries, some parts are not so nice.

Sometimes adjacent strategic space is highly variable indeed: for instance, while the Cotswolds are wonderfully pretty, Swindon, some 15 miles away, is not!

Porter's contention is that these forces will differ for different industries and for the same industry over time, which is observable over time. Consider, for example, the weddings industry, which is chosen as a relatively attractive industry:

- Buyer power: low, as this is an emotional purchase and an infrequent one at that (one hopes: I am trying to keep this to three!). Attractiveness – high.

- Competitive rivalry: medium; most players do not compete vigorously but there is some price discounting. Attractiveness – medium.

- Entry barriers: variable; many venues are licensed so that is one entry barrier, and there are some in reputation, skills etc. Attractiveness – medium.

- Substitutes: low, except when people do it themselves, unbundling the reception and (self-organizing) the photography, the cake. The internet is a sort of substitute for buying the wedding dress from the high street. Attractiveness – high.

- Suppliers: not very important, so low. Attractiveness – high.

So while not perhaps a five-star (all positive) industry, it isn't bad. There were no 'low attractiveness' ratings and three that, with some caveats, were 'high'.

We will be covering the five forces in separate bites: first, a quick overview now of its major features, and second, a more in-depth exploration of its subtleties in our last section of this chapter.

So if we go back to personal experiences, one can see how this impacts in reality. This case is around weddings that I have had in the past and one I had during this writing – in October 2011.

My (then) fiancée was planning our wedding with me. My first wedding had been a conventional one, with around 40 people. The second had been a smaller affair – just the two of us with two witnesses. It was a 'cost leadership' wedding (in terms of the Michael Porter concept), which meant that we still went to a posh venue and had champagne but didn't tell them that it was a wedding, saving £2,000. We had a balloon ride, too. The total cost was £415.50, including the dress, which my then wife-to-be on that second occasion bought in the sale at Dorothy Perkins and negotiated the price down by not paying by credit card (by 50 pence).

My third (and final, I pray) wedding was something in between the two. We had both been married twice before (so after the wedding we would have been married – between the two of us – six times to five different people!). We didn't really want the conventional dress and church scenario – that was out of the question as Carolina is Catholic and the divorced market is not a served-market segment for them. We weren't short of cash but it seemed silly to spray it around like champagne. So we did want something for our money.

I had recently been to my brother's and my nephew's posh and enormous weddings with things like firework displays and a dead roast pig as a late snack in a huge stately home that they had hired (he is in banking), which seemed well over the top as a model for us. Both could easily have cost £20,000 plus, and I calculated that, spread over five hours of 'wedding breakfast' time, that is £4,000 an hour.

I started shopping around and some of the poshest venues in Surrey were up to £9,000 before anyone even touched a drink, which seemed absurd. And as soon as you used the very word 'wedding' the price seemed almost to double. It struck me that this was because of two things: the low bargaining power of the buyers as a wedding is a very emotional thing (like a funeral, but a lighter event), and also because of unconscious price collusion by suppliers (low competitive rivalry).

So then we enquired about photography. We had quotes from around £300 to £900. In the latter case you had the photographer hanging around for four hours – that's over £200 an hour, which I thought wouldn't be that bad for an independent strategy consultant but it seemed very generous for photography. This seemed pointless, so we saved a lot of money by asking a friend with a good camera to do it. We had heard of digital cameras and it occurred to us that even a monkey could get some half-decent shots with 500 pictures and that a human whom we trusted would be better. Do it yourself (the 'substitute' was easy).

What surprises me is that there aren't more lower-priced players in the photography market – for a nice Saturday job. You buy a camera, a suit, and that's almost it. I thought I might do that myself! I had once doubled as the presenter and as the cameraman recording myself in Trinidad teaching MBAs corporate finance....

Next, we set about buying the wedding cake, sorry, no, I should say 'the cake': it is very important to get that right. I told Carolina that she really mustn't say the word 'wedding' – ever – in making the purchase, but she just couldn't help herself and the word 'wedding' slipped out. She had already got a quote of £70 from a deluxe cake shop in south Croydon, which didn't seem massively pricy for only 24 of us (around £3 a slice – but still not cheap, although yummy). We were to do the decorations ourselves.

Unfortunately, I wasn't there in the shop as her strategic minder when Carolina managed to use the word 'wedding' in the shop when ordering, and the cake price suddenly doubled to £140! Carolina said that there must have been some confusion as the price was quoted as £70. The £70 had apparently been for a 'normal' cake. Carolina said that we couldn't do that price and if they wanted to reconsider the price to ring her. After she left the shop, only five minutes later she had a call to say that we could have it for £70, sorry, but it had been embarrassing as there had been other customers around!

So beware what you call things! I had got it dead right: if it's for a wedding the same thing doubles in price.

This case just shows the profound influence that emotional value and its skilful manipulation can have on buyer power, on competitive rivalry and the bottom line, price.

A second contribution of Michael Porter's was his idea that generic strategies broke down into differentiation and cost leadership strategies, and broad versus focus strategies:

- A differentiation strategy is one 'where the company offers superior value to its target customers: this is rewarded by a premium price. Superior value can be real or perceived, or both.'
- A cost leadership strategy is one which 'is based on attaining lower costs than all other competitors'.
- A broad strategy is one 'where the company competes across all or most products and services, and/or market segments'.
- A focus strategy is one 'where the company competes across a narrow range of products and services, and/or market segments'.

A differentiation strategy can be a broad or focus strategy, ditto a cost leadership strategy.

In some ways these generic strategies map onto the competitive landscape that we saw earlier: a differentiation strategy seems to match the more attractive zone of the industry, particularly where there is lower buyer power and less price rivalry. A cost leadership strategy is more common where there is fiercer competitive rivalry, high buyer power, threat of entrants and substitutes: price competition is intense and to remain in business and make money there is an equal downward pressure on costs.

This correlation between the two sets of concepts is at best highly implicit in the literature, and they are typically thought of as largely separate things. Probably these categories of strategies can be best characterized as more 'strategy styles' rather than 'generic strategies' that you can just pick up off the shelf and adopt.

Porter believed that a successful company had to choose between the generic strategies that were available: if it tried to compete across more than one of these, it would lose its way and be more average. If it tried to have it both ways, success would be frustrated and it would get 'stuck in the middle'.

Porter was emphasizing here the very good concept of strategic choice: which meant that in strategy you need to decide what you are *not* going to do: a principle that we subscribe to. But the question remains: 'Why is it not possible to have it both ways and take the best of both?'

This could be due to a number of reasons. From the theory and from experience, problems with 'having it both ways' could arise:

- because of customers getting confused, eg on the brand values, on pricing, on service levels etc;
- sales, marketing and service staff with an outward-facing role could get confused, too;

- ditto with operational staff;
- and also with the board: in terms, for example, of investment and other resource allocation decisions.

So there are good reasons to think that a company will struggle with a mix of generic strategies: and a lot of these are tied up in terms of managing inconsistent mindsets and behaviours.

In reality the generic strategies are in any event an oversimplification. These are often relative, for the following reason: you can have a differentiated strategy relative to companies of a particularly low level of value added, but a cost leader compared with one at a much higher value level. This is possibly one reason why Porter's rule, 'you must choose', seems to fly in the face of everyday competitive facts.

Also, there may be ways of operating with a dual-positioning of one's strategy. An example might be to examine the strategic hypothesis that Tesco, the now global supermarket company, has a three-pronged strategy: firstly, to sell some premium products such as branded goods (and in higher proportions than some lower-priced competitors) and its own deluxe finest ranges (to address its higher-earning customers). Secondly, it is 'me too' in terms of the bulk of its sales – offering no special price advantage. Thirdly, it addresses the customer mindset of 'getting a cheap deal' by making some very good offers (on petrol discounts, two for one etc), alongside having a permanently low-priced value range.

My perception, purely as a customer myself, is that psychologically many customers will accept the parity of mainstream products as this can be offset by many perceived bargains each week, while at the same time offering the possibility (but not the necessity) of buying selected brands, or going up in quality if the inclination takes them. Thus Tesco creates a halo-like effect of 'value' which over-shines its mainstream products, possibly out of proportion to any actual saving.

Coming back again to the issue of whether one has to make a clear choice or not, let us examine a brief case study.

I once did some research into the links between HR strategy and corporate strategy in some financial services companies. One UK bank, owned by the Spanish giant Santander, had a strategy of hiring new graduates to provide more intellectually rigorous input to its people development. Yet its support services were designed to be 'cost leadership' and its pricing very competitive indeed. So service and resource levels were strained.

This all meant that whoever they were, and whatever their skills, bright young things could play only a very limited role and the graduate recruitment policy succeeded only in adding to costs. Also, they tended not to stay very long as the experience was very frustrating and disappointing. Thus there was no beneficial effect on performance and probably a negative effect.

So it looks as if a lot of the difficulty is down to that of corporate inflexibility. The argument could be raised, as indeed it is by Chan Kim and

Mauborgne (2005) in their 'blue ocean' strategy (see later), that with greater organizational flexibility these constraints can be overcome: I wish! The problem is that this is not a very easy thing to bring off. For example, many European companies have 'offshored' back-office functions and call centres to Mumbai, with variable success. Despite the very best efforts of Indian staff, who are invariably patient, polite, intelligent and helpful (different-iators), they lack the technical training, the local culture and, above all, the decent telephone lines to be able to offer a service without 'hygiene factors not met'.

If organizational flexibility is elusive, it may be possible to try to insulate a business unit so that it has a specific generic competitive positioning such that it has enough autonomy to be able to work unimpeded on its mission. There are many examples of this, such as in telecommunications (for example at O_2 Select, where I was a heavy user and had my own personal adviser), or in banking, where one can have similar differentiation. Or within a single business unit one can have separately focused teams targeting different customer segments with different generic strategies. But all this can increase costs through minimizing economies of scale, and present dilemmas of organizational structuring and rivalry, and confusion to customers. Frequently a different model is tried and doesn't work too well, and this then leads to frequent restructurings which dilute competitive advantage – through trying to have it too much all ways.

You guys – managers – know all too well about this problem, but academics hardly recognize these damaging and dynamic effects of organizational distraction and lost energy and momentum.

In some situations, the generic positioning of different business units can be made in an autonomous way locally, and actually work without problems between different units. But there can still be a confused mindset at board level, where there will almost certainly be a dominant style of strategy and mindset. This will confound appropriate strategic decisions and resource allocation, and generate considerable political heat. The above problem can become focused on cross-functional debate, for example when the FD tends to take a cost leadership route, and sales and marketing heads have a tendency to be attracted towards differentiation. Indeed, in any strategy audit/team-building event it isn't uncommon to find a board who have very different perceptions of not only which generic strategy they should be pursing, but which one they actually are!

Let's now take a pause and allow you some time to reflect on your generic strategies.

STRATEGIC EXERCISE 4.1 What is your generic strategy?
– 5 minutes

Using the generic strategy framework, and for a particular business unit, which you are pursuing, rate the following in terms of the extent to which it applies:

	Very strongly 5	Strongly 4	Average 3	Moderately 2	Very moderately 1
Differentiation – broad:					
Differentiation – focus:					
Cost leadership – broad:					
Cost leadership – focus:					

And why do you say that? What contradictions or tensions does that reveal? What are their consequences?

What are the consequences of any strategy being very mixed, for example in brand positioning, customer loyalty and retention, the sufficiency of internal cost breakthroughs, etc?

In conclusion, Porter has left us with some very useful ideas that have stood the test of time but with some demystification and further development to do (see our later section on Porter's five forces).

Rumelt et al

Rumelt was at the very heart of the resource-based theory of competitive advantage. He was able to demonstrate that the majority of the reasons why company performance seemed variable were not so much due to the different attractiveness of the different industry environments, but because of company-specific issues. So while Porter's five forces matter, they appear to matter less than the variation in levels of competitive advantage.

Others who have written much about this topic include Barney (2001) and Grant (1991). These authors all play on a mysterious and murky concept of 'asset heterogeneity', namely that within a particular market the players will have a different mix of resources to one another. This can be due to differences in the amount of particular resources, in their mix, their quality, and in their coordination and alignment. In economic terms, this property helps to explain how there can be very different levels of performance from different organizations working in the same competitive conditions and within a largely common industry mindset.

In terms of the word itself, I feel that the term 'heterogeneity' is rather unfortunate as it is so abstract. I can imagine well-grounded CEOs cringing if they ever heard that word used by their strategic planning director or any-one else! Why on earth don't people come up with concepts that really spell out, and in the simplest of terms, what an idea is really about? Why wasn't this labelled, for example, 'variability'? 'Heterogeneity' is a 13-letter word, of which there aren't too many in the English language. At least 'variability' is only 11 letters. Simplicity is important.

Let's now assume for a while that the idea that internal differences in companies are more important in determining their performance is true. There might be reasons for not getting carried away with that view; for example, there are particular industries where we can show that the stronger/medium-performing companies' levels of return most certainly are corre-lated with the structural nature of the industry. Examples here are funerals (see later), pharmaceuticals, fertility treatments, grocery retailers, car com-panies, satellite television etc. But what is there for the everyday manager to take away from RBT? Otherwise we might fail in our mission to demystify strategy in this area.

Barney and Hesterly (2002) came up with four main criteria for assessing resource-based advantage. These are used as important tests. In their frame-work of VRIO, the resource needs to be:

- Valuable;
- Rare;
- Inimitable; and
- Organizationally embedded;

or, as above, VRIO. (My third wife passes all the tests, my second ex only the third!)

After years of seeing many of my MBA students use this model, I think I have eventually got my head around that acronym – but it possibly isn't one of the best going.

To reframe this, let's see if the following is a potentially more direct and powerful one, which we now explain and expand on, and which we call the 'STRIPE' test (like a pregnancy test, as it were):

- Sufficiency;
- Transcendent;
- Rare;
- Important;
- Protectable;
- Evolutionary.

Sufficiency, here, means having sufficient quantity and quality of the resource to raise the level of competitive advantage on its own up a quantum shift. Transcendent means that it is exceptional, and well above the average. Rare means, essentially, scarce: there is not a lot of it around on the market. Important means that it is very significant relative to other sources of competitive advantage and has a big impact on value, cost, or both. Protectable means protectable against copying, or imitation, or poaching by the competition. Evolutionary means that it has dynamic possibilities and the potential to develop to an even higher level, thus creating dynamic competitive advantage.

Organizations often have the potential to pass the sufficiency test as above but don't quite get there. This is particularly the case in assessing sufficiency where it is important to be able to identify the most critical constraints that are inhibiting competitive advantage.

The advantages of this framework appear to be that:

- it is a lot more memorable and user-friendly;
- it is less academic but still grounded in economic thinking;
- it also has two additional variables: sufficient (in terms of its impact) and also evolutionary, building in the important idea of competitive advantage being a moving target: its dynamic characteristics.

Prior to the advent of RBT in 1991, this general idea was often encapsulated more simply in the idea of sustainable competitive advantage that we looked at in Chapter 1, ie that it is durable. Its sustainability hinges particularly on the aspects of its being rare, as there is not a lot of it around, it is protectable, and it is evolutionary so that attempts to reach it or acquire it will fail to catch up. Here we are capitalizing on the idea of 'time-based competitive advantage' (Stalk, 1990), defined as 'that competitive advantage which accrues solely through being either first or early to do something in the market or to be able to do things significantly faster than the competition'. Time-based competitive advantage is thus an early example of dynamic competitive strategy, which we will be going into in the next chapter.

Tesco and dynamic competitive advantage

Tesco, who we mentioned earlier, have now been experts in time-based competitive advantage for a decade and a half. When I was helping them some 15 years ago on their first, hesitating steps in creating a home-shopping strategy, during the workshop the issue came up as to what was the best name for the sub-brand. We arrived at the very simple but appealing name of 'Tesco Direct'. (Until that workshop, the strategy had been highly emergent.) Three weeks after that meeting, I was shopping in Tesco Bar Hill, Cambridge, and I saw a new sign saying 'Tesco Direct'!

The capacity to move very fast indeed at Tesco was at the time not widely shared by British grocery retailers. Sainsbury, the previous market leader, was in the past a very reactive player. After Tesco had overtaken and outpaced Sainsbury, a national newspaper commented: 'Tesco has one foot flat out on the accelerator but also one foot on Sainsbury's throat.'

Probably at that time only ASDA seemed to have anything like that same drive. So without knocking Tesco's huge success in the UK, particularly from 1996 through to around the 2007/08 period, which was truly awesome, at least a small part of this success could be seen as due to the fact that they were playing against average or weaker teams.

But such time-based competitive advantages are hard to sustain forever. If we fast-forward into today's market, it seems very evident that in the UK supermarket environment as of 2012, ASDA, Sainsbury and even the Co-op have made major strides not just in product quality but particularly in service, as compared to Tesco. For me, every shopping mission is an attempt to pick up strategic data, and my shopping expeditions to all of these stores suggest that the earlier advantages that Tesco enjoyed in 1995 to 2005 in the UK have been partially reversed. Sustainability can never just be assumed.

Post-2008, Tesco initially shook off these effects in the UK throughout the economic slowdown as the consumer has been focusing on cheap prices, which Tesco does deliver on. But should a fuller recovery ever materialize, I can foresee a real 'service quality gap' kicking in and affecting its sales. This was written in 2011 – Tesco's profits warning came in January 2012. That wasn't a surprise based purely on shopping experiences there and elsewhere.

This very morning I was reminded of the dangers of potential erosion in the basis of strategic assets. I did a Google search of the concept 'strategic option grid' to see how many other people had adopted this and were taking it to market. (The strategic option grid is a tool that I developed 20 years ago (see Chapter 6) and has been rolled out in many corporations.) Lo and behold, I found listed a course on strategy which I used to run with IIR and, very prominently, tools such as the strategic option grid, AID and the difficulty-over-time curve as being major benefits of attending that course (see Chapter 7).

Clearly the new tutor has been given my handouts from my course and has copied them in. It is unlikely that they will have suitably attributed them to their true source and it couldn't be surprising that these have been marked 'copyright'. I have seen that happen before, as I have seen a 'C' on other consultants' handouts. I also wouldn't be surprised if they have read either my paper on 'Rejuvenating strategy – the strategic option grid' (Grundy, 2004) or similar material in *Be Your Own Strategy Consultant* (Grundy, 2002b), to enrich their delivery. When I was writing these documents I was mindful that it was quite possible for others to pick up at least some of the tacit advantage from these techniques.

At the time I felt that on balance there were more benefits in sharing more of this knowledge than there were in keeping it closer to my chest. Like most other strategy thinkers, I still feel I made the right choice as I doubt that this competitor would have evolved the process to the extent that I have: but that's an assumption. I still feel that that has been the right choice, particularly as clients like the fact that I am transparent and giving, and also to see that I am very much on the 'well-published' map. But the decision was, nevertheless, a dilemma at the time.

The general point here is that there isn't that much that really is sustainable or durable in markets which are very mobile and in which players are often getting more agile. Advances in the resource base are often quickly eroded and this pace of erosion has got noticeably quicker over the past 10–20 years. This is despite the fact that strategic thinking capability is often not that strong. Somehow, managers pick up environmental signals, often via noticing performance shortfalls, and initiate knee-jerk competitive reaction, and quickly.

The VRIO/STRIPE example above is a case in point. It didn't take very long to re-engineer some general economic concepts into a framework which seems to be a) more effective and b) more accessible. Yet VRIO has remained relatively frozen in time for 20 years. The strategic thinking market is itself a competitive market and is subject to the same laws and influences as any other. Perhaps the RBT theorists will be as displeased by this as I was to learn that my tools were being used – without reference – to deliver a product that I once delivered! That's life, though.

In terms of what the elusive and real sources of competitive advantage are, often these are to be found in the area of distinctive organizational capability. This highlights an important and big gap in much that passes for strategic planning: it doesn't often pay enough attention to the 'competitive software' – the tacit skills of an organization and its behavioural attitude and energy. Indeed, the need to spend time on that competitive software is very great and means that the element of 'human resource strategy' (or, as I prefer to call it, 'organizational strategy' – Grundy, 2003b) should play a prominent role – and not one that is simply a follow-on from the competitive strategy. The two of these should pay a dialectical role together.

So now let's take an example of a strategic asset of a well-known international company, Dell, to illustrate this more generally.

Dell – what it might do for an encore

Dell pioneered a low-cost model of PCs, particularly laptops, from the mid-1990s through to the early 2000s, establishing a very strong position in the market. It was able to make computers to order through clever distribution systems. Dell products were good, reliable and cheap.

By around 2010 a number of other players were trying to match the Dell model. As of 2012, Dell's key strategic asset, its low cost base, was by now:

- sufficient: far less so than in the past;
- transcendent: only to a degree;
- rare: not as rare now;
- important: still playing a role;
- protectable: clearly not in the long term;
- evolutionary: may be the area Dell needs to work on.

Interestingly, I had not appreciated until doing that analysis just how marginal that strategic asset, at least from the outside, had become.

To develop the STRIPE model even more to test how durable competitive advantage is, you can use force field analysis to assess the enablers and constraints underlying each and every branch of this competitive advantage. This will help not only to test the strength of organizational alignment and resource sufficiency to deliver truly sustainable competitive advantage, but also to identify which are the most limiting constraints, and to do something about them. See Figure 4.2 to see the sort of shape that this looks like – with the positive and negative vectors being drawn to show the relative importance and effectiveness of these competitive enablers and constraints.

FIGURE 4.2   Force field model of competitive advantage

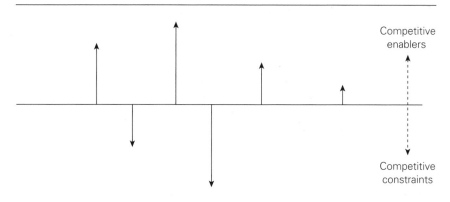

STRATEGIC EXERCISE 4.2 Assessing a strategic asset –
5 minutes

Identify a strong candidate for being a strategic asset in your business. What does the STRIPE test now tell you, perhaps scoring it this time as:

	Very strong indeed 5	Very strong 4	Strong 3	Moderate 2	Low 1
Sufficiency:					
Transcendent:					
Rare:					
Important:					
Protectable:					
Evolutionary:					

What does this tell you about the contribution of this strategic asset to your distinctive competitive advantage? What are the underlying sources of these resource-based advantages? Where are there obvious gaps that can be filled to make this an even more awesome edge? What are the key constraints that are holding each one of these back? What are your key insights – the 'so what's?' – from this thinking?

Kim Warren's work (2008) is also of interest here as it emphasizes the systemic nature of the way that resources turn into economic value. In that book, Warren breaks down the resource-based drivers of performance using systems diagrams – rather like my value and cost driver pictures (see Figures 3.7 and 3.8 earlier in this book), and also the business value system (Grundy, 1998b). He does this skilfully for Ryanair, the discount carrier, and relates this well to RBT through analysing the resource flows through the business – especially those to meet assumed growth. This and my own work suggest plenty of potential in the way of insights through mapping and modelling into how different bundles of resources can suggest better strategies.

Blue ocean gurus – Chan Kim and Mauborgne

About 10 years after the wave of RBT ideas on exploiting competitive advantage came a new force, 'blue ocean strategy' (Chan Kim and Mauborgne, 2005). Blue ocean was a very clever and appealing mix of ideas which were extremely well packaged. Like an evangelical church, the purveyors of its core beliefs set about positioning it as a golden way to solve all the main problems of strategy that was self-contained and based on some very important premises:

- Most competitive strategies are incremental responses to medium-term changes in the competitive environment and will not result in sustainable superior performance on their own.
- Significantly more profitable strategies come from bolder and more imaginative strategic moves.
- These typically exploit not existing, but new competitive space.
- The rewards in that space (the uncrowded 'blue ocean') are naturally much higher than space in more mature and competitively saturated markets ('red oceans').
- In addition, it is then possible to compete for customer value through a flexible mix of differentiation and cost leadership strategies through a special 'value proposition'.

Before we get into dissecting this, I would like to give some comments on my first impressions of this 'new theory'. I had heard about the book at the business school (not Henley then) via my then boss, an economist (who I think saw me very much as a resource, and that if it wasn't 'inimitable' it might be substituted), at coffee where academics were inclined to spend a lot of time strategizing. He was extolling the virtues of the 'blue ocean' market idea. My mind began to drift – I began to imagine an old film that I had seen featuring Nicole Kidman when she was even more attractive, and where she and her boyfriend get kidnapped on a yacht in the middle of the Pacific Ocean, becalmed, surrounded by a vast ocean and nowhere to escape from the psychotic who had captured them. I thought, as my boss was going on and on, that being alone in the blue ocean could actually be quite scary!

My interest had been sparked, however. So when I was next in the bookshop I thought I would have a very quick skim-read of the book. Now I mark an average of three million words of MBA/MSc scripts and projects per year, so I am an extremely quick reader. After five minutes I had read the book and decided that other than the simple notion of 'uncontested space' there seemed to be nothing actually new about it. It did seem somewhat a little like the case of the 'emperor's new clothes'.

But it *was* very well packaged, and that's what would sell the process. Besides the book, and the Harvard Business School articles too, there is a website and even a video with a presentation on YouTube. The book was the joint product of a strategy consultant and an academic, which is an interesting combination bringing together different skills and mindsets – a 'unique set of resources' but one which is in danger of suffering from not being sure whether it is a prescriptive framework or a theory grounded in robust, evidence-based research. Wikipedia gives a good critique. (By the way, Wikipedia is excellent on strategy – oh dear, I just told you a substitute, but I have to be honest – so do dip into this for further research or study.)

So let's now break down the ingredients of the blue ocean theory. In each case we tell you what proposition it makes and then comment on these individually:

- Most competitive strategies are incremental: yes, but we saw that in our critique of logical incrementalism earlier; that's why we need more imaginative strategies that create the future and are cunning, so we have seen that before.

- More profitable strategies come from bolder and more imaginative strategic moves: yes, they should indeed come from 'breakthrough thinking' (Grundy, 1995) – a pre-existing idea.

- These typically exploit not existing, but new competitive space: they should be about 'competing for the future' (Hamel and Prahalad, 1994) – a previous idea.

- The rewards in that uncrowded space are naturally much higher: we would expect that to be the case because these will be less 'perfect' markets and they will have different 'industry mindsets', thus creating cognitive and emotional barriers to entry/substitution; that is clear from existing microeconomic and related theory.

- Differentiation and cost leadership strategies can be mixed together: they are not alone in critiquing these strategies of Michael Porter (1980), as have many others, but to say that you can mix both styles of strategy together doesn't really help much in achieving sustainable competitive advantage – see our previous discussions on this.

So while blue ocean is a useful collection of pointers, we may be better off picking from previous theories and perspectives. Also, there may well be a danger in overemphasizing new competitive space. We have examined the point about differentiation versus cost leadership strategies already in the discussion of Michael Porter and we concluded from this that mixing strategies is a very real challenge for anything other than the most agile of companies.

Two other clever things that these two gurus did were a) to build the models on what appeared to be robust academic research and b) subsume frameworks from other management schools without totally transparent attribution (a number of other strategy models seem to suffer from that). In terms of a), however, they claimed that the findings on performance were based on 150 case studies of bold strategic moves over a very long period of time, although the interpretations of the findings have been challenged – see Wikipedia.

The idea was no doubt to give any lay reader the idea that the evidence was overwhelming. But unless the researchers were open to data that might falsify their hypotheses, which it is not clear they were – for instance, they lacked any control group, they could so easily have selected the cases out of a large population to be ones that were a) major and radical strategic moves and b) ones which were clearly very successful performance-wise. Also, as has been pointed out (eg in Wikipedia), the finer detail of the approach appears to be substantially drawn from pre-existing ideas from other management frameworks, for example Six Sigma, suitably renamed.

Another problem is that if we are talking here about identifying a possible market through visualizing customer needs and potential value added/radical reductions in costs that could be supplied, rather than are being currently supplied, then such a radically different space will be hard to identify and may take some time to evolve into a market. Also, that market, unless it is being served by existing products in effectively a different and inferior way, will essentially lack price comparatives and thus possibly be harder to build up. As Porter pointed out (1980), it is often a facilitator to market growth to have different competitors there to offer customers a choice, based on different offerings where there are price differentials; in other words, there can be 'good competitors' as they facilitate benchmarking, which, if absent, can inhibit the buying process and thus demand.

A further issue is that uncontested space, once served, rapidly becomes contested. In the blue ocean the calm waters can conceal deadly sharks waiting to surface and take advantage of new food, so the analogy is deceptively comforting. We are back in the land of resource-based competitive advantage, which appears far more theoretical but is much more solidly grounded, but unfortunately shoots itself in the foot *vis-à-vis* blue ocean thinking by being hard to penetrate and more poorly packaged for ready consumption.

So we are left with the most powerful idea of the theory as being the simple metaphor of 'blue ocean' and 'red ocean'. These pre-existed in terms of the idea of an 'inherently highly attractive market' and that of an 'inherently less attractive market'. This is a very catchy idea but we shouldn't get carried away with that, just as the pigs and the humans in George Orwell's novel *Animal Farm* did when first they were saying 'Two legs good, four legs bad' and then changed it to 'Four legs good, two legs bad'.

While some of the examples of extremely successful strategies were also examples of original blue ocean strategies, such as Facebook and Google, others were to be found in more mixed waters. So Apple's innovations are step-out but rapidly fall back to redder ocean conditions, and Amazon is competing with the red ocean retail market. So there is more to it than finding uncontested space. As Warren suggests (2008), these first movers need to have established both a more dominant position and a cumulative dynamic so that it would take a new entrant or imitator a long time to catch up.

Maybe a refinement is necessary here: perhaps it is useful to posit a 'green ocean' too: one in which there are existing competitive markets, but ones which lend themselves to new competitive behaviours.

There could also be a 'brown ocean' where there is a mature and well-served market and competitors still manage to make a living – albeit a more modest one – and where this positive performance is very much due to its being relatively cosy, so a more aggressive strategy based on existing styles of competition might secure a real edge. An example of this is the cafés and takeaway snacks market in the UK where McDonald's and Subway are able to make strides in their markets through simple aggression as opposed to any more radical innovation, threatening to turn it more red – or brown with a reddish tinge.

There might also be a 'black ocean' where there is a high level of perfect competition and the industry environment is generally closing in – the effect of the economy, new regulation, late-stage maturity etc, and possibly where there are very high exit barriers. (The volume car industry springs to mind here.) In a black ocean the natural instinct is to exit – unless one has unique and powerful competitive advantages.

So we now have a quite neat continuum of:

- blue ocean;
- green ocean;
- brown ocean;
- red ocean;
- black ocean.

We can use these as a catalyst to our strategic thinking as they encourage us to helicopter back from the industry.

Ultimately it seems to be down to a choice of language here: do we prefer the idea of strategic breakthroughs (Grundy, 1995, 2002b) or cunning plans (Grundy, 2002b) or value innovation to Chan Kim and Mauborgne's bold strategic moves (2005). Or we might choose between future competitive space (Hamel and Prahalad, 1994), uncontested market and blue ocean.

STRATEGIC EXERCISE 4.3 Identifying and exploiting uncontested market opportunities – 10–15 minutes

For a particular business area: thinking about latent customer/market unmet need and potential for value innovation:

- What are the most promising lines of enquiry, looking at it as if you were an alien entering this market for the first time?
- How attractive are these?

- Can a strong competitive position be built?

- Are you well placed to occupy that space with the strategic assets that you have/ would this positioning and set of strategic assets be easy or hard to copy?

- If you did do this, how would or could this fit with the structure?

Porter's five forces

The alternative structures of the Porter model

In this section we now go a lot deeper into Porter's five forces so that the reader can become fully competent in it, rather than superficially. Those totally new to Porter's forces should definitely read this twice. Others will still have to read carefully and digest, because there will be new and interesting things I have to say about it. These things come from using it and seeing it used for 25 years and from experience of it in probably 100 industries.

We have already described Porter's five forces as being:

- buyer power;
- competitive rivalry;
- entry barriers;
- substitutes;
- supplier power.

Figure 4.1 earlier in the chapter shows the traditional picture of Porter's five forces.

This shows competitive rivalry at the centre of the five forces picture, with arrows going into it from the other four forces. This signifies that where any of the other four forces puts pressure on margins, this will tend to increase competitive rivalry and thus squeeze profits. This is a good point, but this representation underplays the fact that all five forces are interdependent and will have an influence on each other. Indeed, the five forces can be redrawn with other forces at the centre to identify these other potentially significant influences too (Grundy, 2006).

One of the alternative pictures showing 'Substitutes' at the centre is shown in Figure 4.3.

For example, entry barriers can lead to customers actively encouraging new entrants or the expansion of lower-priced competitors to increase competitive rivalry. Entrants may try to get round entry barriers by encouraging substitutes. For example, witness my own successful attempts to overcome the high entry barriers into strategy consulting by offering strategy training and coaching and by handing over the process to help clients to 'do it themselves' (as encouraged by my book *Be Your Own Strategy Consultant* – Grundy, 2002b).

FIGURE 4.3   Porter's five forces re-engineered

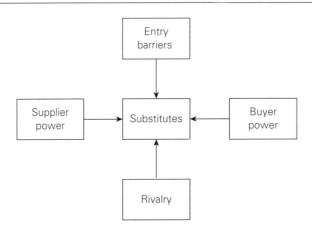

In many industries the existence of high entry barriers is the key to its superior attractiveness – this is a strategic clue: how can entry barriers be raised?

Porter's micro-level forces

Each of the five forces can be subjected to a 'deep dive', entailing breaking them down to their more micro-level drivers. These might include, for example in the case of the bargaining power of buyers:

- emotional value;
- importance within their value systems;
- degree of discretion;
- information about the players and their value delivery.

For example, a) where customers see this as adding a lot of emotional value, and b) this is in areas that are also very important to adding value in their business, and c) which are non-discretionary as to whether and how to make the purchase, and d) there isn't very good information about the players eg value and pricing, then bargaining power of buyers will be low. For example, the funerals market (except the pre-need market) generally exhibits very low bargaining power for all of these reasons.

For the particularly eager reader I also list the other micro forces that I came up with, namely:

- Entry barriers:
  - information (about the market);
  - psychological (attractiveness);
  - economic;
  - physical.

- Rivalry:
  - commitment;
  - mindset;
  - number;
  - similarity.
- Supplier power:
  - resource scarcity;
  - unique knowledge;
  - forward integration;
  - size and number.

Each of the five forces might therefore warrant a more detailed and more structured investigation or, at minimum, holding these in your mind when assessing the various forces. This we call 'deep-dive' analysis – as it involves digging a level down, as we will also see for the strategic option grid in Chapter 6 and in some of the implementation tools in Chapter 7.

Others have hinted that there is more to Porter's five forces at a surface level – for instance, Warren (2008) draws interesting pictures of systems that determine rivalry according to three types of pattern. These effectively map out the sub-forces for rivalry, although that was not what Warren was seemingly trying to do.

Other variables in Porter's five forces

In addition, there are a number of other cuts of the analysis that can also be done here, and which we now cover:

- The five forces and their drivers will change over the life cycle: we may need to do a separate analysis for past, present and future.
- They may change over the lifetime of a customer relationship or over a transaction cycle.
- They may vary over different markets and products and even geographic segments, or even by different customers and different distribution channels.
- They may have a variable impact on individual players: this may be relatively low, medium or high.
- They may vary over the life cycle of the economy.

These bring Porter's five forces far more to life – and lift us into the realms of strategic thinking.

Indeed, these can be represented as a curve of 'competitive pressure' (which it is felt is a more user-friendly term than talking about 'competitive forces'). These are likely to change over time (see Figure 4.4), either for a market as a whole or for a particular customer relationship on its own. This

FIGURE 4.4   Dynamics of competitive-pressure-over-time figure

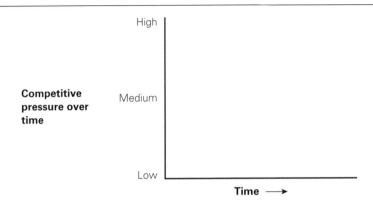

can be done for the aggregation of all five forces or just one: for example, buyer power over time, or entry barriers over time.

We now pick up these points individually.

Changes over life cycle

Generally these will become less and less attractive – without value innovation – as a market matures. Thus the average level of return will tend to decline over time and in an equilibrium state these returns will tend to converge to the average cost of capital. (Where there are high exit barriers – which Porter subsumes under 'entry barriers' – these returns can even fall below the average cost of capital.)

Changes over customer relationship or transaction cycle lifetime

Here bargaining power will generally start medium to high and may then decline as switching costs build up. For example, a consulting relationship which started through a competitive tender will typically have high buyer power, but this may weaken as loyalty is built up and personal relationships grow and as the project moves into phases of higher and higher commitment levels.

Another everyday example is having a meal out. Bargaining power is high when you are window shopping but decreases as soon as you enter a restaurant, as you start to go to sit down or are seated by a waiter (worse), or as time elapses after you have sat down, and particularly after you have placed the order. It is very hard to just suddenly get up and go after that point, just because the service is slow or you have had second thoughts – for example, it is getting too hot or cold, too noisy, there seems to be a very long time to wait etc. But on a number of occasions that is what I have actually done! To achieve that, one has to have great clarity about one's strategy, and to have some way of positioning it which is mannerly: difficult, but not impossible. On one occasion I had the waiter chasing me out of an Indian restaurant to pay the bill when I hadn't eaten and had never even got to place an order for the meal!

Where the purchase is a particularly emotional one, and it is one where bargaining power declines over the time of the transaction, it gets even worse. For instance, I was planning to propose to my partner in the restaurant next to the Airport Hotel, Croydon (yes, Croydon does have an airport): we had had our first real date there so it seemed very romantic – which turned out to be a mistake.

It was empty except for ourselves (which should have forewarned me!), but after the first course, when I was building up to the big question, a guitarist suddenly leapt out from nowhere and began practising. That wasn't too bad in itself, but then he began to use some Karaoke background music to compete with in banging out some rock songs from the 1960s. He also turned his amp up and became more and more enthusiastic. Somehow it seemed to be an unromantic act to ask him to turn it down or to go away, even though we were 100 per cent of the audience at that point. Our bargaining power in terms of getting the value we wanted out of the experience was minimal as I would have soured the occasion if I had brought this to the attention of the restaurant – and made it harder to be romantic.

So I had to wait until we got into the Airport Hotel next door and brave their loud check-in question, 'You have got the £50 deposit for the £90 room?', in front of my would-be fiancée, before I could think of popping the question – the one big thing I forgot.

Both of these experiences are also classic examples of customer value destruction – which we will come back to in Chapter 5 in relation to 'hygiene factors not met'.

Have you, the reader, observed any similar experiences – where you have felt inhibited from taking your normal buying power as a result of emotional issues, such as buying insurance, for example? I would be very surprised if you hadn't.

Variation in the five forces over products and markets

Here it may be useful to rate each of the five forces over a) different market segments and b) different products as:

- very attractive: score 3;

- moderately attractive: score 2;

- low attractiveness: score 1.

This could be drawn as a matrix of the forces against a) these segments and b) these products. This may well highlight significant variation.

Thus it can be potentially misleading to suggest that an industry has a certain level of homogeneous 'market attractiveness' where there are marked variations in the 'competitive landscape' – a fruitful concept.

Another possibility is to analyse the exposure of individual players to the five forces, including yourselves. Here we can develop another matrix which plots the competitive forces vertically, and each of the different players in the columns horizontally, at the top. Indeed, during many managers' early attempts to rate Porter's five forces they will often default to analysing their own business rather than the market as a whole, which isn't the normal convention. That isn't actually a totally wrong thing to do, as it is informative about exposure to competitive conditions, but one does have to bear in mind that this doesn't actually describe the entire market. (For instance, in such a more specifically based five forces analysis a particular company might have a positioning and edge in that market that may mitigate high bargaining power, so that the latter matters less.)

Variation over the life cycle of the economy

The life cycle of the economy is a very important additional variable that will shape the five forces. For instance, in an economic slowdown we will typically see:

- big increases in the exercise of latent buyer power;
- more influence of cheaper substitutes;
- increased competitive rivalry as competitors compete to maintain sales for a greater share of the cake;
- potentially, exits of competitors happening, reducing competitive rivalry, or mergers.

The impact of these shifts is typically felt through price resistance, price reduction generally and specific discounting, competitors offering more for the same price, increased costs of sale, increased difficulty of implementing to new and more challenging standards, etc.

So the lesson from all of this is that Porter's five forces need to be applied in a sensitive and quite sophisticated way, and also that they can't be looked at in isolation.

STRATEGIC EXERCISE 4.4 Analysing Porter's five forces across your business – 10 minutes

---

For some chosen products/markets, how attractive are Porter's five forces, rated as 3 ticks, highly attractive; 2 ticks, moderately attractive; 1 tick, lower attractiveness:

	Product/market 1	Product/market 2	Product/market 3
Buyer power:			
Entry barriers:			

	Product/market 1	Product/market 2	Product/market 3
Competitive rivalry:			
Substitutes:			
Supplier power:			
Overall score:			

Some key questions to consider here are:

- For each of these markets, which is the most important force, and why?
- For each of these business areas, what are the CSFs for the players as a whole?
- How well does your own company stack up on these?
- What options does this suggest for strengthening your resilience?

For example, in the context of the last question, you might consider, in a situation of intensified buyer power and increased rivalry, the possibility, for example, of:

- enhancing the brand or product or service innovation to differentiate and to build switching barriers;
- some breakthrough cost reductions;
- carefully targeted price reductions;
- creating a lower-value budget sub-brand, as Tesco did with its 'Value' products.

So the idea that Porter's five forces analysis is just used for the industry environment isn't valid – it should also be used to develop strategic options too, and thus takes us from strategic analysis into strategic thinking.

A final point is that Porter's five forces seem to assume that markets are essentially combative, but just as in war there are more cooperative situations that exist – such as alliances. That is a fair point, and some have suggested that 'collaboration' should be seen as an extension of the five forces. However, there are arguments for not adding it as an extra force, because:

- Porter's five forces analysis models the influences on the general level of margin in an industry, whereas collaboration has a much more company-specific effect.
- The result would be a more complex, and mixed, model that could be confusing.

To give you a fuller and practical grounding in the competitive forces, let us take a look at a classic case study of the funerals business. This was popularized in the US black comedy series *Six Feet Under*. This featured a somewhat dysfunctional (if not slightly deranged) family funeral company run by the Fishers. This family don't seem to be particularly good at running their business but as they get a steady stream of people suffering usually untimely deaths (always the start to the programme), they still manage to have a very good living. Porter's five forces, as we will see, give funeral directors a protective umbrella of very benign competitive conditions that leave incumbents with generally very good returns.

Case study of Porter's five forces in the funerals industry

The lessons of this longer case on the funerals industry are many and include:

- The funerals industry is a very imperfect market, principally due to the normally very low bargaining power of the buyers.
- This is due to the fact that it is a very emotional time, when buyers are distressed and time poor and might be nervous about buying on price because there is embarrassment if things go wrong. Also, they are vulnerable to being sold extras.
- There are unusually large psychological entry barriers as well.
- The economic attractiveness of the industry might nevertheless attract new entrants in.
- Because existing suppliers are relatively traditional, there is likely to be a lot of latent, uncontested space.
- The internet and the pre-need market offer potentially interesting routes in both entering this market and making it generally less attractive to existing players.

So while the industry's competitive structure is still quite stable, especially because most of the incumbents are very traditional and gentlemanly, there is the potential for more challenge and instability. That is still very important, despite RBT. This industry is thus ripe for strategic thinking.

The case study illustrates really well how important it is to get a sense of the relative attractiveness of the competitive forces in an industry – to judge how profitable it is relative to others, among variation in competitive advantage. It is also helpful in terms of understanding how it has been changing and what changes and shifts could well happen in the future. This all has an impact on industry CSFs.

This analysis can also be helpful in identifying areas of low contested competitive space and this can stimulate ideas for novel strategic moves with perhaps a different, and fresher, 'industry mindset'.

So, looking at this market: first, buyers have relatively low bargaining power. When someone dies, sorting out the funeral and other arrangements is usually an urgent process. Death is what sociologists have described (rather clinically) as an 'unscheduled status passage'. Furthermore, the buyers are in the perhaps unusual position of paying for the burial indirectly – from the deceased's estate. While it will not be their own money that they are using, it will reduce the share they get from the estate.

The buyer(s) (the deceased's relatives) may also be emotionally affected by the death. The buyer is therefore far less likely to be in a state of mind conducive to driving a hard bargain, to shopping around or going for a lowest-cost burial. This might look conspicuous in front of other relatives. In short, this situation of lower buyer power is of clear advantage to players in the undertaking industry and this force *is very favourable indeed*.

As Jessica Mitford (a critic of the funeral industry for many years) explained on the UK's Channel 4:

> The funeral transaction is unlike any other. If you buy a car or a house you discuss it with everybody, you shop around, and you consult. But if you have got a dead body in your living room then this puts a different complexion on things. You are likely to call the first undertaker who comes to mind.
>
> Once he comes in there and gets the body, that's the end of it as far as he is concerned. In other words, you are very unlikely to insist on someone else after that.
>
> The nature of the transaction is that you are probably in a fog of misery. You are not quite in your right mind and very susceptible in fact to all that the undertaker has to tell you; after all, he is the expert.
>
> This is compounded by the fact that when there is a death in the family then there is a lot of guilt feeling around – 'Oh dear, I wish I had been nicer when he was alive' – that kind of thing. And guilt feelings are very much what the undertaker counts on in selling his merchandise.
>
> The fact is that people can be easily talked into something they don't need and cannot afford.

The very low bargaining position of the buyers in a funeral purchase is a constant theme of *Six Feet Under*. The theme of the series is that of black humour. Every episode starts with someone dying – often in very unfortunate and unexpected circumstances. At some point in the episode the next of kin has to buy the funeral, which the Fishers play emotionally, usually to perfection – typically up-selling the relatives into a superior coffin.

Sometimes they are willing victims and, racked by grief and guilt, can't buy enough. In one episode a biker dies from a heart attack and what seems like a hundred friends take over the Fisher home in a massive wake party – they get well paid for the inconvenience. In sum, funerals are an interesting market, very limited in terms of the effectiveness of real competition, but in what we will describe as the 'strategic landscape' there are variations, as in the following episode with Rico and Mr Fisher, funeral directors, and their two clients. A young budding film star overdosed and she is being buried by her two closest friends:

Rico: 'This is my sister in law, Angie.'

Angie: '... Ann Henneka. And this is Berdie Farrell.'

Mr Fisher: 'Are you her next of kin?'

Berdie: 'She was kind of my girlfriend. Her mother died and she was raised by her grandmother who also died.'

Mr Fisher: 'Well, we'll need someone... (to pay for it).'

Angie: 'The cost of the funeral – we're all pitching in... Berdie can do that.'

Mr Fisher: 'Now, do you know what kind of funeral you want?'

Angie: 'Cheap.'

Rico 'Well, we provide a variety of options for the more budget conscious.' [Mr Fisher's mobile rings and he takes the call, which is about a date.]

Rico (very firmly): 'Take it. I can handle it.' [Mr Fisher goes off.]

Rico: 'Well, we could start with the American Eagle casket.'

Berdie: 'I don't think we should bury her – she was always totally terrified of the dark.'

Rico 'We can still have a viewing, in which the casket will never be closed.'

Berdie: 'That's good. And we can scatter her ashes some place she really liked – like Griffith Park, or the Lava Lounge on Le Brand.'

Angie: 'I think that we should just skip the casket.' [Silence as Rico looks very unhappy....]

So in this scene we see the funeral directors working with the emotions of their clients and trying to take them through a structured buying process and yet in a supportive, relaxed way, trying to optimize the value and trying to manage the bargaining power of the buyers – and in this rather spoof case (would that ever happen?), failing.

Second, substitutes to a conventional burial in modern society have not really existed – at least in the UK (except of course the substitutes of going for cemetery versus crematorium options). The do-it-yourself burial is not socially acceptable. Substitutes are therefore relatively unimportant – currently. (In a number of other industries this is also the case, but when using the five forces tool managers spend a lot of time trying to brainstorm substitutes. However, there is a caveat here in that in certain industries, potentially important substitutes can be easily glossed over because managers haven't thought about the industry from the customers' perspective and also deeply enough about innovation possibilities.)

Illustrating the latter point, Jane Spottiswode (UK Channel 4), author of *Undertaken with Love*, recounted a do-it-yourself (DIY) experiment with her husband's body:

Well, the only real difficulty was getting a coffin, because I started with local undertakers and, shock, horror, they said: 'We only provide it as part of our full service.'

So then I tried the undertakers' suppliers, and the same thing happened. But then I found one, they thought it was a bit unusual. I got the coffin. It was chipboard and it was £36 plus VAT.

> Friends of mine had a Volvo, and they didn't want me to pick it up in
> my Mini – it wasn't quite the thing; we put it in the loft until my husband
> died because we knew there was no way he would live – he had lung
> cancer.
> When he died, after various tribulations we put him in the coffin and we
> took it and him to the crematorium. The funeral cost us just under £200 for
> everything.

Apparently (according to Channel 4) in the UK you can bury a body in the
back garden (and don't even need a coffin) – but you do need a death
certificate (but check the legalities first). You may also need to check that the
decomposing remains are unlikely to affect local water supplies. In the UK
there is now even a movement towards DIY funerals – 'The Natural Death
Centre'.

Interestingly, the issue of substitutes highlights that the five competitive
forces are not necessarily the same in each market – either by type of
customer or by geography. For example, on a visit to Egypt I had the dubious fortune to be staying with a family who had experienced a sudden
bereavement.

The owner of the village – a local Egyptian – came running in one night,
shaking. His father had died, and the big issue was how to get his body to
its destination within 24 hours. He seemed overwhelmed with a sense of
urgency (or, more technically, Tom Peters' 'A Bias for Action' [Peters and
Waterman, 1982]) and overwhelmed by grief (no doubt that would take
hold after the funeral).

His imperative was to organize the relatives, the entourage, the funeral,
the grieving – and all within hours (if not minutes). In Egypt, it would
appear, you did not have the option, you had to do it yourself. The fact that
this one force is different causes a whole set of different market dynamics
in Egypt.

Continuing our story, entrants (our third force) may not be attracted to
the funerals industry because of its traditionally gloomy image. On the
other hand, real entry barriers may not be so high, particularly where a
determined player enters by acquisition (as is now happening in the UK).
Acquisitions may therefore enable entry and thereby shift the entry barrier
indicator from being a *favourable* force to one which is *slightly less favourable*.

Howard Hodgson (a former UK undertaker – and now millionaire and
author of *How to Get Dead Rich*) reflects on how business was done in the
industry 20 years ago:

> It was very much a cottage industry. It was very much, other than the Co-op,
> family, small. We needed to buy these (businesses) locally in order for us to
> have a strategy which went from strength to strength. In fact, by 1990 we had
> established 546 outlets in the United Kingdom and were the largest funeral
> directors in the country.

This entry/acquisition strategy yielded some very tangible economies of
scale for Howard Hodgson's business. He continues:

There were considerable economies of scale. The average family firm of funeral directors had to have a hearse, probably two limousines, and conduct five or six funerals a week. The capital equipment was used once a day. By acquiring firms in the area and rationalizing, we were able to get one of these limousines to go out five or six times a day each.

Besides Howard Hodgson, a major entrant is Service Corporation International (SCI) of the United States. Bill Heiligbrodt, president of SCI (a nearly $1 billion company worldwide), said on UK Channel 4:

We have found [in Australia]... that people have chosen to spend more on funerals. I would again emphasize the word chosen – it has been their choice.
  What we are here to do is to offer services and merchandise that make people feel better at a tough time in their lives.... So that fact that our revenues have grown [per funeral] in Australia is because the Australian public desired it.
In the UK that's our goal as well.

Apparently (according to Channel 4), funeral prices since SCI entered the Australian market have increased by 40 per cent. Even where pre-paid funerals are involved, this can apparently increase industry profitability as the supplier reaps the fruit of receiving pre-paid investment funds. Estimates by *The Sunday Times* as long ago as 1995 of the value of just 25 per cent of funerals being pre-paid were put at £5 billion. (It is likely to be much bigger now.) This obviously suggests both a major threat and opportunity for investment institutions such as insurance companies.

Howard Hodgson's strategy seemed to have been very much in the context of seeing this as a brown ocean – which could be exploited by greater aggression.

The pre-need market offers potential not merely for capturing value before death, but also for value added by pre-planning tailored funerals. Apparently in some cultures this has been the norm in the past. In China, for example, over 100 years ago all funerals were pre-planned, with individuals taking up to 20 years to refine the exotic details of their funeral plans (*Mail on Sunday*, 20 May 2001).

Fourth, suppliers may have some bargaining power (especially in restricting space for graves or even for cemetery plaques), but there appears nothing special in the supply of hardware such as coffins, hearses or the provision of flowers. (The one exception is perhaps the availability of land for burials.) This again is a *favourable* force.

Fifth, existing firms in the industry are currently relatively fragmented (few having significant market share, even locally against one another). Also, competitive behaviour is restrained, given the cultural norms of the industry. Thus we would rate competitive rivalry overall as *favourable*, but as relatively important. So if rivalry were to increase significantly, this would have a big impact on the industry.

So, taking the five forces as a whole (see Figure 4.5), it can be seen that the industry is currently relatively *favourable* in providing the conditions for players in that industry to make a good, longer-term profit. Here we use a vector analysis format to do two things in one:

FIGURE 4.5   Porter's five forces vectors for funerals

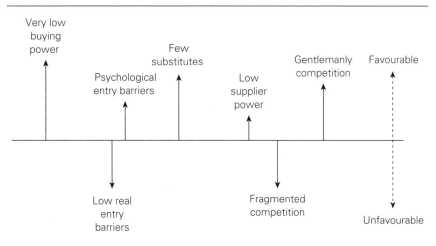

- to sort out whether a force is favourable (upward arrows) or unfavourable (downward arrows);
- to prioritize its importance.

This analysis suggests that:

- if already in the industry, longer-term profit should be good (unless entrants move in and restructure the industry or unless buyer power strengthens);
- if rated against other industries for identifying avenues for strategies for development, it might be considered to be an (inherently) attractive one to enter;
- CSFs such as building one's brand (to keep entrants out) and perhaps seeking a differentiation strategy can be readily identified, and also getting economies of scale (and thus sweating underutilized assets).

The relative attractiveness of the undertaking industry has not escaped the attention of new players. Even as long ago as 1994, changes were mooted in the industry in a feature on 'The new British way of death' appearing in *The Times* (20 November 1994). This feature contrasted the clinical and gloomy British approach to the death business with innovation in the industry in France.

Around 1990, Michael Leclerc (who was part of the Leclerc family famed for their French supermarket operation) opened his first 'Supermarché de Mort' in Paris. By 1994 he had 60 supermarket franchises, 200 smaller shops and one-third of the French funeral business. In 1995 he entered the UK.

Michel Leclerc's business concept was to 'apply the technology of the food supermarket to the funeral industry'. In place of black, the Roc Leclerc colour scheme is blue and yellow, and in place of dim bulbs and heavy velvet curtains are strip lighting and stripped pine shelving. All the paraphernalia of death is on display with a price tag. The main things they could offer, Mr Weller (the UK franchise manager) said, 'are choice, economy and no hidden extras. The business aims to charge between 20 and 30 per cent less than elsewhere but, above all, to offer the widest possible range, which our customers can view without the pressure of having a funeral director at their shoulder.'

Monsieur Michel Leclerc himself said on Channel 4: 'We will try to reduce prices by between 40 and 50 per cent, because to me prices in England are very high, and I think we will quickly expand. I don't see what can stop us.'

As Jane Spottiswode (the Channel 4 expert on DIY funerals) also said: 'Why don't Texas and MFI and all those firms that profess to be DIY experts stack flat-pack coffins; stick-it-together yourself. Again I was laughed to scorn. I received quite a nice letter from Sainsbury's who thought it was a good idea, but not for them.'

Unfortunately, Michael Leclerc's new business did not prosper in the UK, presumably because he overlooked certain PEST factors (especially the 'social' – the very traditional, British culture). Also, he may have entered at the wrong place – Catford, in south London – which was perhaps not the most trendy and innovative place in the UK. Probably this was one of several things of 'the one big thing that I forgot'.

A key lesson from this case is that you do not just have to have a good strategy – it has to be implemented at the right place, at the right time, and in the right way.

Coming back to the opportunities for expanding the very narrow, DIY substitute niche, one might be surprised to discover:

- In principle, if one were able to secure a cheap burial site one could achieve a 'lowest cost' grave for 'as little as' £300 (including a cardboard coffin for £49.50). To this you would need to add the funeral service itself – still coming in at the cheapest at £645. The lower-cost burial options have been exalted as 'environmentally friendly', saving the burning of hundreds of thousands of coffins each year.

- Alternatively, you might opt for a more conventional and, by comparison, up-market burial for over £4,000 (with an expensive oak coffin at around £2,000).

- Burial at sea is a novel proposition – this operation saves the graveyard or cemetery cost, but requires 'boat hire with precise navigation equipment' (presumably to avoid the coffin turning up by mistake on a public beach) – a minimum of £3,000.

- There are other ecologically friendly ways of disposing of the body, eg 'shake and vac' in Scandinavia where the body is freeze dried to near absolute zero, shaken rapidly and becomes dust, and any mercury in fillings drops out so that there are no poisonous fumes on cremation.

- Burial of ashes in space (maybe as a side business for Virgin Galactic, a vehicle for budget space flights)?
- Being converted into a diamond.

The idea of being converted into a diamond may not be so crazy but sensible. For example, in the comedy film *Due Date*, one of the anti-heroes is on a journey to bury the ashes of his father and keeps the ashes in a coffee jar. He and his travelling companion have to be rescued by an old friend who takes them back to his home and both of them sleep late that night. Unfortunately, they are still asleep when the friend wakes up. The friend fancies some coffee and he makes a cup from the jar. When the two anti-heroes wake up he mentions to them that the coffee was a bit 'weird', to the horror of the anti-hero who lost his father.

On a more serious note, each one of the above bullet point strategic options looks very much 'blue-ocean'-ish.

In addition to these innovations, there are many others that have been mooted over the years to cater for different segment needs, and to exploit new ways of doing things. For instance, there are possibilities of:

- exploiting the internet for expanding choices;
- reaching the pre-need market either directly or via insurance companies, insurance brokers or solicitors and will writers;
- using this to develop a distribution network that doesn't have to have an expensive and unnecessary retail high street presence;
- providing other services such as being able to set up e-mails to go out after your death! (see the site 'Life Without you.com').

What emerges therefore from our industry analysis is a cosy industry structure ripe for innovation and restructuring, offering better quality at a much more acceptable price. This is the classical uncontested space of blue ocean thinking.

For example, to go one better than the Leclerc business concept, one might even imagine the possibility of a telephone-based funeral service or 'Funerals Direct plc'. This concept might offer the advantages of speed, simplicity, openness (about price) and flexibility. To update this to the dotcom era, perhaps this could be entitled 'Directdeath.com'.

Another competitive force which might change in this industry is the bargaining power of customers. There is near local monopoly or oligopoly of undertakers. An assumption here is that bodies cannot really be moved around very far because of the twin problems of refrigeration and speed (why do funeral vehicles never seem to exceed 5 to 10 miles per hour? In Egypt the funeral cars seem to do a minimum of 60 miles an hour, such is the sense of real urgency). There appear to be no physical reasons, however,

FIGURE 4.6   Industry mindset

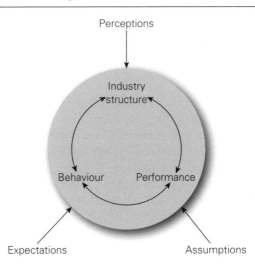

why bodies cannot be transported quicker (if colder) to a central location prior to collection for the actual funeral. Even cost would not be a major issue if one had a national network with high market share (supplementing the 'Directdeath.com' concept above). So there are real possibilities for innovation.

Finally we can use this rich case study to illustrate how there may be a need for a sixth force, the 'industry mindset' (Grundy, 2002b) (see Figure 4.6), which psychologically conditions many of the competitive dynamics that go alongside the five competitive forces. We define the industry mindset as being 'the shared perceptions, expectations, and assumptions about an industry that drive competitive behaviour and investment'.

Strategic thinking entails having to be able to detach from the current industry mindset and experiment with new and different ones.

This definition has three main ingredients:

- perceptions: about its relative profitability and CSFs;
- expectations: about where it might be headed in future;
- assumptions: about who the competition will be and what their relative strength will be, and also how they will be competing.

These are generally shared and thus influence behaviour across all players. In the case of funerals, these assumptions were, and still are:

- The industry will continue to be profitable.
- There will be slow innovation and minimal new entrants.
- It will continue in its present competitive shape, with a very small number of bigger players such as Dignity and the Co-op and a large number of very small, fragmented players.

- The rules of the game won't change much, with gentlemanly rivalry and low price competition, branding will play a minimal role and customers won't tend to shop around much.

The industry mindset here, if it does hold, will continue to maintain it as a cosy industry, but if this is challenged by a new player there is the potential for a shake, and a shake out.

The industry mindset also influences the more specific forces, for example through:

- buyer power: through conditioning the attitudes of buyers – for example that they should negotiate in a very tough way;
- entry barriers: by attracting new players or by actually building up psychological barriers to deter them;
- substitutes: by influencing buyers to either consider or not consider substitutes;
- competitive rivalry: through shaping the vigour and focus of rivalry;
- suppliers: by influencing their bargaining mentality and any integration down the value-added chain and closer to the customer as they expect there to be more profits from that market.

Further applications of the five forces model are to look at it from the perspective of the department, the project, or even at the individual level. At the project level it can be applied to, for example, the bargaining power of internal stakeholders, the competition from existing and new products or other ways of delivering the goals (substitutes), or the ease of acquiring resources from internal suppliers.

There are analogous issues that come out of using Porter's five forces at the project level, too. Here we see the forces as being:

- buyer power: of the project sponsor;
- entry barriers: the threat of new projects coming in and taking away resources and attention;
- substitutes: finding other ways (either internally or externally) of delivering the value that you do;
- competitive rivalry: between your project and other existing ones;
- supplier power: the extent to which internal suppliers are willing to give sufficient resources and support to you.

For instance, at the departmental level it can be used to look at the buyer power of internal customers, at other ways of doing this or new structures being set up to serve it. Also, there might be direct rivalry with existing departments, or internal suppliers who are hard to influence or control.

But perhaps one of the most interesting uses of Porter's five forces is in applying it to the individual executive. Here we can translate the forces into:

- buyer power: of your boss, his or her boss, and other key stakeholders that you add value to;
- entry barriers: to hiring someone else to do things similar to you;
- substitutes: finding other ways of delivering the value that you do;
- competitive rivalry: between you and your peers;
- supplier power: the extent to which suppliers to you internally can be difficult or keep you waiting.

That is a most interesting piece of work. Try that now.

STRATEGIC EXERCISE 4.5 Using Porter's five forces on your own role and position – 5–10 minutes

Given your organizational role, how would you characterize the internal Porter's five forces that impact on your situation?

	Favourable	Neutral	Unfavourable
Bargaining power of buyers:			
Entry barriers:			
Substitutes:			
Rivalry:			
Supplier power:			

Now apply similar thinking to that at the level of a specific strategic project.

STRATEGIC EXERCISE 4.6 Using Porter's five forces on a specific strategic project – 5–10 minutes

Given a specific project you have in mind, how would you characterize the internal Porter's five forces that impact on your situation?

	Favourable	Neutral	Unfavourable
Bargaining power of buyers:			
Entry barriers:			
Substitutes:			
Rivalry:			
Supplier power:			

In conclusion, I feel that we have repositioned a now long-standing tool of competitive strategy which was threatening to become more peripheral owing to the resource-based theory of competitive advantage. We have also shown that there can be a lot more in Porter's model than might be seen at first sight and that, in particular, it isn't just about managing what is there now, but thinking strategically about our options for dealing with it and changing it. There is a lot more that one can do with Porter's five forces than is often realized.

The industry mindset is an important and, I feel, missing element in the picture of strategy. It helps to illuminate the economic world of competitive forces by introducing a more dynamic factor – essentially cultural. That broader industry culture also conditions the cultures of specific organizations. The dynamic model of competitive pressure over time was also useful, as was the micro analysis of the sub-forces behind Porter's original set of five.

In final conclusion, we have covered some wide-ranging themes of economic analysis in this chapter and that has led to some rich insights – as we see below.

Key insights from the chapter – general

- Different industries and markets will have different degrees of inherent economic attractiveness.
- This is due to structural differences as exemplified by Porter's five forces.
- These are to do with: buyer power, entry barriers, substitutes, rivalry, supplier power.
- These forces change over time.
- They have a huge impact on prices, margins, profit and economic returns.

- Companies can use different strategic recipes or styles for competing: differentiation, cost leadership, broad versus focus strategies.
- What is behind this is that one really does need to make a clear strategic choice as to one's positioning: this also means choosing what we are *not* going to do.
- It is hard to mix these up without being a very agile company.
- A complementary theory of strategic performance is that of resource-based competitive advantage: here we focus on the strategic assets of a business – and where these can leverage us.
- These can lead to the evolution of new strategies: so we are competing 'inside-out', and these can be found in some less tangible skills that can be hard to copy.
- These thoughts mean that it is useful to test against: is that strategic asset valuable, rare, inimitable (or hard to copy), organizationally embedded (or VRIO)?
- Or is it as an asset: sufficient, transcendent (a cut above?), rare, important, protectable, evolutionary (ie offers dynamic potential) (or the STRIPE test)?
- Time (or speed – especially of implementation) can be a key source of competitive advantage.
- 'Blue ocean' strategies suggest that we should try to find uncontested competitive space.
- But this space can be rapidly discovered by others, so we need to do a rigorous test for sustainability, again bringing in Porter's forces and RBT, eg the 'STRIPE' test.

Key insights from the chapter – Porter's five forces in depth

- Porter's forces aren't fixed constraints: they offer opportunities for getting around them, for example in reducing and getting round entry barriers.
- Porter's forces are drawn with 'competitive rivalry' at the centre. But all five forces are actually interrelated and this invites a more sophisticated system.
- Each of the forces can be broken down to a more micro level: for example, for things such as emotional value etc for 'buyer power'.
- In many industries the existence of high entry barriers is the key to its superior attractiveness: this is a strategic clue – how can entry barriers be raised?

- Also, where there is potentially a lot of emotional value, this can suggest ways of achieving high customer value capture (higher prices/selling more products).

- There might even be 'blue ocean' possibilities beyond the existing patterns of competition to be explored – industry attractiveness is not necessarily a given.

- The forces will vary over the competitive terrain, or the strategic landscape of different products/market segments/geographies, and this all needs mapping.

- To talk about the attractiveness of an industry or market is thus potentially misleading. One can find attractive niches in almost any market: selectivity is key.

- Also, these forces will change over the industry life cycle, the economic life cycle, the transaction life cycle and the relationship life cycle: and this can be represented as 'curves of competitive pressure' over time.

- In addition to the five forces, there is a related force: the industry mindset, which is the shared perceptions, expectations and assumptions that shape competitive behaviour.

- Understanding the industry mindset can lead to spotting opportunities for identifying uncontested competitive space, and especially to identify where and what the sustainable options are.

In the next chapter we turn to look at more dynamic models of strategy than many of those that we have explored to date, which gives us a fresh perspective on strategy and makes even more use of the more fluid processes of strategic thinking than many of the tools that we have seen so far. This is because we have to time-travel a lot more in our imagination.

But before we end here, a thought struck me that by now some of my readers may be feeling that there are a lot of ideas, frameworks and perspectives to get one's head around, as indeed there are, just as there are many regions and aspects of life in France – that's in the nature of the beast. But that doesn't mean that one needs to be always talking about strategy in complex ways – not at all. Indeed, to the contrary, as once the models link up nicely in your thinking and become tacit, you need to refer to them only infrequently and unobtrusively – but they are always there.

Porter's Postscript in June 2012: I tried to hire a barrister for a family court case – a very emotional purchase. The quote was initially for '£3,000–£4,000' for just nine hours in court plus £1,250 for 'refreshers' (what were these?). 'Refreshers' subsequently turned out to be 'thinking time in the evening'. The total cost was £6,000 plus VAT. What do you think I did – represent myself!

Porter's five forces: witness the importance of emotional value in shaping them, and margins.

05 Dynamic competitive positioning

Introduction

In this chapter we take a look at the more dynamic competitive positioning. This should enable you to cope with the much more fluid strategies that are needed in today's competitive world. First of all we will take a quick look at what some of the gurus say about competing in a very dynamic competitive world, and then look at a variety of models that we can use to cope with that. We take a look at the example of Pfizer's drug Viagra in illustrating competitor profiling and how its profile can shift. We will then look at how role playing can be of help – for competitors.

Finally we use the Bikram yoga case to illustrate, and in an international context, how important it is to evolve one's competitive advantage as well as to track subtle but important shifts in the competitive environment. Even though Bikram yoga is phenomenally successful globally, there are still many promising ideas for its further development that come out of strategic thinking on it.

What the gurus say

In this section we will look at a number of useful sources of insight from the gurus:

- Kenichi Ohmae's the three C's;
- Hamel and Prahalad's future three C's, or competing for the future;
- more dynamic models, including my own and ones like those of Tovstiga, at Henley.

The original formulations of competitive advantage go back a long time to the 1980s. One wonders what words were used before then to describe this strategic position, other than 'strong', 'average' or 'weak'. The abstraction of market attractiveness from competitive position was being used at Harvard, but competitive strategy was in its infancy.

The three C's: customers, competitors, the company

Competitive position was still thought about in a relatively static way as well. Kenichi Ohmae (1982), in his classic little book *The Mind of the Strategist*, used the expression 'the three C's' of:

- customer value;
- company;
- competitor;

in the model that we see in Figure 5.1.

FIGURE 5.1   The three C's

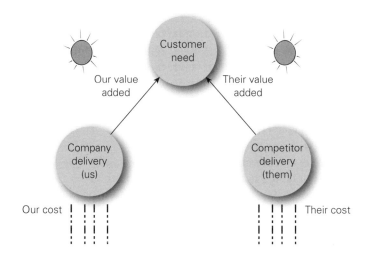

This pictures the company as adding real and perceived value to its target customers and striving to add more value to them relative to that added by competitors to them. Or the company is able to add similar value but at a lower cost. So here we are back to the dimensions of Porter's generic strategies once again. This is a nice little picture to remember, as it highlights that we can have a competitive advantage for some segments and not for others. Again, it is tough to be good at delivering superior value to everyone.

Also, the perception of value is a very subjective and variable one. One only has to look at the shape of contemporary cars, for example. I once hired a Ford Focus to drive 500 miles. I wasn't told this, but the model the garage had was some sort of stretched and huge version: a 'Ford Unfocused', I thought to myself.

I couldn't believe my eyes: I wanted something nippy and economical, and now I was faced with driving a small bus to Cornwall and back! And with all that mass it was heavier on petrol than my 3-litre Alfa Romeo sports car! But I had to keep thinking to myself that there were other people on the planet and they would have enjoyed such a roomy and flexible car, and even the boxy shape: it is all about conditioning.

So value is very contingent on whom you are targeting. It is also variable in terms of the context: for example, if I go to a café in Croydon for an English breakfast, I am not expecting deluxe settings and instantaneous service, so that expectations have a big role to play in this. But if I am paying £100 for a meal for two, I most certainly am – although I might be less likely to get it! So there are groupings of similar buying experiences that will be automatically compared with one another, while discounting experiences that aren't associated psychologically as being in the same *competitive space*.

Also, value assessments are conditioned by what people generally expect from the supplier. For example, I always expect estate agents to be driven by their own agendas and to be double agents – if you are selling your house they will spend as much time knocking your price down as finding a buyer and getting a better price, and you are paying them! Also, if you tell them you don't want something, for example 'on no account send me details of bungalows', you are certain to get them sent to you. But one expects that kind of behaviour from them, so it is not the end of the world.

You wouldn't complain to Ryanair, the discount airline, that they had long queues (unless you were me, of course – where they are obviously half an hour long I have shown them red cards to symbolize a disqualifying level of service, which you can buy from The Referees' Association, Coventry – you don't have to be an actual referee).

But where delivery, either in quantity or quality, falls well outside expectations, there is bound to be trouble. For example, at the time of writing we are moving house. An electricity company contacted us (tipped off by the estate agent that we were moving, a cunning plan), and they were trying to sell us electricity and gas. They then rang me in the middle of a meal and the price comparison was that they were 3 per cent more expensive than the current source of supply. So I asked them: 'Why should I pay 3 per cent more for that power? Is your electricity any more powerful or does the gas smell any sweeter?' They said: 'But you can always get through quickly to our call centre, and it is actually in the UK.' I opted to go with the existing and cheaper point of supply. But the problem was then that I had in my head the industry mindset that these things were commodities, so why pay more for the same – I was wrong.

So what might be a real turn-on sufficient for me to switch to this player, or if I am with them, to make it psychologically very difficult for me to switch (called the 'motivator factors' – Grundy, 2002b)? Also, what are the basic areas that need to be met well that would otherwise cause value destruction or the 'hygiene factors not met'?

Figure 5.2 represents that for a particular example – of a senior executive thinking of buying a BMW and who is concerned about the number of

FIGURE 5.2 Motivator-hygiene factor analysis

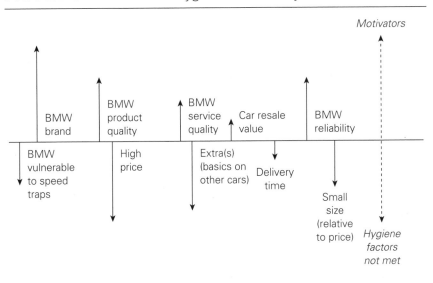

extras on the car (you typically have to pay more for a lot of things that get included on many other cars).

Going back to the case of the electricity company, it proved very difficult to get through to them to open an account. The internet wanted an account number already so I couldn't sign up online, and there was no address to post anything to on the website. The contact centre wasn't answering – there were interminable queues. So I decided that we would go with the company that rang me up – and pay the extra 3 per cent. They signed us up but told us that owing to the regulations we would have to wait four weeks to open an account.

Of course, the power was still connected to the house and was supplied by the existing supplier. We tried again to activate an account and the same frustrations occurred. I was able to e-mail them and got an answer that they would respond to my query in 10 working days!

The call centre had a message to say 'Oh dear, we are very sorry but the waiting time is long because we didn't hire enough staff – we are 600 people short'. I was perplexed: any new customer would have the same frustration and would not sign up with them: they were committing competitive suicide!

So while I started with the commodity-industry mindset as my basis for decision making, that all went out of the window. I now wanted service, and would happily pay 5 per cent more for a better service experience. Here my value context shifted as a result of the *value destruction* that they were causing.

Here we define value destruction (which I often call 'VD' – as you really want to avoid it!) as 'the inadvertent loss of value caused by inept service or by a product which is deficient in a fundamental way, or charging for something which really doesn't add value at all, and which could be free if value were delivered in a different way'.

An example of value destruction in the latter case was that of vacuum cleaners which, before the Dyson, came with bags that cost money and were inconvenient to obtain. Dyson's alternative machine operated with a cyclonic cylinder so you no longer had to have a bag. So Dyson's original competitive advantage was built on *avoiding value destruction*, as opposed to *adding incremental value*. Indeed, I have often said that at least in the UK, where service is generally poor anyway, you can achieve competitive advantage to some extent merely by avoiding the competitive disadvantage through value destruction that is characteristic of most of the players. This is an important message.

STRATEGIC EXERCISE 5.1 Customer value destruction – 5 minutes

Pick an everyday experience that you have had of customer value destruction:

- Did value get destroyed?
- How?
- Why?
- What were the consequences, eg for repeat buying?
- How could it have been avoided?

STRATEGIC EXERCISE 5.2 Diagnosing value destruction – 5 minutes

For an area where you suspect that there is some value destruction in your own business:

- What value might be being destroyed?
- How?
- Why?
- With what consequences?
- How could that be remedied?

In addition, customers will tend to associate a supplier with being a member of a particular 'strategic group'. We can define a strategic group as being 'a group of similar minded and configured suppliers, of similar size'. So the comparisons of customer value will tend to look at a supplier *vis-à-vis* other members of the strategic group that it seems to belong to.

Another element in the three C's which is often neglected is that of costs. Indeed, it should have been named the four C's as we would now have: customers, competitors, company and costs. Cost-based competitive advantage can be very important, and again there is a dynamic here. In conventional cost management we typically see there being a highly tactical process in which cost reductions are targeted in terms of relatively arbitrary and short-term, year-on-year, round percentage cost reductions. Here there is relatively little thinking about what the longer cost base should be, given changing competitive pressure, price points, and the downward shift in costs of competitors and new entrants. Yet all of these are important factors which require thoughtful and careful consideration.

Competitor profiling

One very good method of comparing oneself with the competitors or with new entrants is to use the competitor profiling technique (see Figure 5.3). This plots some of the key aspects of competitive advantage down the vertical axis and then rates these according to their strength or weakness *vis-à-vis* the competition generally. This can be done as zigzag curves which plot your company against each one of the key competitors – one at a time so that the picture doesn't get too complex or confusing.

FIGURE 5.3   Competitor profiling

	Very strong 5	Strong 4	Average 3	Weak 2	Very weak 1
Brand image					
Product performance					
Service quality					
Innovation drive					
Cost base					
Supporting systems*					
Support skills*					

* These are both within- and cross-function

The criteria listed are very generic and ideally are listed for your own company. These can be arrived at with help from the environmental analysis – particularly with Porter's five forces – and also some motivator-hygiene factor analysis. In terms of the definitions we have:

- brand reputation: the relative strength and appeal of the brand;
- product quality: perceived and real value for money;
- service quality: self-evident;
- innovation drive: both external and internal innovation – its effectiveness, speed, and typical value added;
- cost base: unit costs compared with competitors (not to be confused with price);
- supporting systems: IT and non-IT processes;
- supporting skills: general management, marketing, operations, IT, HR and finance.

This kind of analysis can really help to position the company in a more objective way than mere SWOT analysis. SWOT analysis typically takes place without doing really clear testing out of strengths and weaknesses: when you are comparing yourself with specific competitors it is much more difficult to miss or ignore competitive disadvantages.

Competitor profiling can be a major spur to identifying possible areas of strategic breakthrough, either by focusing on areas which are not only most critical but also where you are very strong, or where it is evident from the profiling that you are relatively weak.

STRATEGIC EXERCISE 5.3   Competitor profiling – 10–15 minutes

- Where are you likely to shift on the basis of current changes and current strategies?
- For one of the product/market areas that you are in, what is the competitive position of your company?
- For one of your key competitors, what is their position?
- Where are you likely to shift on the basis of current changes and your current strategies?
- Where are they likely to shift on the basis of current changes and their current strategies?
- To what extent are they a threat, or even an opportunity to attack?
- Generally, does this analysis suggest any areas where there might be strategic breakthroughs, either offensively or defensively?

As an example of a competitor analysis, let us take the pharmaceutical company Pfizer's business in the erectile dysfunction market. In the early 2000s Pfizer launched its blockbuster drug Viagra to a welcoming world. Originally developed as a circulatory drug, it was observed that it had interesting side effects in terms of erection capability. Many patients suffering from what Pfizer chose, cunningly, to name 'erectile dysfunction' could regain their libido in an impressive way. Viagra was thus at least in part an emergent strategy.

In launching this drug Pfizer was very good at cunning planning. There were many reinforcing aspects of its cunning plan – which created a very strong opening competitive position:

- The effects of the drug were dramatic and, for its users, life changing in terms of their ability to enjoy a normal sexual life to the full.
- The choice of the brand 'Viagra' was inspired – this became synonymous with that kind of treatment.
- Similarly its packaging as the innocent 'little blue pill'.
- Pfizer went out of its way to make it acceptable, by recruiting the services of Bill Dole, former vice president of the United States, who had needed to take the drug, to endorse it, as well as the famous World Cup footballer Pele.
- The company even went as far as getting the approval of the Catholic Church.
- To increase market scope, Pfizer was able to sell, perhaps unintentionally, to the recreational market.

Pfizer established a first-mover, initially dominant competitive position in a highly attractive market. This must have been extremely profitable for it. In relation to the competitor profile it was thus estimated as:

- brand: very strong – 5;
- product performance: very strong – 5;
- service performance: strong – 4;
- innovation drive: very strong – 5;
- cost base: at least strong (economies of scale) – 4;
- systems – probably the same – 4;
- supporting skills: assumed as strong – 4.

In short, an extremely strong position overall.

Viagra was protected by patent and also this market has very big entry barriers, so it looked very much 'blue ocean'. But by the latter part of the first decade Viagra was challenged by two very strong competitors, Cialis from Lily and Levitra from GSK/Bayer.

Taking Cialis as an example, this had one key and overwhelming advantage: it offered an effectiveness for up to 36 hours compared to Viagra's much more limited 5 hours. This offered more flexibility and more potential occasions to have sex per pill – so was cheaper. Where the drug was pre-scribed, this was a major advantage as it was obviously cheaper. Levitra is also effective for only around 5 hours but can be taken where people have higher blood pressure, and it works well with the elderly. It is also claimed that it has fewer side effects, which can be a problem with other drugs. Levitra was around before 2004 and was even then building substantial market share – so there was simultaneous development of competing prod-ucts in parallel with Viagra. By 2011 Cialis was catching up fast (Wikipedia) and by 2011 had overtaken Viagra (medical-specialists.co.uk, IMS data) according to US-collected statistics.

Viagra comes off patent in 2012, which will clearly be an encouragement for generic drugs – and that will affect all players.

So by now this is very much no longer a blue ocean and Pfizer's position in that market is far less secure. The scores that we saw above will have shifted product performance-wise from a 5 to a 3 or even a 2.5, and some edge might have been shaved off the brand strength; also, two other players have proved innovative, so we are now at a 4 or 3 there. All in all, this is a big adverse shift, which nicely illustrates the nature of dynamic competitive positioning.

In terms of anticipating the moves of competitors it may be a good idea to think of doing some competitor role playing. To do this you have to take an out-of-body experience of the possible intent of a competitor – which means seeing the world through their perspective. To begin, compile a one- or two-page competitor analysis listing:

- its overall strategy;
- its competitor profile;
- other data on resources and skills.

You then look at its possible intent. Insights here can be gained from:

- the 'optopus' (see Chapter 6) – in its strategic degrees of freedom;
- the strategic option grid – the attractiveness of its options;
- its stakeholder analysis – for particular options;
- its mindset and leadership.

In terms of data collection both for competitor analysis and generally, the internet is very powerful for obtaining rich insights. This should be used in very focused ways, for example to understand the financial performance and position of a particular competitor, to identify its strengths and weak-nesses and also to begin to imagine its intent, based on its degrees of think-ing (optopus) and the likely perceived attractiveness of any of its possible strategies (strategic option grid). Sometimes there are analysts' reports or other reports on industry trends, as well as commentary in the business and financial press. This can also reveal key top-level appointments, which may be suggestive.

In terms of doing competitor analysis generally, perhaps an important point is that many managers seem curiously reluctant to actually do this. One possible hypothesis is that this may be due to a reluctance to get customer feedback in order to get good data – that is probably valid.

So coming back to our original point, the idea that competitive advantage is easily measurable is not really valid. It is contingent on a variety of things, including mindset, expectations and the changing perceptions over time. In Chapter 7 we look at the 'value-over-time curve' and we see that it helps us to plot the dynamic of value creation as it changes. The more frequently we make a purchase, the quicker we will be to judge that changing value, and unless value is generally delivered with reliability we will quickly alter our buying decisions and be more cautious with our commitment levels. The same goes for where we have a history of buying such things, so that if something has been around for some time then our discernment levels will be higher. This type of behaviour is modelled by Warren (2008) too.

To really manage costs strategically we then need to search for the long-term strategic cost breakthroughs that will deliver such long-term competitive shifts. Where an industry is in maturity and searching for blue oceans isn't looking very plausible, costs may offer real potential for competitive advantage. There is nothing mucky about that if it is really the case. In that event, very similar breakthrough thinking is required, which elsewhere has been called 'strategic cost management' (Grundy, 1996; Grundy *et al*, 1998b).

Just briefly, the key tenets of strategic cost management are:

- Cost must never be managed in isolation: one must also look at value.
- Costs must always be managed to enhance and not undermine competitive advantage.
- You should always seek to deliver your strategic objectives at the lowest cost and not jeopardize them.
- Costs must be targeted long term, and require cost breakthroughs to arrive at targets.
- Competitors' costs, now and in the future, need to be thought about.
- As with broader-based strategic planning, the diagnosis phase is separate from the option creation and option evaluation stages.
- It is a multidisciplinary process.
- Many of the tools are the same as in strategic thinking generally, such as the strategic option grid and the cunning checklists (see Chapter 6).
- It commonly entails a big emphasis on stakeholder and change management.

So while it is useful to have a model of competitive advantage as per Kenichi Ohmae in one's head, there are dangers in ignoring both the psychological context and the dynamics and the life-cycle effects: these are important, too. We shouldn't operate with a very fixed and static model here.

The next main input is from Hamel and Prahalad (1994). They took Ohmae's (1982) simple three C's model and said that what we should really be doing is looking at it from a future perspective. So we should be considering:

- future customers;
- future value added;
- future competitors;
- future company competences;
- future costs;
- future competitive environment;
- and thus, future competitive advantage;

thus introducing more of a dynamic perspective.

This is a very simple but nevertheless a very powerful thought, as it emphasizes the creation of new competitive space and thus blue-ocean-type thinking. This naturally brings in our different curves of competitive advantage and competitive pressure over time. Thus, for example, if we take Dyson's bagless carpet cleaner, in the late 1990s Dyson should have been considering its future basis for competing after competitors had imitated the cyclonic technology (which began around 1998) and thinking about the future design and brand-based areas of hard-to-imitate customer value and a reduced cost base through offshoring its manufacturing to the Far East – which we saw it competing on only much later, towards 2010, some time afterwards. The Dyson product looked very much like blue ocean but self-evidently was fundamentally leaning towards red, or at least pink.

The sweet spot

The final ingredient that we will look at is the idea of the sweet spot (not to be confused with the 'G Spot'). This is an elaboration of the three C's. Here one identifies that strategic space where one addresses one's customer needs and value added far better than one's competitors, or better still where the competitors simply don't address those zones of value at all.

According to Wikipedia, a sweet spot has its origins in sport, particularly in golf, where the key thing is to hit a golf ball in absolutely the right spot: 'A sweet spot is a place, often numerical as opposed to physical, where a combination of factors results in a maximum response for a given amount of effort.'

I like the idea of the sweet spot a lot, because it is simple and conjures up a very precise picture in people's heads, so that if they are deluded that they have a sweet spot it is not too difficult to wean them off the idea. It is linked to both the three C's and motivator factor analysis.

For illustration, choosing one of the markets that I am in (strategic facilitation), the areas where I would claim to have a sweet spot are:

- Speed: I have processes that get to the result much, much faster than larger consultancies because I do not have to dump my time on the client as I don't need to sell big pieces of work to keep busy and earn a living.

- Processes: mine are eclectic and are part of a total system, and I am prepared to pass those and the knowledge on to my clients: larger consultancies generally won't want to do this in order to encourage a dependency.

- My processes are endorsed through publications and through having academic credibility.

- Positioning: I am quite happy not even to appear to be a consultant at all, as helped by academic connections I can distance myself from that strategic group. I can help clients to 'avoid strategy consultants' and the embarrassment of having to lean on outside help in that kind of capacity, so all I am creating is the unique competitive space of the sweet spot (Tovstiga, 2010).

But sweet spots decay over time. Even the sweet spot that I have claimed can shrink over time. This could occur because:

- The business model becomes frozen: one of my reasons for writing this book is that it gives me the reflective space to have new thoughts, to freshen up my publications, to capture the lessons of any previous accounts of the process, particularly over the past 10 years. Even the very best value delivery needs freshening up: virtually all forms of intellectual knowledge will decay in value over time, and it is hard to keep achieving that sense of freshness and vitality.

- Also, competitors will imitate it: for instance, I recently searched Google for strategy courses and found a supplier that worked with me offering virtually the same course with the same tools that I had developed and was passing these tools off as being those of the new presenter.

- There may be substitutes: although facilitation is hard and strategic facilitation is even harder, these skills are attractive ones to acquire and this is an attractive area for companies to develop themselves. So the number of opportunities for doing this may decline as companies will often try the DIY approach. Even if they often don't do it terribly well, the fact that they think they can do it, and do it well, can amplify this substitute activity.

- Owing to the variability of customer needs, it is superficial to make the general claim about a sweet spot. Some managers and some in-company clients do not want the complete set of strategic tools as they find it a challenge to be faced with quite a number of them.

So they offer a dumbed-down approach from people who are not as rigorous and as stretching, and sometimes actually prefer a simplified model, because they can hang on to that. So one must be very careful not to assume that just because some customers love what you do, this is representative and you have all that competitive space to yourself; through no fault of your own, that sweet spot is shrinking.

STRATEGIC EXERCISE 5.4 The sweet spot – 5–10 minutes

- Does your business have a sweet spot?

- Why and how does it exist?

- Is it changing over time, and why?

- What might be done to sustain it or refresh and extend it?

Coupling this kind of thinking with a more dynamic perspective, Tovstiga (2010) also looks at two other important variables:

- future market opportunity, as against
- future competitive advantage.

Tovstiga's thesis is that the attractiveness of a particular market opportunity declines over time – there is a dynamic profile implicit in there being a window of opportunity. And the company will take time to build its competitive advantage to address that particular opportunity. Ideally the attractiveness of the opportunity doesn't fade rapidly over time, and an astute player ought to build up its competitive edge quickly, so the time to realize the opportunity is short. It can therefore secure a time window of opportunity and a strong competitive position quickly. In this situation, speed is in itself an aspect of competitive advantage. This has been called 'time-based competitive advantage' (Stalk, 1991). This is a useful strand in thinking, not only because it is dynamic, but also it raises the significance of softer organizational competences. Warren's work also looks at the way that the resource base needs to move slightly ahead of ceiling constraints to facilitate growth, while minimizing the risks of over-capacity (Warren, 2008).

In terms of an example of a sweet spot, Facebook is an obvious one. Facebook was a key player in the expansion of social networking, which is itself a key environmental factor that is shaping how buyers behave (and their choices), and which companies need to think about, not to mention things like the smartphone which has many implications for the consumer market, particularly for retail.

Facebook worked backwards from customer need by enabling technology to create new social relationships and to shape existing ones. Being on Facebook – and things like the number of Facebook friends – became a status enabler, particularly with the young. The incredible speed of Facebook's expansion gave it a very powerful competitive dynamic that built entry barriers and barriers to imitation too. This was a truly blue ocean.

To summarize the key learnings from the gurus:

- The three C's model is a useful framework for thinking about competitive advantage.
- The hidden or fourth 'C' is often equally important: 'costs'.
- Comparisons of relative competitive advantage can be too simplistic and require deeper thinking about segmentation and the competitive context.
- It is often more important to think of how the three C's will be in the future.
- The three C's is too much of a static model.
- The sweet spot is a useful concept as long as one does not delude oneself over its size and zone of applicability.
- The sweet spot will decay over time and needs freshening up.
- More dynamic models, such are competitive-pressure-over-time and competitive-advantage-over-time curves and the time window and speed to realize an opportunity, are important in a dynamic context.

We will now seek to illustrate these ideas in the context of a very interesting, if unusual, case study on hot, or Bikram, yoga.

Bikram yoga case study

Bikram yoga is a very particular form of Hatha yoga that has a huge international appeal globally. Bikram yoga is practised especially in Anglo-Saxon countries, including the UK, the United States and Australia. Millions of people practise it each year. If Mr Bikram hadn't been there to invent it, it might have been called 'urban yoga'. But he did invent it so it is distinctive because of its very strong brand: there is definitely a very strong 'guru' element to it. Typically it is practised in trendier areas of large, urban conurbations: there are now 13 centres in London: trebled in 10 years.

Using the Bikramyoga.com website and my own ingenuity (the site ignores studios in England?), Bikram yoga is practised in 38 countries in North and South America, Europe and Asia. It is highly concentrated in North America, with 76 in Canada and around 390 in the United States – that's 466! I made it 33 in continental Europe and 19 in the UK – or 52 in total, and a remaining 37 in South America, Asia and Israel. Of the total of around 555, there are 83 per cent just in the United States and Canada.

The number in Canada is scary – compared with the population, pro rata. And if, simplistically, there are 4 times as many people in the United States as in the UK, the UK could have 390 divided by 4 or around 100 studios – and it has only 13 at present. There are 30 studios in the New York area alone. Interestingly, two-thirds of the UK studios are in London – a little surprising, but this seems to be a younger urban phenomenon.

The writer is an addict: he has practised it for 11 years and had over 400 classes – that's 600 hours. That is not 600 hours of normal life, Bikram yoga is HOT! – Very HOT. It is practised in a room heated to just over 100 °F: almost a sauna. And it is very strong yoga, so there is a very intense cardio-vascular experience: it is a very intense workout indeed. As a spin off, it is also a detoxification: one has to drink around a litre and a half of water to replace the sweat, during but preferably mainly after the class. Indeed, after a particularly hot class one can still be sweating an hour later: it can be a bit pointless showering just afterwards.

To get the most out of this case, I would suggest that you Google 'Bikram yoga on YouTube': there are some great clips of some of the sequences, with the students looking as if they are really, really stretching themselves.

As part of writing the case study I interviewed Olga Allon who owns and runs several studios, including Fulham, Balham and the newly opened London Bridge. I first met Olga about eight years ago at Queens Park studio and I talked to her then about her plans to open one in Fulham. She still practises Bikram and now has a family, and she looks the exact same age as when I met her: one of the key benefits of this yoga is its rejuvenation effects.

Bikram yoga is operated under licence from Mr Bikram and he has the say-so on who ends up opening a club on a specific site, so it is an unusual network of owners and a regulator type of holding company. There is thus some competition between studios.

Bilkram yoga is a fascinating strategic case as it exemplifies not only competitive advantage/resource-based theory, but also we are back to how highly attractive markets are created and sustained. In addition, it illustrates how further strategic innovation might be feasible.

Bikram yoga is a classic example of how we can use the system of competitive advantage or SCA (developed from the onion model of competitive advantage). We have already got the ingredients of:

- sweaty heat;
- detoxification;
- international reach;
- the guru element;
- trendy, urban focus.

Bikram yoga was formulated when Mr Bikram suffered a major knee injury when he was young. Using a series of strengthening postures (probably the 'awkward posture' where you stand on your tiptoes for a very long time), he rebuilt the strength in his body. Bikram went on to devise a system of 26 very carefully sequenced postures that have a very particular and powerful effect on the body and on the experience itself.

Now, for those readers not familiar with yoga there are probably about 1,000 different postures that can be practised – it is more complex than the Kama Sutra! So mathematically, there must be billions of combinations of possible yoga systems like Bikram. But this particular system is very special. Bikram decided that he would evolve an optimal system and once he had got there, that would be it: so simple an idea, but this gave huge competitive advantage over yoga teachers who do a different sequence each class, so the students never really know what is coming next! By contrast, after the first few sessions you do know what the sequence is and that enables you to concentrate much harder.

So to the sequence: this breaks down into two halves – like a football match: the standing series and the floor sequence. The standing series is split into:

- warming up: a breathing-in exercise to oxygenate the body (pranayama) and 'half moon' – which is an extremely strenuous spine-bending exercise;
- standing – balancing: on tiptoes, crouching, and both, kicking out and bow;
- standing – forward stretch and triangle;
- floor – digestinal postures;
- floor – back strengthening and locust;
- floor forward and backward bends, stretches;
- finally spinal twist and rapid detoxification breathing (pranayama).

With the exception of half moon, the earlier postures are a gradual opening up and warming up in preparation for the latter. It is almost like going through a session with a chiropractor, as the stiffness and tension go and the posture is straightened. In addition, there are a number of compression and pressure postures which stimulate the thyroid and other centres, the colon, and many other glands in the body, so that natural health is promoted throughout the body.

I have analysed each one of the 26 exercises to see what their prime focus is. The areas of benefit or focus are:

- arm strength;
- shoulder strength;
- chest muscles;
- upper back;
- middle back;
- lower back;
- tummy;

- hips;
- legs;
- spinal twisting;
- internal organs and glands;
- cardiovascular;
- balance;
- breathing;
- concentration/relaxation.

This makes 15 in all.

What is very interesting is that most of these exercises cover a large number of benefits. For example, 'triangle' posture, where you take a big stride so that one leg is at a perfect right angle to the floor, the other is straight and you bend in an extreme way like a windmill, both arms like sails. There is a simultaneous spinal twist so that the chest opens up. This complete 'master' posture thus covers:

- upper back;
- middle back;
- lower back;
- arms;
- chest;
- balance;
- tummy;
- spinal twist;
- legs.

This accounts for nine of these areas. While triangle isn't a posture unique to Bikram, most of the postures have a lot more to them in terms of what they do for you than the average yoga posture. This made me realize that that was a line of enquiry – that to list these out would be a powerful incentive to conveying the system's benefits, potentially.

In most London Bikram studios, class numbers vary from around 20 off-peak to as many as 75 at the peak time of 10 am on Sunday. Bikram yoga, which is £15 a session for a drop-in class – a premium, plus £1.50 for a towel and £2 for a bottle of water, cannot fail to be anything other than profitable, while other yogas really struggle here. Probably the average secondary sales from water/towels are about 50p a person. The average yield is lower – at around £10 a session, as most students have monthly or longer passes, and at around £99 a month and 10 visits on average that would even out. (It is probably more, as there are drop-in members paying more.)

If one takes a typical class schedule of 6 sessions a day (5 on a Friday), that's 41 sessions a week, and if we assume an average over the week of

25 students per class, that's around 1,025 students at an average of £10.50 a time net of VAT, or £10,750 a week with VAT. Allowing for shorter bank holidays, at 51 weeks a year that's around £548,000 a year – quite a lot, especially for a yoga studio.

If we compare that to, say, a typical health club with a turnover of, say, £1.2 million a year but with about four times the space, then that is 0.55 divided by 1.2 times 4, or 1.83 – that's 83 per cent more revenues per square foot. Also, there is virtually no equipment, no real sales costs and minimal maintenance, so resource-wise it is very efficient and is a substitute to that market. (I used to pay for a health club myself until I realized that most of the benefits were to be had from the yoga, so I cancelled my membership.)

Bikram claims to have used this yoga system to turn round the health of many sick people around the world. One might discount some of his claims, but there is evidence of its effectiveness from class members. For example, after one class, one of the students was saying that he had been advised to try Bikram yoga for high blood pressure, and after a month his high blood pressure had disappeared. It almost certainly extends the time that one will have a good and young-looking, fit and healthy body: mine feels like I am about 40 – in fact it feels a lot better – and that was 17 years ago!

Another ingredient of its business model is the flexibility with the 'drop-in' option: this means that, unlike a normal health club, you can 'pay as you go', which fits in well with many customers' needs. It also helps to get newcomers to establish it as a regular and committed habit.

So let's add some further aspects of its USP:

- the beneficial effects on the glands;
- cardiovascular benefits;
- strengthening the muscles;
- weight control to converge on a more natural weight (slimming for larger people and putting on muscle for those who were skinny – like me);
- postural improvement;
- relief of stiffness and alleviation of back problems;
- acceleration of healing after injuries.*

---

* In terms of the latter, a month ago I had what could have been a quite serious accident: I was standing on top of a small monument at a very nice view on the Downs and decided that I would just leap from that onto the car park wall. My foot slipped and I went diving down into the car park. It was a short flight and I crashed to the ground, breaking my fall with an outstretched arm. I could easily have broken a wrist or my arm or nose, but fortunately I cushioned the fall with my arm and emerged just with bad bruises to my hand, a knee and my shoulder – and a strained shoulder and chest ligaments. After just one yoga session 10 days later I was able to see much restored shoulder movement and began the process of restoring the strength to my left side. After a month it is 95 per cent better.

Speaking of muscle strength, the effects of cumulative practice over a long period are impressive as well. For example, after hundreds of times of doing the balancing posture (the awkward posture), I had developed incredible strength in the foot muscles, which are very underdeveloped in most people. These came in very useful when I managed to avoid another major accident around 2003.

Around that time I had become slightly concerned that I had the habit of zooming around London and getting across very busy roads where if you made one false move you could get hit by a car. I don't know whether I had a premonition or what, but the thought occurred to me one day that 'I should be more careful – or one day I might easily get hit by a car'. The evening before I had a very close encounter, I was watching a war film on TV, *Where Eagle's Dare*, and I saw a man being nearly crushed by a tank, but he just managed to leap out of the way. I thought to myself that if ever I were in that position I would do something very similar, and by using the strength in the muscles in my feet.

It was an exercise in scenario storytelling, and in the back of my mind's eye I was thinking of the assumption that 'I will not get hit by a car in the next month' as one that was both actually very important and potentially high risk too, on the uncertainty grid (see Chapter 6), ie watch out!

The next day I was on a sales mission to sell a strategic workshop to Honda in Swindon. I decided to go a slightly different way from my normal route and went via Farnham Common, so that I could go to a post office. The queue was slow and I was aware that I might be late for my meeting, so when I came out I put on a burst of acceleration... to 8 mph. Unfortunately, I hadn't noticed that I was actually on a road area – it was cobbled and the same colour as the previous pavement. I hadn't seen a four-wheel-drive car coming out of a side entrance of a car park, also doing 8 mph. We were about to collide head-on at around 12 mph!

Instinctively I leapt into the air and twisted around so that my impact with the car was actually on its bonnet and with one twist I landed to the side of the car on both feet, perfectly, like in a Kung Fu movie. I looked at the shocked driver, who seemed in a much worse state than I was, and after a brief damage report I said, 'collision with a four wheel drive and not bad – only a scratch'. I continued on my journey to Swindon to meet Honda – the journey was very boring by comparison.

While not quite as many students have reported similar experiences to that one after Bikram yoga, they have many others of the benefits it has brought them.

Now, continuing with the case study, yoga is often known as well for its meditative practices. While Bikram yoga isn't obvious for this and is a very secular experience – at least on the surface – there is a strong focus on concentration and on mind-emptying. This is done through:

- the fact that there is always the same sequence of postures and so it has a hypnotic quality;

- the teacher encourages one to focus exclusively on one's own practice and this is helped by the fact that there is a wall-to-wall mirror at the front of the class so that one can track one's posture and make small adjustments;
- halfway through and at the end there are opportunities for systematic relaxation;
- talking is a no-no so this encourages concentration as well.

Most students won't realize this, but they are getting some basic training in meditation: this is highly stress relieving.

There are also benefits through the sense of psychological and physical challenge and the sense of achievement, as one can suddenly begin to do things that really weren't possible or very difficult at first.

So all in all there are some huge and interconnected benefits of the system over other yoga practices in the context of the Western market. In terms of the teaching, this is most rigorous and is controlled by Mr Bikram himself. As this is a very standardized sequence the skills of the teachers are developed to a very high and consistent level, and this is unusual in yoga classes. This is another area we can add to the SCA.

Because the classes are very demanding, the challenge is to get students through the initial comfort barrier. New students are coached specially and are encouraged to give it a proper trial, as they could until recently get un-limited classes for 10 days for £15. While many become converts, the fact that there are generally a couple of new students leads one to suspect that there is quite a high 'try this and drop out' rate.

Socially it is a good interest to talk about with friends and people that one bumps into. While it isn't an obvious way of meeting new people – it isn't an obvious dating event, although sometimes there are people there who are old-timers so looks are sometimes exchanged – there is a very strong culture of a common purpose and belonging to a group. I normally go when my wife goes to church on a Sunday, and I think of it as being similar!

As Olga said to me: 'It is still something that people can and do talk about a lot as it still has a lot of novelty. But looking forward I can see a time when most people will have heard about it so that those conversations won't be quite so novel and interesting.'

The sessions are delivered by the yoga teacher standing at the front simply using a monologue to guide the students, done through a micro-phone, so that a class of whatever size can still hear well. He or she rarely demonstrates the postures and teaches through group-level or individual interventions to adjust the postures. (The monologue, at which the teachers are word perfect, is also very meditative as well.) The most experienced students work at the front so that they provide a visual role model for the rest of the class.

Some teachers do their classes at regular times in the week so that they get a personal following, but overall they are very interchangeable and one learns things from different teachers – unlike conventional yoga, which is always with the same teacher, which can get predictable and boring.

That model makes the 90 minutes very efficient as there is little down-time: often yoga sessions have about half the practice time as the yoga teacher has to do his or her own demonstration before each posture – which is inefficient and boring.

In terms of positioning, Bikram is a very clear differentiation/focus strategy. As Olga said: 'We have to be really clear about what we do, and why. For example, when we first opened I thought about not covering all those times but even though some sessions wouldn't pay for themselves it was still better that people could choose to come when it suited them, and overall that was a better model. We only needed about 10 students to make that more or less viable.'

A complete list of the SCA is now as follows:

- sweaty heat;
- detoxification;
- international reach;
- the guru element and its strong branding;
- trendy, urban focus;
- premium pricing;
- it is flexible: you can 'pay as you go';
- secondary sales;
- the beneficial effects on the glands;
- cardiovascular benefits;
- strengthening the muscles;
- improved balance;
- weight control to converge on a more natural weight (slimming for larger people and putting on muscle for those who were skinny – like me);
- a better-looking body;
- also one that will stay younger longer and can be rejuvenated: it is never too late to start;
- postural improvement;
- relief of stiffness and alleviation of back problems;
- acceleration of healing after injuries;
- lower stress;
- meditative benefits;
- concentration;
- psychological and physical challenge;
- sense of achievement;

- a unique interest to talk about;
- social spin-offs;
- very efficient and a non-boring process;
- consistently high level of teaching;
- very effective use of space;
- many classes so you can always go;
- it is highly addictive!

An awesome model of competitive advantage: all in all, 30 elements – most businesses would be lucky to say they have even 3 to 5.

So that I don't forget, if any of my readers are now inspired to try it out, please don't eat in the previous hour – you are likely to feel sick! However, don't go without breakfast as you will run out of fuel halfway through: hot and hungry is not a good combination.

As this yoga model is very likely to be relatively profitable, it raises the issues of rivalry and new entrants. Bikram also had a career running businesses earlier in his life, so has copyrighted the system and has in the past been involved in legal cases against those who have tried to copy the process. This appears to have been highly successful. Nevertheless, there have been some attempts to do this. For example, a studio three miles away from me in Beckenham, London has a centre called 'Urban Yoga' which has 'Hot yoga' and 'Hot Pilates'. I trialled this once and it seemed to have around 18 of the Bikram postures – sufficient to make it seem perhaps not too obvious a copy. But I never went back as this seemed sadly lacking. However, this would have a real appeal to students who wanted something less gung-ho, so that threat should not be discounted.

Without even resorting to legal cases Bikram has built very powerful barriers to entry and imitation. Even if very high-quality teachers were available to health clubs wanting to put on a class, they would still have to invest in the special heating equipment to begin to compete. Also, the very great strength of the brand itself and the ready availability of classes throughout the week at a Bikram studio give it much protection: this is far from being a 'perfect market' in economic terms.

Bikram is thus still very much in the blue ocean of uncontested competitive space, so this looks an unusually attractive market and sustainably so. This seems mainly limited by the suitability of the local geography and sufficient concentration of its target socio-economic segments, which seem mainly in the age range of 25 to 40, and consist of relatively health- and look-conscious, affluent and professional people without young families.

Surprisingly to me but probably not to my readers is the fact that it is highly concentrated on females at weekends, who typically make up between 80 and 85 per cent of the class. I would say that as I am a male myself and I know that potentially it has strong macho appeal: potentially it could have a much stronger male following than it currently has. Apparently the males surface in number on Monday, Tuesday and Wednesday evenings.

Olga confirmed: 'Overall, there are about 40 per cent males so we are attracting that market.'

Another feature that is almost not represented at all is the 'grey market' of over-50s. I am now over 50 myself (although when dating a while back I had memory lapses and was quite a bit younger!). I would say that in most classes I am the oldest or nearly that, so with a class of 50 there are about 4 per cent of us who are over 50, with a very high percentage of the attendees 25 to 50, so only 4 per cent is actually grey! This segment is also generally more cash and time rich, another line of enquiry.

Other areas of opportunity might be:

- pricing and packaging, eg off-peak discounts for the over-55 market;
- systems: more efficient check-ins with automatic swipe cards;
- internet marketing/making more of YouTube;
- competitions (more);
- certification of what level you are at, like the belts of Karate;
- more advanced classes (sometimes there is one a week, but this could be developed);
- more explicit focus on the meditative aspects;
- building a Bikram yoga social network;
- more Bikram yoga holidays;
- encouraging more frequent use;
- e-mailing people who haven't been for some time, and tempting them back;
- reducing the fall-out rate of new customers: this is of the order of 75% (success rate 25%);
- promoting the special benefits more – say the top ten – as a list;
- getting the students to be its free sales force by suggesting that they invite a friend or their partner (especially those of the women regulars);
- a special introductory package as a gift voucher;
- capitalizing on the 'feel guilty' post-Christmas/New-Year's resolution market more explicitly;
- occasionally having classes that are even hotter for those who love the heat – the Vindaloo classes (that opens up the possibility of sub-branded products – Mr Bikram would frown on that!);
- exploiting the merchandising possibilities of the Bikram brand – which is trendy;
- milestone celebration: for example, doing 100, 200, 300 classes;
- an alliance with a health insurance partner;
- making the medical benefits more explicit: eg helping insomnia, headaches, the various organs that are worked on, benefits for joints;

- alliances with purveyors of massage, healing and other stress-relieving services, fitness assessors, chiropractors – the Bikram notice board;
- links with local GPs: referrals;
- alliances with local restaurants and bars, eg they hand out free leaflets and studios do the same in return;
- added at the end is the possibility of listing the postures against their benefits.

And there are plenty more, especially in terms of further product development and development of underserved segments. Bikram yoga has hardly changed in 10 years – and that might be the plan – and so may be ripe for taking it up to a slightly higher level.

Olga said of this list that:

> There are plenty of interesting ideas there. We are looking at quite a few things, including simplifying our pricing and changing the introductory offer so that it encourages a longer period of trial to build up more commitment, and social networking. We want to increase the frequency of use and build an even more thriving business. I would like to see our (three) studios at the very forefront of Bikram and making it even more that extra special.

There is therefore rich potential for strategic thinking in this market in terms of option generation.

A final and obvious point is regarding the international concentration on Anglo-Saxon countries: in the longer term China would seem an excellent prospect – and also Japan. And why are there only four studios in France? What happened to Spain? Two in Italy? There are obviously some thoughts to be had here.

Before we begin to come out of this experience it is worth focusing on two things: Porter's five forces and the STRIPE test of its strategic assets.

Porter's five forces:

- buyer power: very low, it is addictive and has an appeal at mental, emotional and physical levels;
- entry barriers: high;
- rivalry: low but possibly increasing;
- substitutes: medium to low – medium for new students, low for addicted devotees;
- supplier power: low – there is an excess of talent wanting to teach Bikram yoga.

Verdict: this segment of the yoga market is very attractive on the basis of the five competitive forces: it is quite unlike almost all of the others. The only shadow is the one cast by competition. Olga's take on that is: 'We are increasingly competing with other Hot Yogas, such as Urban Yoga and Yoga Haven, who aren't Bikram. Also, as there are more and more Bikram's opening up then at some point that will cause some competition as a result of overlapping catchment areas.'

Coincidentally I was in a nightclub at the weekend and met an Indian guy called Wikram who seemed very interested in Bikram yoga – could he be the new guru and launch something even better – 'Wikram yoga'?

While having a big served market, there appears to be plenty of market growth potential and the growth drivers are very positive. Being addictive, it is one of the last things that people will cut when money is tight, so it is not so much affected by economic cycles. It is also in alignment with leisure and health trends and is resilient to the PEST test.

Reflecting on this analysis, OIga's view was that: 'It is very comforting but I am always thinking about the market in terms of "How long will this last?". I am a worrier but you have to think "at what point does this ever get affected by what else is going on around us all?"', presumably referring to the continued economic clouds of the time of the interview.

Now, going back to the STRIPE test that we saw earlier on, Bikram yoga passes this with comfort and ease:

- Sufficiency: it has 25 elements in its system of competitive advantage.
- Transcendent: the effects are demonstrably outstanding.
- Rare: it is tightly controlled legally and any copies are likely to look cheap, and it is very strongly branded.
- Important: all of the strategic assets that it has are relevant and impactful.
- Protectable: it is copyrighted.
- Evolutionary: only on this count does it seem weaker, other than through the dynamic of geographic expansion.

So, in conclusion, it holds not only a very strong strategic position indeed but one where there is potential for more development (from the cunning plan to the stunning plan). During this long case we have seen:

- The importance of having multiple and mutually reinforcing sources of competitive advantage – or the system of competitive advantage.
- Besides these being hard to copy individually, they are even harder to copy as a systemic whole: this gives a much higher level of true sustainability.
- It has some very useful resource- and cost-efficiency aspects.
- It is also in tune with the wider environment and is less threatened by it.
- Its Porter's five forces are a rare example of very low levels of competitive pressure, and margins and returns should be very good.
- It also passes our STRIPE test with ease (see above).
- Even in a mature and very successful business model there is typically still a lot of breakthrough potential.

One needs to be very mindful of the possible life-cycle effects on the business.

Bikram yoga thus illustrates very well many of the strategic concepts that we have been exploring to date, and especially those of Chapter 4 and this one. The case also gives us many lessons in the key ingredients in finding a very successful competitive strategy: unique and valuable customer experience, a simple business model with a clear focus, naturally low costs positioned in a naturally very attractive market that we can control well. It is almost a dream business. It has also been an opportunity to show how easy it is to take an everyday phenomenon and to interpret it strategically: this is truly being your own strategy guru.

A final word on the yoga is that if you think you need stamina for a Bikram class, you will need even more to listen to a talk by Bikram himself. He gave a talk in London in the spring of 2011 which I attended. He didn't start on time and after half an hour I tried to go to the loo but the doors were being locked. The talk lasted two and a half hours without intermission: I was beginning to worry about the last train home – fascinating, but regrettably I had to leave.

STRATEGIC EXERCISE 5.5 Evaluating strategic options for Bikram yoga – 10 minutes

---

- Using the optopus (see Chapter 6), what further options for strategic development can you think of? (You may choose to think about any more degrees of freedom that can be identified, such as events, the media, smaller but wealthier areas etc.)

- Using the strategic option grid (see Chapter 6), what is a first-cut evaluation of its criteria?

- Revisiting these scores with your cunning implementation plan, do these scores improve more?

So, in terms of the lessons from the Bikram yoga case we see:

- Bikram yoga definitely hits a very good sweet spot.
- But this might corrode, albeit imperceptibly, over time, through freezing and not refreshing the business model, through it eventually becoming less novel and trendy, and through competitors – other Hot yoga and Hot Pilates, which strengthen the inner core, and substitute high-calorie-burning, intense and challenging classes with other weight-burning and endorphin-stimulating exercises.

- Its resilience is to be found in its system of competitive advantage with its many reinforcing aspects.
- That sweet spot will always be strengthened by its powerful brand and by the charismatic Mr Bikram himself (when I listened to his talk I felt there were a good 20 years left in him – could someone please reduce his energy? He must be around 70 plus, but looks under 60!).
- Bikram yoga has first-mover advantages, economies of scale and a developed distribution network.
- The product is such that it sells itself easily by word-of-mouth, which is real competitive leverage.
- There is very little value destruction: I must have had 50 different teachers over 12 years and they are remarkably consistent and high value added in their delivery (that said, there are one or two who, for me, go too far as one ends up too well cooked by the end, although, in defence, there is a big segment who like it that way – somewhat Vindaloo. But after feedback they do listen and adapt so that the heat plateaus a bit more).

Speaking of unintended disadvantages, if there has been quite a hot class one can still be quite red in the face the next day. I once went for a chat with an old ex-colleague of mine when I was at KPMG, Peter Hogarth, with whom I have done a lot of work and who now does board-level reviews for FTSE top 100 plcs. Peter is a real fan but I could just see in his eyes, last time we met on a Monday morning after Bikram yoga on the Sunday, that he was thinking to himself: 'I wonder if Tony is OK? He is *very* red today. Too much wine – I wonder? Er, I am not sure that I could wheel him out in front of a big plc that needs some strategic help.' I think that my out-of-body experience of Peter's thoughts was probably spot on. So I have learnt to drink a vast amount of water afterwards, and definitely not wine! I think he will enjoy that story: I should send it to him.

Humour aside, the above story is a reminder that one's sweet spot can easily be damaged by impressions.

STRATEGIC EXERCISE 5.6 Learning from Bikram yoga – 5 minutes

In this exercise, learn from the successful ingredients of Bikram yoga, eg:

- building an awesome brand;
- delivering distinctive customer value;
- exploiting possibilities for emotional value;

- getting lock-in, ideally to addictive levels;

- encouraging the buying habit;

- building and maintaining very high entry barriers;

- clarity and consistency of delivery;

- having a lean cost model;

- understanding the value drivers really well, eg the rate of attrition of new students and old students, the price sensitivity of demand etc.

What clues do these give you for your own business?

Key insights from the chapter

So, to summarize and integrate the key lessons from the gurus and from our discussions of the Bikram yoga case, we have:

- The three C's model is a useful framework for thinking about competitive advantage.

- In it the hidden or fourth 'C' is often equally important: 'costs'.

- Comparisons of relative competitive advantage can be too simplistic and require deeper thinking about segmentation and the competitive context.

- It is often more important to think of how the three C's will be in the future.

- The three C's is too much of a static model: we need to think of the dynamics of shifts in relative strength over time.

- The sweet spot is a useful concept as long as one does not delude oneself over its size and zone of applicability.

- The sweet spot will decay over time and needs freshening up.

- More dynamic models, such as competitive-pressure-over-time and competitive-advantage-over-time curves and the time window and speed to realize an opportunity, are important in a dynamic context.

- We must also ensure that no areas of value destruction that undermine the sweet spot come up.

- Life-cycle effects need to be tracked and anticipated, as in the Bikram yoga case, and the business model refreshed.

- New strategic opportunities for strengthening and extending the sweet spot also need to be investigated.

In conclusion, many of the original ideas of competitive positioning were relatively static. We have now learnt that a much more dynamic model of competitive advantage, and one that is much more sensitive to the different competitive context, is needed.

In our next chapter we will move on to the theme of developing and evaluating strategic options, much of which is based on the notion of dynamic competitive positioning and thus more fluid and strategic thinking, Shortly we will be entering the terrain of the most obviously practical and value-added strategic thinking techniques.

Designing and evaluating options

06

Introduction

In this chapter we use a single framework, the strategic option grid, to help give clarity, imagination and insight into strategic decision making. This process was first applied by the likes of Tesco plc, a now global retailer, and later in companies such as HSBC and Microsoft. A more sophisticated model of the process has also been implemented by Diageo, the global drinks company, and throughout Eastern Europe by Raiffeissen International Banking Group. We will focus on this more advanced approach in this account.

This framework is at the very heart of strategic thinking. I have known of managers who chose this as their core tool and on the back of that became competent strategic thinkers.

So, to begin with, the strategic option grid – probably like most novel management techniques – was developed in an accidental context. A small division of (what was then) British Rail was about to be privatized. While it had a then-turnover of around £2 million, its costs were £4 million – leading to an annual loss of £2 million. The business unit was responsible for servicing telephone enquiries.

Unsurprisingly, the senior management team faced some rather difficult dilemmas. At very first sight, the business was obviously non-viable. But should that business have been closed down, besides the loss of 50 jobs this would have led to a loss of service to the rest of the railway network.

Indeed, closure might have resulted in some significant disruption – not only operationally, but also politically – to the privatization process. Had the media become aware of any proposal to close down this essential service, there might well have been some adverse publicity.

In order to help the team to come up with a new way of thinking about the business, I suggested: 'Perhaps we should look not only at a number of options – and as many as we can – but also we may need to set down a number of criteria for judging these options against.'

I am not alone in realizing the need to use a number of criteria to evaluate options against. One framework is that of Johnson and Scholes in their wide-ranging textbook *Exploring Corporate Strategy* (1987) (Johnson was my mentor once, and I worked with Scholes on a book titled *Exploring Strategic Financial Management* (1998b)). Their criteria for strategic decision making are:

- suitability;
- acceptability;
- feasibility;

where suitability means having a strategic fit to the existing business, and is based on the company's competences and competitive advantage. Acceptability means a combination of strategic desirability, financial attractiveness and fit with stakeholder needs. Feasibility is about implementation.

Another very similar framework taught to Henley MBAs is the AFD framework, or 'acceptability, feasibility and desirability'. Here the difference is the focus on desirability as opposed to suitability. I marginally prefer desirability as a term as it emphasizes the strategic attractiveness in a more direct way. Also, for many managers, suitability, without a lot of teaching, is a more amorphous concept.

The students are taught, as they are with the strategic option grid below, to score these somehow, and to break them down into sub-criteria, which is a must-do. Unfortunately, even in a very detailed analysis one sees that important elements such as 'uncertainty and risk' are either missed off or are only one of five or more sub-criteria, and thus get lost. From the past 20 years of personal experience I do think that uncertainty and risk warrant a lot more attention than this.

The five criteria which I suggest are generally the best (see Figure 6.1) (Grundy, 1995, 2002b, 2004):

- strategic attractiveness;
- financial attractiveness;
- implementation difficulty;
- uncertainty and risk;
- stakeholder acceptability.

We will define these terms in the next section.

I believe that these are close to many of the tacit criteria that an intuitive strategist will operate with. I also believe that they are definitely along the lines of what should be used, and formally as well. This process has been used in well over 50 organizations and has been taken over as a core strategic process, lock, stock and barrel, by many leading companies over the years, such as Tesco, Mothercare and Microsoft's European Operation Division.

These are also founded on theory, in that a number of key literatures support this, namely those on:

FIGURE 6.1 Strategic option grid

Options\nCriteria	Option 1	Option 2	Option 3	Option 4
Strategic attractiveness				
Financial attractiveness*				
Implementation difficulty				
Uncertainty and risk				
Acceptability (to stakeholders)				

SCORE: 3 = very attractive, 2 = medium attractiveness, 1 = low attractiveness.
* Benefits less costs, − net cash flows relative to investment

- strategic attractiveness: competitive strategy;
- financial attractiveness: financial theory and value-based management;
- implementation difficulty: organizational behaviour, change management and project management;
- uncertainty and risk: scenarios and risk management;
- stakeholder acceptability: organizational politics.

So we are embracing other intellectual inputs beyond strategy.

The AFD and the Johnson and Scholes methods also tend to be taught by strategists, who, although they are familiar at a general level with the other areas such as organizational politics (except, perhaps, the ins and outs of finance), will typically focus on the more qualitative and strategic aspects, rather than on the more nitty-gritty which I believe is also important.

Before we begin in earnest, I should emphasize that the discussion of the criteria and the scores shouldn't be abstract at all but should be specific enough to give us quite a clear picture of what is entailed; for example, in the market, in how we will address it, and in how we will operationize that, too. The reader might also notice that by including 'implementation difficulty' in the mix of criteria, we are making sure that we don't run away with what seem to be attractive ideas which we will really struggle to deliver on. I am reminded here of a story from an insurance company.

When I was running a workshop called 'Strategic Change' with some more senior executives, and was telling them about the strategic option grid, we had a visit from one of the directors, who was giving a talk on strategic planning. I had previously been stressing to these executives that they must always include some assessment of implementation difficulty in their evaluation of strategic options.

When the director did his talk he was describing an away day where the top team were looking at some areas for strategic thinking, and it seemed that the debate was all about future direction and not really about implementation feasibility. He was asked by someone in the Q&A, 'so how do you deal with implementation?', to which the answer was 'Implementation? – Well that's down to all you guys...' in a rather dismissive way.

We were all a bit surprised (if not shocked) by that answer. Even if implementation difficulty were only weighted as 20 per cent of importance in our overall criteria, that's a very big gap not to be considering it. I believe that it is actually criminal to think that strategic thinking isn't essential in implementation – and also that it is also criminal not to factor in implementation difficulty to the strategic thinking process.

Typically each criterion is scored as:

✓✓✓   – very attractive

✓✓   – moderately attractive

✓   – low attractiveness

or sometimes with half-ticks.

In the course of the next six hours the team managed to come up with not just three or four, but as many as *nine* different strategic options. One, in particular, actually met the strategic objectives of the business and also had a highly attractive score summed across the five criteria. This particular strategic option was a combination of:

● price rises (to reflect the true value added to its customers);

● cost reduction;

● and also, increased subsidy, from central sources, in order to sustain the consistency of the former service – both during and after the privatization process.

But while one particular strategic option *did* achieve the required threshold level of attractiveness – in terms of making business and financial sense – the decisive factor in the decision-making process turned out to be stakeholder acceptability. Once the full consequences of closure were thought through and spelt out, and when looked at from the perspective of certain stakeholders, closure did not seem to be an attractive decision.

Figure 6.2 now illustrates these scores. While each criterion normally has an equal weighting (for simplicity), clearly in this case 'stakeholder acceptability' was of major importance, making it even more unattractive to choose the closure option, as opposed to a continued strategy to run the call centre with more subsidy.

FIGURE 6.2   Strategic option grid – worked example

Options Criteria	Cut costs (1)	Increase subsidy (2)	Closure	1&2 & new service
Strategic attractiveness	//	///	/	///
Financial attractiveness*	///	///	///	///
Implementation difficulty	//	/	/	//
Uncertainty and risk	//	//	/	//
Acceptability (to stakeholders)	//	/	//	//
	11	10	8	12

SCORE: 3 = very attractive, 2 = medium attractiveness, 1 = low attractiveness.
* Benefits less costs – net cash flows relative to investment

This particular organization still exists today – nearly 20 years later, although many of its staff are now offshored to India, and there has also been an attempt to automate many of the calls using voice recognition, which is only partly successful. (For example, you may be asking to go to Aberdeen and might be given instead a train stop in the Forest of Dean.)

It is perhaps doubtful, if its senior team had just looked at the financials at the time – in their narrowest sense – and tried to evolve incremental strategies to the business, that this would have been accomplished.

Having looked quite generally at this technique, we can now look much closer at how you might actually use it, and for what. In this chapter we now look at:

- how to use it in more depth;
- interdependencies and the deep-dive techniques for creative option generation;
- the optopus;
- testing the scores – or the 'challenge and build' process;
- practical applications and implications of the strategic option grid;
- future possibilities;
- conclusions.

How to use the strategic option grid in more depth

The strategic option grid can be used for:

- market development;
- product/service development;
- new technology development;
- geographic entry strategies;
- strategic account management;
- sourcing decisions, eg outsourcing, offshoring;
- acquisitions;
- divestment;
- alliances;
- diversification;
- turnarounds;
- strategic financing decisions;
- IT investment;
- organizational structuring options;
- organizational change;
- strategic projects;
- departmental strategy;
- HR strategy;
- regulatory strategy;
- cost breakthroughs;
- contract negotiation;
- competitor intent modelling;
- career strategies;
- strategies in everyday life (even holidays, dating opportunities…).

This is a very long list!

The example in the earlier case study of the strategic option grid now highlights its effectiveness in a number of ways:

- Visually, because the strategic option grid has columns for four, if not more, strategic options, this in itself can generate greater creativity among senior managers.
- The definition of specific decision-making criteria allows managers to think about options in a more objective way.
- The specific choice of the five criteria – although originally set instinctively – appeared to reflect very closely the unconscious and

informal decision-making heuristics which managers use – especially the criteria of financial attractiveness, uncertainty and risk, and stakeholder acceptability. The two criteria of implementation difficulty and strategic attractiveness may be slightly lower down at least some managers' prioritization preferences – in a financially driven environment. (Note that high implementation difficulty and uncertainty and risk are scores of one and not three ticks.)

- Each of the criteria can be checked out/or supported by other, more specific techniques (which we call later the deep-dive techniques). By spelling out these criteria separately, they do not merge all together as a single criterion of attractiveness.

The technique also seems to alleviate some of the worst difficulties of politics, because of stakeholder positions and agendas, besides being an excellent medium for communicating strategic ideas.

In terms of using the strategic option grid, the following need to happen:

- We need to explore what options might be available.

- This can be facilitated by looking at the degrees of freedom that might be available.

- Having produced a good menu of possibilities, these can be further enhanced by considering options for 'how' a strategic option might be done, and the timing options.

- For each option we then develop at least a working model of the cunning plan.

- We then do the evaluation scores, based on what is behind these criteria, and by using any deep-dive tools as appropriate.

- After that it may be time to check out any facts – some data gathering in the area which the option grid evaluation looks most sensitive to.

- Finally we may need to revisit the cunning plan, and to ask the question 'what's the one big thing that we have missed?'

When using the strategic option grid it is quite often the case that there is a lot of discussion on the rationale for the scores: on a practical note, it is a really good idea to write some notes alongside the scores or somewhere else at the time. Even the next day, what the rationale of some of the scores actually was starts to get slightly fuzzier. This can be especially the case when there were a number of factors discussed and some offset one another.

In terms of the five criteria, we define these in the following way:

- Strategic attractiveness: this is the external market attractiveness and the relative competitive position. Market attractiveness is based on things like the growth drivers, Porter's five forces (see Figure 4.1) and perhaps PEST analysis. A simple technique which supports the judgements on strategic attractiveness is the GE grid (or General Electric grid – see Figure 6.3).

- Financial attractiveness: these are the long- and short-term returns from the option (or possibly its economic profit) – ultimately this should go down into the value and cost drivers (see Figures 3.7 and 3.8), and the financial model.

- Implementation difficulty: this is the sum of difficulty over time to achieve the strategic goals.

- Uncertainty and risk: this is the extent of the volatility of the assumptions underlying a specific strategic option (see Figure 6.5).

- Stakeholder acceptability: this is the extent to which stakeholders favour, disfavour, or are neutral regarding that option (see Figure 3.1).

Stakeholders will frequently shift over time and these trajectories need to be plotted on the stakeholder acceptability grid against different scenarios, requiring a good dose of strategic thinking.

Also, there is a time dimension to be explored here. First, this needs to be set so that there is no confusion as to what the timescales under consideration here are. Second, where there is perceived to be a differential attractiveness over time, this should be discriminated somehow. For example, one might split some of the boxes into two, to differentiate the shorter term from the longer term. This may be helpful, especially in looking at situations where, for example, there may not be a short-term financial attractiveness, but there is one longer term, or vice versa. Alternatively, a change management project could be hard to implement initially, but once established, easier, while maintaining the status quo might be the opposite, easy at first but then progressively getting more difficult.

This again argues for us to have at least in our minds the model of the 'attractiveness-over-time curve', at least for the aggregate of the strategic option grid scores.

STRATEGIC EXERCISE 6.1 Using the strategic option grid
– 10–15 minutes

For one strategic decision or dilemma facing your organization or yourself:

- What are the key strategic options?

- What is the most cunning way of implementing them?

- What are their scores on the strategic option grid?

- How can these scores still be improved?

- What do you see as being their resilience?

In terms of the interpretation of the scoring and the mechanics, two issues are:

- What is the significance of the scores?
- Should we weight them, and if so, how?

First, as a broad guideline, for the significance of scores we have:

- 12 to 15: these appear to be attractive strategies on the face of it: they still need testing;
- 10 to 11: these need more refinement and are probably lacking cunning in some respect;
- 8 to 9: these need a lot more work on and would be unacceptable at that level;
- 5 to 7: these are weak and unless they can be completely rethought are off the menu;
- below 5: don't touch with a bargepole!

These scores will move up and down quite a lot as one goes through the 'challenge and build' process and tries to make them more cunning, so that shifts of ±2 in the scores are not unusual.

On the last point above, when a strategic option can be seen from quite a different perspective the shifts can be far more dramatic: for example, a year into my lecturing experience at Cranfield School of Management I was finding that I struggled to adjust to teaching the full-time MBAs there, as my style was so different from my colleagues' and also my perception was that these students were not much interested in practical issues but more in abstract academic theory, and getting high marks was an end in itself. As a strategy (and then I was part-time, so this was only part of my work portfolio), I had scores for my first year of:

Strategic attractiveness:	score 2
Financial attractiveness:	score 1½
Implementation difficulty:	score 1
Uncertainty and risk:	score 1
Stakeholder acceptability:	score 1½
Total:	7

So I put it to my then boss that I would like to withdraw from MBA teaching – not a risk-free move – and do executive teaching instead. He agreed, and I went on to develop and run one of the most successful courses ever at Cranfield on 'Breakthrough Strategic Thinking' as well as one on 'Strategic Consulting Skills', and also a whole variety of in-company courses. There were many spin-offs outside this as well for me, which, in those more enlightened days, Cranfield then encouraged.

The result was a wonderful score for my new area of involvement, as follows:

Strategic attractiveness:	score 3
Financial attractiveness:	score 3
Implementation difficulty:	score 3
Uncertainty and risk:	score 3
Stakeholder acceptability:	score 3
Total	15

... or a full house!

So there is a lesson here for those who might interpret their scores in a simplistic and too mechanistic way. What you certainly don't want is the scores going the other way, as they might well do for existing strategies where life-cycle effects kick in, there is greater competition and an eroding sweet spot/competitive complacency, maybe topped off by a stagnant economic environment. This might sound all too familiar to many companies reviewing their strategies as I write in autumn 2011. Here, scores of 10+ previously can easily drop into the below 7 range.

Second, in terms of their weighting, the process is as follows: suppose that we want to weight scores so that there is 20 per cent more importance than the average for the first two criteria and we will reduce the importance of the third and the fourth proportionately, and keep the fifth one, stakeholder acceptability, the same.

Then we will be adjusting the weightings in percentage terms as follows:

	From	To	Old score	Old score weighted	New score weighted
Strategic attractiveness:	20%	24%	2.5	0.5	0.6
Financial attractiveness:	20%	24%	2.5	0.5	0.6
Implementation difficulty:	20%	16%	2.0	0.4	0.32
Uncertainty and risk:	20%	16%	1.5	0.3	0.24
Stakeholder acceptability:	20%	20%	2.5	0.5	0.5
Totals				2.2	2.26
Times 5 (as there are 5 criteria)				11	11.3

which demonstrates that unless more dramatic weightings are made, there isn't a huge impact on the result. It would take, pro rata, an increase in weightings of the top two criteria to over 60 per cent of importance and the bottom two to proportionately less in order to arrive at a score one point higher.

There are three circumstances where the weighting is so important that these may need to be worked out quantitatively, rather than through a more qualitative overview:

- Where one of the criteria seems less relevant, eg using it for strategic cost management at Scottish Water we used the option grid to evaluate about 30 options for breakthroughs/continuous improvements. Strategic attractiveness wasn't really relevant, but financial attractiveness was, so we allocated the latter a double weighting.

- Where one of them is far more relevant: for instance, where it has a big bearing on the outcome.

- Where there is a (rare) extension to the criteria: for example, many years back the RAC (one of the two biggest vehicle breakdown services in the UK) was contemplating diversification strategies. Working with the board we identified two further criteria that we needed to consider: complexity and degree of distraction; sadly, while they got very excited about funerals (the ultimate breakdown?), that might have been distracting both inside and outside the organization.

Generally speaking, it is probably better to stay with the simpler number of five criteria. The RAC experience is the only one in over 20 years where there seems to have been a real need here. The only criterion which generically has competed in my mind on occasion is that of 'timing', as that can be very important, particularly where a market opportunity is fluid, embryonic or fast moving, or is highly affected by the economic cycle.

STRATEGIC EXERCISE 6.2 Weighting your strategic option grid scores – 5 minutes

- For the exercise that you just did above, what relative importance do you place on each of the criteria?

- Were you to weight your criteria as we discussed, would the overall score and evaluation shift significantly?

Finally, where an option criterion looks to be really not good at all, or simply didn't qualify, one is challenged to give it a half-score, and maybe only a zero. The question arises in the latter case as to whether one should still add the scores together or whether the option loses all of its points: possibly the latter is a valid approach. (I once rated one of my ex-long-term relationships as a zero on one criterion.)

That also raises the issue of minimal threshold criteria scores: for example, we may decide that for one criterion we really do need a score of, say, 2. This can be of a lot of help in dealing with any dilemmas.

Returning now to the other possible things to be aware of as a newcomer to this idea, typical weaknesses of first-time use of the strategic option grid are:

- Strategic attractiveness may be scored without any real thought about the environment and things like Porter's five forces.

- Financial attractiveness may be viewed as more about the short and medium term, not the longer term, too.

- Implementation difficulty may be largely a subjective and emotional impression based mainly on the kind of general strategy that this is, rather than about any detailed thinking about enablers and constraints, and particularly how these will change over time, and may also lack much real thinking about the 'how'.

- Uncertainty and risk may be merely a global assessment and lack any granular thinking about what the specific assumptions are and how volatile these are.

- Stakeholder acceptability may be done at a global level without thinking who these all are, and also how their agendas differ, and individually.

- There may not be a cunning plan at all, or for what will be done and how, and so many of the scored boxes may have moderate or weaker scores, not because they are inherently not so good but because of a lack of truly inventive thinking.

- Implementation difficulty and uncertainty and risk may be frequently underestimated. Strategic attractiveness is also frequently overestimated, leading to biased initial scores.

- Unless stakeholder analysis can be done alongside having a true out-of-body experience of imagining that you really are those stakeholders, the picture can be inaccurate and misleading.

Even for much more experienced users it is likely that they are lapsing into a number of these, so it is useful to revisit them. There is no substitute for practice here: you really need to do it three times at least to really begin to internalize the fuller process and protocol.

Where you are looking at a more internally focused strategic option, the criterion of strategic attractiveness needs some reinterpretation. 'Inherent market attractiveness' is no longer applicable here, but in its stead we should consider:

- impact on competitive position;
- shift in capability;
- contribution to the strategic goals of the business;

so it is still relevant. This can apply, for example, to cost breakthroughs, restructuring, culture change and other interventions, investment in infra-structure and in IT.

Besides its use on more deliberate strategies, the option grid can also be used for more emergent and detergent strategies within the strategy mix.

Another important thought is that the option grid can be used to simulate the attractiveness to players in the game other than oneself. These might include:

- in any alliance, the vendor and competing bidders;
- the other partners in an alliance;
- the regulator or the government;
- other external stakeholders;
- any other parties to a deal of any kind;
- customers;
- competitors and new entrants: in exploring their intent and possible moves;
- suppliers.

If you are doing this, you will need to imagine all the main impacts that doing something might have on someone else but also simulate their mindsets and see that opportunity entirely through their lens, and not your own.

Working with Sykes Outsourcing Group, who were huge fans of the strategic option grid (or as they called it, the 'SOG'), they developed a double option grid which had:

	Our score	Client score
Strategic attractiveness:	X	Y
Financial attractiveness:	X	Y
Implementation difficulty:	X	Y
Uncertainty and risk:	X	Y
Stakeholder acceptability:	X	Y

as a useful format to highlight where the main differences were likely be in terms of perspectives so that they could work on these.

Interdependencies and the deep-dive techniques for creative option generation

There are some important interdependencies between the five key criteria of the strategic option grid, which we see below. This partly explains why managers, particularly those using the strategic option grid for the first time, may find that they sometimes confuse the criteria. This can lead to some scores being biased and to confusion and double counting. The main things to watch for are:

- Strategic attractiveness is all about whether an opportunity has an appeal, or is desirable: this is actually more about stakeholder acceptability.

- Financial attractiveness is considered lower because the option is financially risky: no, that is to confuse it with uncertainty and risk.

- Implementation difficulty is high because it is uncertain as to how easy it is to do: again, that is more to do with uncertainty and risk.

- Strategic attractiveness is lower because of the uncertainties: no, again, as the former operates with 'the most likely' view of the world, whereas the latter operates with more volatile states of the world.

A number of the key interdependencies are as follows:

- Between strategic attractiveness and financial attractiveness: the environmental assumptions and those about sustainable competitive advantage – these are both crucial in determining sales growth, operating profit margin, and the investment levels which drive net cash inflows, returns and economic value.

- Between strategic attractiveness and uncertainty and risk: in highlighting which variables are key and most volatile and how these might interact under different scenarios.

- Between strategic attractiveness and stakeholder acceptability: through the perceptions of stakeholders, given their view of the level of attractiveness including opportunities and threats.

- Between financial attractiveness and stakeholder acceptability: in shaping stakeholder agendas through financial perceptions.

- Between uncertainty and risk and financial attractiveness: in looking at the volatility of returns.

- Between implementation difficulty and uncertainty and risk: through the risks which are associated primarily with implementation.

- Between financial attractiveness and implementation difficulty: in enabling or frustrating the implementation through unclear and unrealistic financial targeting and resource allocation.

- Between implementation difficulty and stakeholder acceptability: in deciding the level of acceptable implementation stretch and challenge.
- Between uncertainty and stakeholder acceptability: in shaping the risk aversion of the stakeholders.

There are thus a number of complex interdependencies at work underneath the surface of the strategic option grid.

Each of the five decision criteria can now be tested out with a number of deep-dive techniques, as we now see.

For instance, strategic attractiveness (for an externally facing strategy) should be checked out primarily with the GE grid (see Figure 6.3).

FIGURE 6.3   GE grid

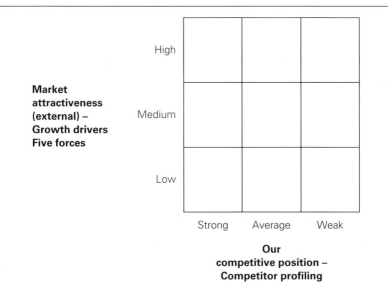

The GE grid distinguishes between the external attractiveness of external markets, and also competitive position. Market attractiveness can be supported by second-tier techniques such as PEST factors, growth drivers and Porter's five competitive forces. Competitive position can be supported by customer value analysis, by competitor profiling, or by these two techniques in combination with relative cost analysis.

In terms of the GE grid, the positionings of different businesses tend to shift quite considerably over time. For example, as a market matures and becomes more competitive, there will tend to be a downward shift in market attractiveness. Also, if a particular player harvests its position and doesn't refresh or rethink its sweet spot, it can slide, or slip from being in the north-west quadrant to the centre, or even to the east, either way coinciding with a decline in financial performance. Again, as we saw in the last chapter, competitive positioning is a very dynamic thing.

Clearly this requires (potentially) a significant amount of thought, and this in turn entails a lot more thinking than more superficial strategic fit. (Sometimes strategic fit is a tautological concept – a strategy is seen as attractive because it fits what we want to do strategically, which is a circular argument – this concept is hardly an objective justification or evaluation for the strategies.)

Managers have to be continually convinced and persuaded *not* to short-circuit their thinking on this first criterion of strategic attractiveness – and to support it with the GE grid and with its second-tier techniques – such as growth drivers and Porter's five forces.

STRATEGIC EXERCISE 6.3 Using the GE grid – 10 minutes

- For a number of business units, where would you position these on the strategic option grid – in the different columns?

- What do the resulting positions show you about the strategic attractiveness of your business?

Financial attractiveness means essentially those factors which (in combination) will deliver a return on investment, or perhaps the more sophisticated concept of 'shareholder value creation' will add incremental economic value.

This can be arrived at by analysing either:

- the value and cost drivers (which we saw earlier in the book); or
- the value-over-time curve (a dynamic tool).

Figure 6.4 (the value-over-time curve) now helps us to get a feel for *when* net cash flows (and thus economic value) will be captured. Using this technique

FIGURE 6.4 Value-over-time curve

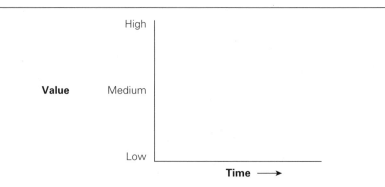

over many years has highlighted that many managers – prior to using this technique – appear to lack a detailed view of *when* they expect to get an economic return from these strategies, especially during the crucial phase of the formulation of a strategy or the definition of a strategic project. They often find this technique particularly helpful at this juncture.

Besides the more qualitative thinking about financial attractiveness, you should also be accompanying these 'judgements' with some detailed financial modelling, and this must include some modelling of the uncertainties and risks.

Note that the value-over-time curve has additional important uses:

- to help in the analysis of customer value, eg over a transaction or customer experience life cycle;
- to devise new ways of innovating in adding value to customers, as we saw with the funerals industry and also with the Virgin Galactic case that we see later on in this chapter;
- as a facilitation device to help a team track its value added in strategic debate;
- to help monitor strategy implementation and project management.

Implementation difficulty: this can be addressed either using force field analysis or through the difficulty-over-time curve, which we see in depth again in Chapter 7 on implementation.

Uncertainty and risk is arrived at by using the uncertainty–importance grid (Figure 6.5) (Mitroff and Linstone, 1993).

FIGURE 6.5   Uncertainty grid

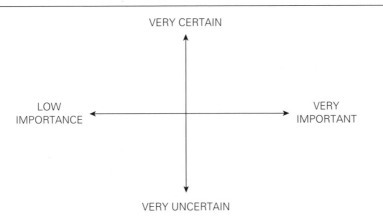

First, some of the most critical assumptions about the strategy actually working out alright are identified (perhaps using Post-its). Then we begin to position them in terms of their relative importance, and also in terms of how certain/uncertain they are perceived to be. A cluster of several assumptions in the southeast part of the grid (the 'danger zone') would suggest a highly uncertain strategy (or one tick).

In looking at uncertainty and risk generally, one needs to consider different types of risks (or 'uncertainty and risk segmentation'). This means looking at the different ways that uncertainty and risk can be brought about, for example:

- economic;
- regulatory;
- competitive;
- the customer;
- technical;
- operational;
- organizational.

(I feel that my MBA students should think a lot more broadly about that: they often just list 3 to 5 risks without any clear search for 'what are the real drivers of risk' when what they are actually advocating for a company can have 30 or more.)

It might help, to get a more complete picture, to use the format of the optopus, which we come on to below, and to do this with dimensions like the list above in mind, suitably tailored.

Finally, stakeholder analysis allows us to judge how for/against the stakeholders are likely to be, given their degree of influence (again perhaps using Post-its). This requires taking the stakeholders' own perspective either by asking them directly or, second best, by estimating their positions by imagining we are them (the out-of-body experience). Again, we will pick this up in depth in Chapter 7.

Once again, it is worth reminding ourselves that while there seems a lot to do in going through this process (for a single option), this process has been applied, and successfully, in a number of companies (for instance at Diageo).

Indeed, the deep-dive techniques do raise some dilemmas – as one example experienced by Diageo managers shows:

A bottom-up approach: a) Should one use *all* the deep-dive techniques for all the boxes of the strategic option grid *and then* do the scores; or

A top-down approach: b) Should one fill in the scores tentatively *and then* do – either completely or selectively – the deep-dive techniques?

My own personal preference is to do b), as in practice there are many options, and it may be better, therefore, to perform some overall evaluation of *all of them*, rather than to spend a lot of time evaluating a small number of options – only to find that they were not the best ones. (This is especially important where the deep-dive techniques lead straight into significant data collection.) Inevitably, there are trade-offs in how best to use managers' available time.

So, to summarize, in terms of the tools that we might use, these are:

strategic attractiveness: the PEST factors, growth drivers, Porter's five forces, competitive benchmarking, the GE grid;

financial attractiveness: value and cost drivers, return on capital, net present value etc;

implementation difficulty: difficulty-over-time curves, force field analysis;

uncertainty and risk: the uncertainty–importance grid, and scenarios;

stakeholder acceptability: stakeholder analysis.

STRATEGIC EXERCISE 6.4 Using the uncertainty–importance grid – 10–15 minutes

For an option of your choice:

● What are the key external assumptions?

● What are the key internal assumptions?

● How do these break down into sub-assumptions?

● How important are these?

● How uncertain are these?

● Where these are both 'very important' and 'very uncertain', are these so closely and mutually dependent that the uncertainty effect could be magnified?

● What might you do to counter, avoid or minimize the effects of those most volatile assumptions?

Note: in the above case you might decide to plot the high-level assumptions on a single grid and then take the main ones and break these down by sub-assumption – on a separate sheet (as if you are zooming in on Google Maps).

Finally, before we leave the strategic option grid for the time being, I will say a few important things about different ways of applying it. This can be done:

● at the individual level;

● or group or team level;

● or multi-groups.

For a new user it is obviously somewhat harder to do it solo rather than as a group. In a group there is always some danger of 'groupthink', so here it is good to have some facilitation or challenge from a sponsor, or from other groups working in parallel. 'Groupthink' (Janis, 1982) is where being a member of a group results in several members converging either in what they say they think, or in what they really do think, to maintain group consensus. This phenomenon is particularly dangerous where there has been an escalation of commitment, and this has become concretized in the political agendas.

Secondly, the strategic option grid can be used for:

- purely private analysis – not shared with peers;
- communicating strategic views;
- influencing;
- facilitating the thinking of others (having used one's own thinking first).

For example, one might just present one's results to get a debate, and where one's output is largely there to be endorsed (that's how most managers see it). Or it can be used much more as a starter for 10, and when debated with other stakeholders one has no hesitation at all in changing the scores: they will warm to that and influencing becomes easier. Or one might work through the tool from scratch to see what they come up with (obviously with one's 'challenge and build' questions being informed by the private analysis that one has done oneself). These strategies are along a spectrum of challenge, and of skill level.

The optopus

Options can be generated creatively for the strategic option grid at both a macro and a micro level, as we will now see using the optopus. This greatly enriches the strategic thinking process by typically doubling or even trebling the range of strategic options that we can imagine. Effectively, using it means that you are much increasing your 'competitive space' from where you thought it was – and thus strategic elbow-room.

At the macro level one can use the strategy optopus – see Figure 6.6 to tease out new possibilities. The optopus has eight generic dimensions of choice – or degrees of freedom.

These include:

market sectors: the different types of market that one might serve: private/public;

customer segments: the different types of customer with different needs;

value creation: the different ways in which value is added for the customer;

FIGURE 6.6 Optopus

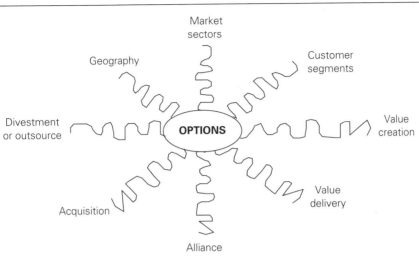

value delivery: the technologies, media and distribution to take it to
market;

alliance: different partners and different types of alliances, doing
different things;

acquisition: different types, different targets, to do different things;

divestment and outsourcing: alternative ways of configuring value-
adding activities/scope;

geography: nationally, regionally, and globally.

As can be seen from the above, each of the eight lines of enquiry that we
have listed here contains many branches and sub-branches, so a well-developed
optopus could be quite large and easily cover a whiteboard. Flip chart paper
soon runs out.

It is also possible to do a totally bespoke optopus. Taking one of my
favourite examples, that of considering options for holidays – a topic to
most definitely apply strategic thinking to, just take a look at this example,
which actually has nine dimensions:

- where to go (country, region, place);
- how to get there (car, bus, train, ship, aeroplane);
- what to spend (premium, value for money, budget);
- when to go (peak/off-peak, time of year);
- what to do when you are there (activities/chill out);
- how long for (fortnight, 10 days, a week, mini-break);

- where to stay (hotel, all-inclusive/non-inclusive, rental);
- how to buy it (package, internet);
- who to go with (solo, with partner, family, extended family, friend/s, group).

Interestingly, when I had only recently met my partner/wife she said to me, 'I don't suppose that you will take me anywhere exciting.' I said, 'where do you want to go?' and she said, 'where can I go?' We used the optopus process to identify a wonderful holiday that was very, very special. We bought a flexible package to Cuba for a week, with two nights in Havana and five in a wonderful five-star all-inclusive brand-new hotel with its own beach down the coast. We searched on the internet and cut out the intermediary travel company, which saved nearly £400. That eventual decision came out of probably a hundred options identified using the holiday optopus above, during which we considered holidays in Hawaii, Thailand and the Red Sea coast.

The lines of enquiry of the optopus can be explored separately, or perhaps through possible interdependencies. Taking a particular example, possible strategic options to enter the funerals business (see the earlier case study in Chapter 4) in a quite innovative way using the optopus (or 'Fabulous Funerals') would be:

Customer segments:	agnostic/atheist/ethnic
Income:	rich, 40–60 years old
Value creation:	the pre-need market, personalized funerals to celebrate death as a positive event, rather than as a negative one
Value delivery:	sold via solicitors – wills, or by satellite TV advertising, or by media publicity
Alliance:	with the basic functions of handling and storing the deceased's body outsourced
Outsourcing:	to existing undertakers
Geography:	initially the UK, perhaps on the south coast where there are more elderly people.

The above idea was generated in around five minutes simply by picking aligned options from a set of eight separate brainstorming outputs from the optopus's eight dimensions.

While these eight generic lines of enquiry are very widely applicable, they can be refined and adjusted or added to. For example, two that I always have at the back of my mind are brand options and pricing options. Pricing options are particularly interesting in the case study below on Virgin Galactic.

These can involve thought experiments of much greater or much lower pricing, or pricing on a more flexible basis. For example, there was once a restaurant in Swiss Cottage, London, with no prices on its menu. The idea was that you had the meal and paid them what you thought it had been worth: generally people paid slightly more than what they did before they had a 'no prices policy' – I did eat out there and it was very nice.

This idea is very much in line with one of the cunning checklists, which says that we should try to find things that are 'irresistible' to customers.

Searching for it on the internet revealed that the owner of that restaurant had started up again in Farringdon, Central London. According to *The Times* (20 December 2009):

> There is a blackboard outside the Little Bay restaurant, in Farringdon. Chalked upon it in large letters are the unambiguous words: 'No food bills – pay us what you think the food is worth.'
>
> The owner is playing a game of chicken with his customers: how little can you pay me without losing your self-respect? Three weeks ago the restaurateur, Peter Ilic, stripped all the prices from his menus. It's a fascinating experiment that has sparked international interest (Ilic has been filmed by TV crews from Japan, Brazil, France and Mexico, and been written about in newspapers on at least four continents): will British reserve, and the fear that we will shame ourselves by paying too little and appearing parsimonious, outweigh self-interest?
>
> It's a repeat performance for Ilic – 24 years ago he did exactly the same thing at a restaurant that he then owned a few miles away in a well-to-do North London suburb. 'Back then, people ended up on average paying more for the food than they would have done if the menu had been priced,' he says. 'I remember one occasion when seven people came over. They were in London for a conference and had been staying at the Savoy. They paid £50 a head in 1985 [which works out at £110 in today's money] for food and drink that would have cost them maybe £15 [£33].'
>
> That was during an economic boom. It's not like that this time around. Over a glass of red wine, Ilic surveys the tables around him. The Yugoslav proprietor – he came to London 35 years ago – is amusingly candid about his experiment. 'People are paying a little less than the regular prices at the moment.' There's a wry smile. 'I've somehow attracted a few students. But it's early days. They can only come once and pay a little – next time, they may be ashamed, I hope.'
>
> Before the prices disappeared, the typical spend here was £18–£20 a head, including wine. Now the average figure is about £15 a head (before drinks), Ilic claims. He says he treats his customers the same, whether they leave £20 or £50 – but then he would say that, wouldn't he?
>
> 'The lowest amount I have seen anyone leave is two pence. They had tap water. I think they came for a joke more than anything. The most anyone has left is £35 a head, without drinks for two courses.' Given what they ate, that was two-and-a-half times what they 'should' have paid.
>
> My small and unscientific survey suggests that the amounts being taken tonight may be a little lower than Ilic's claimed £15 a head, but one thing is certainly true: turnover has shot sky high. By 9 pm, the place is full – many tables for a second time. Ilic says he will do 2,000 covers this week – double his normal total. ... While his margins may be down, his profits are heading north.

Suspending the normal assumptions about pricing is a major departure from the industry mindset and is a classic example of strategic thinking by focusing on the customer's perspective.

In my own industry, consultancy, there is an analogy: 'value-based fees', not seen as yet much in Europe, but nevertheless a possibility. Interestingly, fear is a strong mindset inhibiting experimentation with alternative price bases, so while on the one hand I am attracted to that concept, the fears that one would get paid less are a turn-off. The fact that it is emotional is obvious when I do the thought experiment of trying that out when I don't really need the money: I know that considerable economic value is created from such work, so one might well get a lot more money.

While subsequent research revealed that the restaurant had reverted to a more normal pricing strategy, the publicity must have got a lot of business in its start-up phase.

The optopus can help to provide some prompts/structure to option generation at a macro level – for competitive strategy, partly de-skilling the creative process and extending the possibilities of strategic options.

Another quick case example where we can explore the potential of the optopus is Virgin Galactic. Around 2008 a BBC *Money Programme* ran a documentary on this business model. Essentially, the idea behind it was to develop a technology which was capable of delivering a number of independent passengers into space for a sub-orbital flight. Travelling at a height of around 50 miles, these passengers would then enjoy a short while of seeing the earth from a distance in its glory and in a state of weightlessness. This was going to be made available at a low budget cost of $200,000.

This was to be made possible by launching a quite small but light space vehicle from another launching craft to reach sub-orbital flight in two stages. This followed the idea of the reusable Space Shuttle, but with one important difference: the craft would not have a heavy heat shield to avoid it burning up on re-entry to the earth's atmosphere. That meant that it wouldn't need as much fuel and a separate stage to get into space.

The cunning plan was to design a large fin that could be put up like a sail which would gently and gradually allow it to re-enter the atmosphere without burning up.

The concept allowed for only a relatively short journey of 90 minutes (the duration of a football match or of a Bikram yoga class). Allowing for at least an hour to get up there (as the launcher craft that carries the spaceship up into high altitude had to reach maximum height before the real launch) and back (the glide down would take a lot longer than a conventional re-entry), this didn't leave a lot of time to enjoy the view.

Around that time the business model was relatively simple, with the idea to charge a flat rate, to market it to 'wealthy people' and to make provision for passengers to float around the cabin for a few minutes of weightlessness.

The craft had flown successfully 72 times by the end of August 2011 without incident, which is comforting!

I visited Virgin Galactic's HQ at the time and brought with me a whole stack of ideas which ran as follows:

- Market sectors:
  - End customer corporate, eg as city bonuses, corporate entertaining, acquisition deal meetings
  - Governments – eg to promote ecological awareness, and promoting world peace
- Customer segments:
  - Business millionaires – by industry
  - City dealers
  - Celebrities/wives (footballers/pop-stars etc)
  - Footballers/sportspeople
  - Not so rich – by sponsorship or via a lottery
  - The unfortunates/disadvantaged
  - Gays
  - Religious groups
  - The larger person (charge by the weight? – excess baggage)
  - The general public (lottery)
  - Politicians
  - Groups of individuals
- Value-creating activities:
  - Astronauts club/season ticket holders
  - Present (a very big one!)
  - Differential pricing (premiums seats/service)
  - Differential pricing: for latecomers pay more (as airlines do) or a big premium – first flight
  - Extras: eg for technology-based enhancements of the experience eg advanced telescopes
  - Space parties
  - Two or three flights at once – like *Star Wars*!
  - Corporate networking opportunities and deals in space!
  - Space walks
  - Simulated space wars (two or more craft)
  - DVDs etc
  - Remote conversations with earth friends
  - Webcam links
  - 50-mile-high club!

- Experiments in space
- Enhancement of Virgin Brand generally
- Weddings/dating
- Funerals (again!)
- Easy payment terms
- Life insurance
- Value delivery:
  - Media (TV Channel) eg celebrity knock-out programme in space
  - Alliances
  - NASA
  - Virgin Airlines
  - Media company
- Divestment/outsourcing:
  - Different aeroplane manufacturer
- Geography
  - By customer – eg United States, Europe, Middle East, Japan, China etc.
  - By flight – anywhere – subject to launch sites (world network)

A total of over 40 options in all. It certainly has potential for being a global business.

Another thing to consider is to look at both a deliberate and some relatively random combinations of options, for example:

- Deliberately:
  - China/India
  - Lottery
  - Not so well off

Or:

- Very rich
- IT business founders
- From California to China and back
- Ecologically aware
- Business networking/deal making.

A more random mix would be:

- The disadvantaged
- Lottery
- Space walks.

Each one of these options or bundle of options could then be evaluated using the strategic option grid.

Of particular interest is the possibility of charging a lot more than $200,000, which would come up if we had used 'pricing' as an additional strand of the optopus. What about charging $500,000 for the inaugural flight, for example? Or one might have one flight at $200,000 a seat for a more basic trip, say over the United States, with an extended flight to the Caribbean for $300,000. Apparently Richard Branson was very keen on keeping the price to $200,000, but that did restrict one of the degrees of freedom of the venture. Why not set that as the base price and then have packages on top of that?

In that kind of situation, the main constraint is stakeholder agendas – so one needs a cunning plan to address that. For instance, what about giving Richard two envelopes – one with the base plan where the price per flight gets eroded in value through inflation and revenues are restricted, and another where this isn't the case and there is plenty of value innovation which gets paid for. The economic value of the value innovation option is 50 per cent higher – so you say: 'Richard, are you really sure that you don't want this, given that your core flight price is still $200,000?' A cunning influencing plan – see the cunning checklists coming very soon below, especially on challenging constraints.

Interestingly, when I spoke to Virgin Galactic some years ago they reported customers asking for customized things, but other than that they hadn't – in those early days – thought about the opportunities in the more holistic way encouraged by the optopus. Even when a business is in its formative phase it is all too easy to settle for a business model which meets original goals and is working – rather than to think about optimizing it (as opposed to 'satisficing' it). So even early on, strategic thinking can get switched off and limit the model.

The main 'so what?' out of this analysis is the sheer richness of opportunities that the technique reveals within the Virgin Galactic context. There is the potential here to get most of the cash flows from sponsorship and media opportunities.

In conclusion, the optopus is a very rich way of generating strategic ideas indeed. It is far more effective than purely basic brainstorming. It is not unusual to be able to generate between 50 and 100 possible options if there are a number of subgroups working on the same business.

STRATEGIC EXERCISE 6.5 Applying the optopus –
15–20 minutes

For a particular business area of your choice:

- Taking each strand of the optopus in turn, what are the options that you can generate?

- Now, using the 'pick and mix' approach, what bundles of very plausible option groupings exist?

- Also, taking some implausible options and the same 'pick and mix' approach, what potentially interesting possibilities of an unlikely nature come to light?

- For a number of these ideas, how do they appear on the strategic option grid?

STRATEGIC EXERCISE 6.6 The optopus

- Using the optopus, what lines of enquiry can you generate for your business?

- What further combinations that might be interesting can you come up with via a 'pick and mix' approach?

The strategic option grid scores are only as good as your creative thinking and especially your cunning plan. While the optopus helps to generate more imaginative *content*, managers will also need help with the process of being more imaginative. To help to improve the scores at a micro level we have therefore established a number of recipes for creativity (originally developed for Dyson Appliances). These are grouped as follows:

- challenging the constraints;
- working backwards from customers;
- beating your competitors;
- challenging the industry rules;
- creating greater degrees of freedom.

These are illustrated wherever possible with examples from the Virgin Galactic case.

The cunning checklists

While I can't tell you exactly how to think strategically, more than I have done, the cunning checklists can more than anything get you into the more imaginative and agile cognitive mode required by strategic thinking.

Challenging the constraints

Challenging the constraints can invariably lead to some fruitful lines of enquiry (see Goldratt, 1990). These prompts help you to step outside your current frame of reference. Many of the resistances to strategic thinking are due to taken-for-granted constraints.

If there is a constraint, think why it is there and how it can be avoided

More specifically, it may help (rather than by resorting to simplistic brainstorming) to consider why a constraint exists in the future. In the same breath, by determining why it is there you are probably halfway to avoiding it.

In Virgin Galactic's case it appears that Richard Branson had set himself the target of not selling any seats for over $200,000. But this might be challenged, as some segments might be happy to pay more and also there is some potential for product and service differentiation (the equivalent of first class – in that event you might even be able to justify taking the seats out and putting in posher ones for a particular flight, as the revenues per flight are so great).

Another humorous example came from a Sky satellite documentary series on space: in one of these, sex in space was featured: this appears to be troublesome as there is zero gravity, so a special space suit was invented so that a couple wouldn't keep flying apart! – I guess that could come in handy on a very long flight, say to Mars.

Focus on constraints one at a time, always beginning with the most critical one

Instead of focusing on all constraints simultaneously, it is necessary to pick them out one at a time, to challenge and dissolve them, usually beginning with the hardest. If that one is simply too daunting, pick off a number of the easier ones first.

Working backwards from customers

Customers are potentially an important source of strategic inspiration for the strategic option grid – and one which is frequently ignored because it is felt embarrassing to ask customers what they think you could or should do.

Customers are a wonderful source of strategic thinking. It has been put by some that they are managers' unpaid strategy consultants.

Be your own customer (physically)

In most markets you can actually *be* your own customer. This is easiest in retail, financial services, leisure, publishing and telecommunications. But even in the business-to-business market you can make an enquiry to your own company (or to a competitor) and live through at least the front-end of the process. The main reason why companies do not use this approach seems to be down to fear – fear that one might find out that one is not as good as the average. But discovering such a thing is precisely the kind of learning which can lead to strategic thoughts.

How can you add more value to your customer?

Following on from an out-of-body experience, now think about how you can add *even more* value to your customer. If you were them, what other needs do you have which either are not currently being supplied or are being poorly supplied? Are you delivering value throughout the customer's main phase of consumption? What experiences both before and after that core phase can you also service?

Here the list of areas for much more value-added flights above contained things like space walks, the 50-mile-high club etc.

How can you avoid destroying or diluting value?

Most writers on strategy focus on value added, but by simply avoiding the destruction of customer value, or even merely its dilution, this can in turn generate real competitive advantage.

One could imagine that if you were kept waiting on the runway for three hours before take-off, that would be a big drawback of the Virgin Galactic experience.

If you are creating lots of value, capture more of it

Interestingly, many companies create value but sometimes fail to fully capture it. This might be due to highly competitive market conditions, or it might be due to a lack of innovative positioning and pricing.

When is most value created/least value created over time (plot a value-over-time curve)?

That would be a most interesting way of targeting and monitoring the Virgin Galactic experience.

How can something be made more convenient to buy?

By just taking away the difficulties of buying something, this can lead to increased sales. Alternatively, by making it easier for the customer to buy more (mentally, emotionally and physically), this can facilitate sales volume.

How can something be more absolutely irresistible to buy?

More stretching still, set yourself the mental goal of making your proposition so compelling that it actually becomes irresistible. This can often be achieved by skilful management of the buying experience – and its psychology – on top of an already highly attractive product and service base.

In the context of the Virgin case, one can imagine a lot of people really fancying the idea of space travel but just not quite being able to make up their mind: so something like the astronaut club might be interesting.

Beating your competitors

Competitors, too, can be a source of significant inspiration – not merely to copy them but (ideally) to get tangibly better than them.

Your competitors are equally fertile territory for you to generate new strategic thoughts.

Study your competitors – but then do things even better

Competitive analysis is not particularly done well by many companies. Some do no formal competitor analysis at all. Doing competitor analysis is, however, only the first stage to asking the question: 'How can we do things even better – that is, either better than how they do it or better than how we do it now?'

Learn from how things are done in other industries

Other industries can be fertile grounds for creative thought. For instance, many years ago I helped the British Post Office to think through how it could protect its cost centres, by organizing a lunch with Securicor service managers who were able to suggest not building bullet-proof centres but ways of deceiving criminals so that they did not actually know where the real cash was.

This is a really valuable one in the context of Virgin Galactic, as one can imagine models like that from the football industry really proving insightful. In this case I imagined that I was, say, the CEO of Manchester United who had gone to run Virgin Galactic. Almost certainly that person would have been straight onto the opportunities for sponsorship and the media and merchandising opportunities. Indeed, at the time (2008) Virgin Galactic hadn't really addressed these areas.

Can you build barriers to imitation?

While all of us strive to create competitive advantage, it is not always so obviously important to protect against imitation. The best forms of protection are to create a system of competitive advantage naturally reinforcing competitive advantage (once known as the onion model of competitive advantage). Here, while in theory each level *might* be imitated, copying all the parts of the competitive advantage would be very difficult indeed.

In the Virgin case there was one area that might concern us somewhat. Even as long ago as 2008 there was another potential competitor – a French rocket called Ariadne. Also, when I was running strategy skills workshops all around Eastern Europe in 2007 to 2008 with my banking friends, there were some guys who knew Russia well and they were upfront in saying that the Russians would be well placed to enter that market. They also had, at least in those days, a lot of domestic demand from rich Russians.

Challenging the industry rules

Challenging the ways in which value is created and captured – and how resources are managed – typically provokes powerful lines of enquiry.

How can you change the rules of the game?

The rules of the game are not fixed – and you can change them. Imagine, for example, if you were starting an estate agency industry from scratch at the present time. Would you have expensive BMWs for your senior sales agents? Why not provide them with cheaper SMART cars?

If the rules of the game are changing in the future, how can you do this now?

Rather than respond negatively or defensively to industry change, use scenario storytelling to see into the future. Then work out ways in which you can manifest that future yourselves – to beat competition.

In this case there was an issue with the possible threat from environmental issues: I only had a relatively short period of time with the strategic planning director of Virgin Galactic before I had to leave, and as I was going down to the Underground I remembered about the green issues. Clearly the spacecraft would need to burn up a lot of fuel and produce emissions as a luxury product. It was, *par excellence*, an area of conspicuous consumption. In the longer term it could come under all kinds of pressures from environmental activists or be taxed at a punitive rate: was this a 'one big thing we forgot?'

Creating greater degrees of freedom

Abandon any existing mindset (at industry, company and personal levels)

Begin by letting go of your existing mindset. Forget not only how the industry does things currently – and the company – but also how you do things and even *think* about things.

Have a 'strategic amnesty'

A powerful approach is to spend some time (even if just 20–30 minutes) with the team to talk about, and to let go of, past strategic failures. Usually there has never been the time or the safe opportunity to do this. By calling this a 'strategic amnesty' it is easier to flush things out and to let them go.

Imagine you just started in the organization today

This is a similar thought process to having strategic amnesia. Here you forget your own experience, agendas and thought patterns, which you have been socialized into by the organization. At the same time you can still access the knowledge you have gained from your experience – so you can have the best of both worlds. Besides being a fruitful line of enquiry for competitive strategy, this is also helpful in doing a strategic review (for yourself) of your own role. Coupled to this is an experiment of 'if we were not in the market already, how would we now enter it and with what business model?'

Where you have apparently low influence over something important, how can you get more influence?

In any situation our attention is likely to be drawn to those areas over which we have most apparent influence. It is less obvious that in fact one can often get further at a creative level by focusing instead on at least some areas over which we have little influence – and then trying to work out cunning plans for gaining more influence over them.

Forget that anyone might be against your solution – deal with that later

Stakeholders can sometimes be troublesome, and this can crowd out your thought space to think differently. One tactic is to simply forget that they might either be against you or even that they exist. While influencing stakeholders is, of course, very, very important, this needs to be handled mentally quite separately.

This can be related to the Virgin Galactic case as any price premium would be a no-no for Richard Branson, but there may still be merit in working this up into a viable and attractive business case, and then saying to him: 'Look, we know that you don't want to do that, but this is the prize you are turning down, and this is how it can be done without most of the disadvantages you imagine.'

Create 'white space' – set aside exclusive time to focus solely on the problem

A major problem is frequently the perceived lack of time for strategic thinking. The result of this perception is that managers flit from problem to problem but find it difficult to spend sufficient time to actually resolve any specific problem. Instead, one should focus on a single issue at a time. Also, you do need to allocate sufficient time, which is *completely clear* of other concerns, to address it.

If you can't think of a creative idea, who might?

This prompt is *absolutely not* a last-ditch one. Indeed, you should *always* think about who might be able to get you to your goal of having strategic thoughts about a particular issue.

Look for analogous solutions from other spheres of life

Many people unconsciously draw help from analogies in other domains of thought, for example from military action or from sport. This is really quite helpful and can actually cast new light on a problematic situation. What you are in fact doing here is constructing an analogous model with refreshingly new and powerful characteristics.

Imagine you are your own consultant, advising yourself

Here it may pay off to conduct a special version of the out-of-body experience – of imagining you are your own management consultant. It is useful to couple this with, say, a thought experiment that you are starting your first day in the organization, or that you are re-entering the industry from scratch.

Look for a process of solving the problem first, not necessarily the solution

Einstein once said that the essence of genius was not to solve a problem but to understand the best process for solving it. In a detective-like context, this is about working out recipes for generating fruitful lines of enquiry (for example, here we think about the possible motive for a murder, identifying all of those who might have known the victim, was there anything in the victim's life or recent activities that seemed dubious or out of character?).

Another important thing to discover and remember is that not only are there different strategic options, but there are also different ways of implementing them, and different option timings. Indeed, I have observed so many situations when there have been far more options for *how* you might do something than for *what* you might do that it reminded me of that famous book, the Kama Sutra.

This means that strategic options need to be explored in three dimensions: the what, the how and the timing of the strategy. This can produce a myriad of possibilities, well beyond most managers' mindsets.

Above all is the need always to be on the lookout for a cunning plan. A very recent example of that was reported on Sky News, which carried the story of a couple who got engaged on a train. Adam King asked Louise Rogers to marry him on the 7.57 pm train to Watford Junction. He did this in a very non-average way by smuggling an entire choir – the Adam Street singers – onto the train and merging them with the regular commuters.

Halfway through the journey the singers began to sing – out of nowhere – *Lovely Day*. They then got up and circulated up and down the carriage. As this went on, more and more of them joined in so that half the carriage around Ms Rogers was singing the song.

Some of the other commuters looked quite uncomfortable with all of this and seemed to be wishing that they had caught another train.

At the end Mr King got down on one knee and proposed to Ms Rogers, who, red as a beetroot, fortunately said 'Yes'. She hadn't cottoned on to what was going on until that very moment and seemed quite overwhelmed by the experience. The full sequence is shown on YouTube if you search under 'Videos – Lovely Day'.

Apparently the whole project was nearly jeopardized when Ms Rogers told Mr Adams that morning that she wanted to drive back and not take the train – so Mr Adams disconnected the car battery. That was nearly the 'one big thing that he forgot'!

The moral here is: never do things that are at an average level – always do things with at least some degree of cunning.

STRATEGIC EXERCISE 6.7 Applying the cunning checklists
– 10 minutes

Having identified an important management problem or opportunity, consider:

- which of the cunning checklist items seem to be most suitable;

- taking each one in turn, how might addressing each of these generate new strategic ideas or options?

Testing the scores – or the 'challenge and build' process

While one might have hoped that (from the last section) the strategic option grid now tells us the best possible thinking about each option, often this is not the case. Frequently there is further scope to outline the options to make them better – to make them cunning (or more highly innovative) or (with further refinement) even better, or stunning.

To achieve this, it is often useful to narrow the field of attention down to a small number of boxes on the strategic option grid – perhaps, for example, to focus on:

For Option 1: implementation difficulty

For Option 2: uncertainly and risk

For Option 3: financial attractiveness

For Option 4: stakeholder acceptability.

By going back over the creativity checklists (see the previous section) it may be possible to improve the scores – maybe by one or even (sometimes) two ticks – by thinking of better ideas. This can also be done in conjunction with the deep-dive techniques, or perhaps with further data collection. This is known (as it is at Diageo) as the 'build' process.

Equally, it may be appropriate to 'challenge' the scores, either through specific focus on the uncertainty and risk box (with the uncertainty grid), or by asking 'what is the one big thing we have forgotten?' across any box. A final approach is to test for the resilience of a particular strategic option against different possible states of the world (or 'scenarios'). Here the *same* option is scored across the different columns – each one reflecting a different alternative future.

Practical applications and implications of the strategic option grid

The strategic option grid can be used for a range of applications:

- competitive (or corporate-level) strategy options – new strategies;
- implementation strategy options (for different 'what' options);
- to compare *existing* businesses – as a portfolio analysis;
- to rank strategic projects;
- for organizational restructuring.

Also, the grid can be used not merely to drive out data requirements for further data collection, but also to prioritize them.

Further possibilities

In terms of generating new thinking on the scores in the strategic option grid, the following are all helpful in shaping new scores, so that the initial evaluation is highly tentative:

- the deep-dive techniques;
- the creativity management prompts;
- the optopus (Figure 6.6);
- the generation of options for how you might implement a particular strategy/timings;
- scenario approaches to storytelling.

In particular, scenarios can be used either to put a range of possible scores into each box, or to do separate columns for each one of the scenarios (see Chapter 8 for more on scenarios).

Besides having analytical and creative benefits, it also has benefits in terms of much improved management process, more aligned behaviours, and even political benefits. In the latter respect it typically has the effect of helping managers explore their agendas, and also is able to help their decision process and cope with these agendas in a reasonably well-controlled manner.

It is also helpful in making clear and concise presentations – giving managers more confidence in making these presentations, and making them more digestible at the receiving end. Equally, using it will help take managers a long way towards writing business plans, and also in writing more tentative position papers or draft accounts of the state of their strategic thinking at a particular time.

A further benefit is that it will help gain a much clearer picture of the strategy and of its value and cost drivers *before* doing any financial quantification. By including both financial attractiveness and stakeholder acceptability in the criteria, the grid captures both shareholder value management and also the softer influence of stakeholders. Besides its use for strategic decision making, the strategic option grid is invaluable for helping senior managers develop their strategic thinking skills through formal, management education and development programmes.

Besides its use on new strategies, the strategic option grid can be used for existing strategies as well. This can be really helpful, particularly for identifying those strategies which need more attention, or are in need of a more 'detergent' approach. This is especially useful in the context of doing any strategic audit of the business – see Chapter 9.

Key insights from the chapter

- The strategic option grid is applicable across a very wide range of decisions.

- To make strategic choices we need to have some criteria. These are: strategic, financial attractiveness, implementation difficulty, uncertainty and risk, and stakeholder acceptability.

- Strategic attractiveness is the external market attractiveness and the relative competitive position. Market attractiveness is based on things like the growth drivers, Porter's five forces and perhaps PEST analysis. Competitive positioning is a quite separate thing from this but is also a key part of strategic attractiveness.

- Financial attractiveness: these are the long- and short-term returns from the option (or possibly its economic profit) – ultimately this should go down into the value and cost drivers, and the financial model.

- Implementation difficulty: this is the sum of difficulty over time to achieve the strategic goals.

- Uncertainty and risk: this is the extent of the volatility of the assumptions underlying a specific strategic option.

- Stakeholder acceptability: this is the extent to which stakeholders favour, disfavour, or are neutral regarding that option.

- The scores on the option grid are only as good as the cunning plan.

- Besides its use on more deliberate strategies, it can also be used for more emergent and detergent strategies within the strategy mix.

- The scores can be tested through the deep-dive techniques, or through scenario storytelling.

- The option scores can be weighted and given threshold and qualifying target levels.

- The options can be scored not only from your own perspective but from the perspective of other players, too (the double option grid).

- Besides the more qualitative thinking about financial attractiveness, you should also be accompanying these 'judgements' with some detailed financial modelling, and this must include some modelling of the uncertainties and risks.

- The options should be as specific as possible and should have clear parameters (eg within financial attractiveness, what sales growth and operating profit margin is assumed, over what time?).

- In terms of option generation, there are options for what you do, how you do them and when you do them.

- The strategic options grid can be used to appraise not only new options but also existing strategies, eg as part of any strategic audit.

- Another important thought is that the option grid can be used to simulate the attractiveness to players in the game other than oneself.

- In generating options it is far better to use the optopus rather than less structured brainstorming as you will get a much broader range of options.

- The dimensions of the optopus can be adapted and added to: for example, with brand and pricing options.

- The ideas can be further developed and enriched by the 'pick and mix' of different combinations of ideas.

- The cunning checklists can not only be used to generate new options in their own right, but also to make them a lot more cunning.

- The benefits of the grid are that besides having some systematic criteria which are very relevant and that it helps generate options, it is useful for presentations, position papers, influencing, defusing politics and for identifying key questions and data needs.

In conclusion, the search for options is a natural, essential and most valuable part of the strategic thinking and planning processes. In writing this, an obvious thought I had was 'what proportion of planning processes have any formal options generation and evaluation process?'. Over the past 22 years of independent consulting I have always insisted on this as a discrete part of the process. But this is by no means the norm. So it must be the case that many managers aren't used to operating that way. Indeed, the way in which managers have welcomed this as 'new thing' strongly suggests that if this stage of the process ever did exist, then it was blurred into the detailed planning part. It was certainly not given the time and attention that it really deserved.

I do not typically work mainly with SMEs but with a wide variety of usually much larger companies and my observations apply to the majority of them.

So it is worth taking seriously this creative and evaluative phase in order to widen one's degrees of strategic freedom, to come up with truly cunning strategies and to check their attractiveness and resilience.

In the next chapter we explore the menu of implementation techniques that serve as part of the deep-dive process of option evaluation, besides being applied to the more detailed implementation planning and change management.

07

Implementation

Introduction

Implementation has often been called, and rightly, 'the graveyard of strategy'. Many strategies get decided on and implemented even without satisfactory testing for implementation feasibility.

In Chapter 6 we looked at how one of the key criteria of the strategic option grid deals with 'implementation difficulty', our fourth key criterion. We now take this further by considering how the 'deep dive' can be done to explore this much more fully. This is essential in order to form broader strategic thoughts into more concrete, detailed and resilient action plans and project plans.

Almost no books on strategy put very much emphasis on implementation and yet it is acknowledged as being as important as strategy development. And even fewer deal with implementation tools other than perhaps with force field analysis. I do really believe that we supposed strategy experts should show a real interest in what managers actually have to cope with on the ground in delivering real results from strategy.

As an example, a while back I was working with the board of John Menzies plc on its corporate strategy. At the time its core business was still newspaper distribution, which crudely speaking was a 'cash cow', and it had diversified into a number of areas, including the Early Learning Centre, which didn't really fit and was subsequently sold on, and now belongs to Mothercare (where I encountered it again in its reincarnated existence in 2011). Its then turnover was around £1 billion. It had also got into some other odd diversifications, such as an operation to distribute video games for a Japanese company, and a then fledgling and very promising airport distribution business. In the course of the review Menzies made a very big acquisition in that latter area, as well as deciding to divest the Early Learning Centre and the other odd businesses.

At the time I wasn't really sure that, having come to some decisions within the review (through the strategic option grid etc), they *would actually do it*. At that time I was working with the Metropolitan Police and, prompted by that, at my last workshop with Menzies in Edinburgh I said to them: 'I am really worried that you will not actually do what you say you have decided to do... in fact I warn you that I will come back up as the "strategy police"! Yes. I will pay my own fare and off fees and check out that you actually did it.' They all went quiet – I felt something had registered.

About nine months later I was running a three-day strategy programme in London and had popped out for a walk after lunch, near Victoria. I was just going down a subway when I heard an anonymous cry from behind: 'Tony! Tony!' – my first thoughts were that it was one of the participants wanting an extra consultation. I looked round and it turned out to be none other than the ex-corporate development director of John Menzies plc.

He said to me: 'Tony, after the review the board did everything – and I mean everything that was in the strategy – that's the first time in my life that I have ever seen that happen. Normally very little action comes out of strategy reviews – somehow that gets lost.'

That hasn't often been my experience – whether this is because of the tools that you will see, or the process, or simply my own personal passion and quirkiness I don't know – but I would say that if you can really get it across that implementation is in effect the second half of the football match, that can make a decisive difference. I originally came across this very simple notion while working with a Swedish strategy consultant called Lars at PA Consulting nearly 25 years ago, who called this: 'Strategy times implementation equals performance.'

But the other main ingredient that I would like to add, as we are now in the very dynamic second decade of the 21st century, is how long it actually takes both to arrive at a strategy and to actually mobilize its implementation. So I will add the dimension of time.

To summarize this mathematically:

The Value of a Strategy = Quality (of Strategy) × Quality (of Implementation) divided by the time it takes, T

Or VS = (Q)S × (Q)I / T

So this chapter now sets out to demystify not just one or two implementation techniques, but eight, including:

- fishbone analysis;
- wishbone analysis;
- FT analysis;
- how–how analysis;
- AID analysis;
- force field analysis;
- difficulty-over-time curves;
- stakeholder agenda analysis.

These techniques thus help us considerably with the quality of the implementation and the time that it takes.

But we begin by taking a close look at how the strategy implementation process fits into this. Figure 7.1 defines the five key stages of the strategy implementation process:

- Diagnosis: what is the scope of the opportunity (or threat)? What are its objectives, and possible benefits, costs and risks? What is the overall implementation difficulty and who are the key stakeholders (at a high level)?

- Implementation options – and the cunning plan: what cunning options are available for implementation?

- Planning: for these options, how attractive are they versus difficult to implement? What key activities are needed, and with what resources?

- Implementation: is the actual implementation proving effective and, if not, why not? What new implementation forces and stakeholders have come into play, and how might these be handled? Do the original objectives need revisiting and are these more easily met by other strategies? And if so, what are the costs of refocusing efforts?

- Learning and control: is the implementation on track in terms of its intended competitive, financial, operational and organizational effects? Did you achieve what you set out to achieve? If not, what were the factors you might have controlled, or attempted to influence, but didn't? Or, do you need to revisit and change your recipes for developing strategies for growth (or for their implementation)? Finally, were the implementation difficulties much greater than envisaged and, if so, why?

FIGURE 7.1   Strategic implementation process

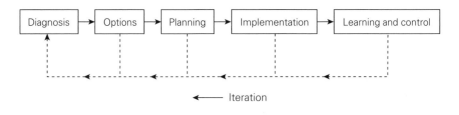

To summarize which strategic thinking techniques are appropriate in managing each stage of the implementation process, consider the following:

Diagnosis	Implementation options	Planning	Implementation	Learning and control
Fishbone analysis	AID analysis	Value and cost drivers – see earlier in book	Force field	Fishbone analysis
FT analysis	Stakeholder analysis	How–how analysis	Difficulty-over-time curve	Wishbone analysis
Force field analysis		AID analysis	Stakeholder and agenda analysis	FT analysis
Stakeholder analysis			Force field and stakeholder analysis	Force field analysis

The techniques which we have already explored are as follows:

Diagnosis	Cunning options	Planning	Implementation	Learning and control
PEST factors	Wishbone analysis	Gap analysis	Wishbone analysis	Gap analysis
Growth drivers	Strategic option grid	Wishbone analysis	Uncertainty grid	Wishbone analysis
Competitive forces	Uncertainty grid	Uncertainty grid		Uncertainty grid
Competitive profiling				
Gap analysis		Value-over-time curve		

STRATEGIC EXERCISE 7.1 Diagnosing past implementation
– 10–15 minutes

For a past area of implementation which you have been involved in, ask the following questions:

● What were the strengths and weaknesses of each phase of the implementation process, particularly:

  – diagnosis;
  – cunning options;
  – planning;
  – implementation;
  – learning and control?

● What 'dos and don'ts' can you distil for the future? Look at some tools for diagnosis, for creating cunning options, for planning, implementation, and learning and control.

Fishbone analysis

Fishbone analysis is a very effective way of going behind the more superficial aspects of the problem or opportunity. For instance, Figure 7.2 takes the example of a manager who lost the plot – in a TV documentary on 'The Complainers' produced within the *Cutting Edge* series. This is an absolutely classic video which has the potential to both shock and, as it is surreal, amuse.

FIGURE 7.2 Fishbone analysis

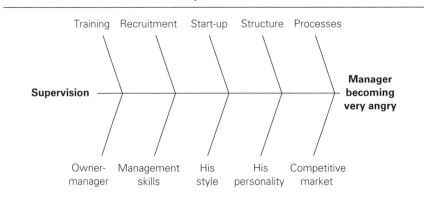

There is a real scene from that programme (so it wasn't being acted out – the camera just happened to catch it on film) in which the many frustrations and stresses of a manager come to the surface when it comes to light that his staff have been less than mindful about their work and this has given rise to a number of customer complaints about the business. (As context, he is the owner as well – and it is evidently a new and vulnerable business operating in a very tough and competitive market.)

In the fishbone we start at the right with the symptom of the problem. This is often the most difficult thing to pin down as often there are a number of things competing for attention. For example, there might be something such as 'like-for-like sales are down', or it might be more general, such as 'we are in strategic decline', which is slightly upstream in the causal chain, and also a broader symptom, or it could be 'we are getting outpaced by the competition'. All three of these symptoms were associated with one particular problem that was being faced by a plc and the 'symptoms' were ambiguous, like this. Each fishbone would have dragged up slightly different things, so it is important to consider what to start with, and maybe piloting it. The fishbones are simply the root causes of the problem. They are placed on the fishbone in no particular order. There is no special significance of the fish's tail, for example.

In the video, which is awesome, the dialogue runs as follows (edited for swear words):

Manager: 'Look, look, it says [in the complaint letter]... "we have just received a copy of your magazine issue, which as you know carried a double paged copy of our advert plus a competition page reply on behalf of our client. Unfortunately, we were not pleased with the advert as there is no reply page as suggested on page 65 as quoted at the bottom of page 29." What is going on???'

Employee: 'I was on holiday.'

Manager: 'What! This is £8,000 of our money! It is a good client – we are getting them out there...' [Second employee now unfortunately walks into the room.]

Manager: 'Where the hell have you been!' [getting even angrier]

Second employee: 'I have been out to lunch.'

Manager: 'Three things, you have caused me a lot of aggravation, sit down, sit down!'

Second employee: 'Could you calm down?'

Manager: 'No I won't calm down. – Three things. £8,000! I have had three calls for me today (about you)... number one, invoices wrong – sixteen hundred quid, no, sixteen thousand pounds for an ad! – What are we? – the *International Sunday Times*? No, it's not f. funny either. Its f. not.

'Number two – about all this aggravation: have you read our ad? What's the most important ad in the magazine – ours?'

Second Employee (agreeing): 'Ours.'

Manager: 'Who wrote it – Rupert the f. bear? – It is not happening, it is not happening.'

Second employee: 'Oh, this is no... (good).'

Manager: 'No, £8,000, eight grand because you went off early partying up to Birmingham, every time, every time. – I have got a pile of CVs that high [gesticulating], that f. high, begging to do your job. I want real people to work for me, not idiots who make mistake after mistake that cost the company money when we are trying to start the company up.'

Second employee: 'No, I know where you can f. stick those CVs...' [Then the manager grasps hold of his office table and throws it in the general direction of his employee – and there is a near miss.]

Manager: 'Get out! Get out! You are sacked!!! Get out of the office now – and don't ever come back!'

After he is shown spending some moments trying to rebuild his team, he is then interviewed later in quiet reflection, presumably revisiting his CSFs: 'It is about three things, three things, credibility and the money... we are not there yet', suggesting that the emotional storm has narrowed his cognitive attention down not just to only three things (Miller's Law), but to two.

When we look at a situation that has gone as wrong as this, it is normal and natural to get sucked into the symptom of the problem – which we have put, neutrally, as 'manager getting very angry'. But underneath that are a number of root causes that a fishbone can be used in quite a calm, clinical and objective way to analyse – at a number of levels. In the fishbone analysis that we see in Figure 7.2 there are things like:

- training;
- recruitment;
- processes;
- he is an owner-manager;
- management skills;
- his style;
- his personality.

Looking at these 'root causes' invites us to take the fishbone down to a more micro level – for example, did the manager have any traumatic events in his life, as were revealed earlier in the video, which may have given him some anger management issues? (That's not to say that his anger was unjustified, necessarily.)

This case study not only highlights the use of fishbone analysis generally, but also its specific use on complex behavioural issues that are often on the critical path of getting the value out of strategic thinking and implementation. Generally, audience reaction to the video is that they often recognize this rather extreme situation in less dramatic and more subtle ways, but nevertheless at work in incidents that they have seen in their management careers.

Management is an emotional thing and there is a lot at stake. Even if emotions are channelled under the surface they are still there, and they are still at work. Management books clearly over-stress the rational and under-stress the emotional in the strategic decision and implementation processes (see Chapter 2).

Coming back to the fishbone analysis tool itself, the following are some important guidelines for using it:

- Identify the symptom of the cause and position it over towards the right-hand side. Where there are a number of possible symptoms you might need to analyse several problems (and thus draw up several fishbones). Or, you may need to summarize a number of issues into a single, overarching fishbone.

- Make sure that the root causes are the real root causes (or at least quite close to their being root causes). If you can still ask the question 'why?', you are still at the level of a symptom.

- Use your common sense to understand at what point you should cease going back up the causal chain. Thus 'lack of leadership skills' for most purposes is a satisfactory root cause rather than going back to 'the board appointed the wrong leader' or 'there were no really suitable candidates'. (You do not necessarily need to go back to the dawn of time to scope and diagnose a problem.)

- Ask yourself at the end: 'What's the one big thing that we missed?'

The don'ts are:

- Don't worry about whether the fishbone causes should go vertically or downwards. There is no special priority in where they are positioned – they are all equivalent. Most fishbones are more complete if they are drawn up in a creative flow, rather than in some pre-structured manner. If you do want to prioritize the fishbones, write the root causes on Post-its and then move them around, perhaps in order of priority or difficulty, or degree of influence, or perhaps their attractiveness.

- Don't forget to consider the external causes as well as the internal root causes, and also the tangible versus the less tangible causes of the original symptom.

- Don't clutter up the analysis with sub-bones off your main fishbone on the same sheet of paper. This produces a visually complex, messy and hard-to-interpret picture. Where appropriate, do the analysis of a particular mini-fishbone for a particular cause on a separate page.

One extra check that can be done to ensure completeness is to use a condensed version of the 'Seven S's' (Peters and Waterman, 1982) to ensure that you have thought about all the key organizational systems that have contributed in a causal way to the problem. These core systems are:

- strategy;
- structure;
- style (or culture);
- skills;
- systems.

In the case of the very angry manager earlier, we can see that this might give us a more complete analysis of the root causes and also surface many of the interdependencies possibly at work. Systems models are very helpful as support to the fishbone process.

It is often asked, around this point, what value does fishbone analysis add? (This is generally sometimes raised by those who appear sceptical of the value of strategic thinking tools.) Our main responses to this view are that the fishbone is an important tool for understanding underlying causes by asking the question 'why?' and then 'why' over again until you get to the end, or root causes. This generates much deeper diagnostic thinking and understanding of the causal chain that has led to an issue or a problem than conventional analysis, which mixes up symptoms, causes and possible solutions in discussion – all at once – so you get an unclear 'problem soup'. This is so particularly as:

- Each fishbone can usually be traced back to its sub-fishbones, as suggested in the case of the manager who got very angry. (With a list, each point is usually the end of the analysis and thus is not analysed in greater depth.)
- Subsequently each fishbone can be prioritized using, for example, AID analysis (see later). This effect can be powerfully shown as an overlay of two pictures, one on top of the other, the first picture being the fishbone and the second one on top being its prioritization. Here one diagnoses the fishbone first and then moves on to look at its prioritization.

If you just do a simple list, the symptoms tend not to stand out from the root causes. Also, a common tendency (without using a fishbone) is to talk around general issues rather than real causes. The fishbone is also a highly visual device, making it easier to communicate (especially to top managers) and generally of much more interest.

Another thing worth stressing here is that without something like the fishbone and without paper it is virtually impossible to remember the root causes, as a typical fishbone will have a dozen or more root causes. Also, by using it as a visual picture you can create a cognitive and emotional distance from it, so you are helicoptering above it. This is especially helpful when dealing with a problem that has some emotional implications.

At a practical level, the key benefits of fishbone analysis are that it:

- helps diagnose a problem in much greater depth, helping to scope strategic issues much more effectively;

- usually goes halfway (at least) towards suggesting solutions;
- reduces the tendency for managers to talk about the same issues over and over again – just using different words creates greater confusion and slows progress significantly;
- communicates the scope and key reasons for the problem in a politically neutral way – it is an essential technique for managing upwards;
- provides a means of linking strategic analysis with implementation (for example, by taking a gap between yourself and a competitor – and using a fishbone to tease out the detailed causes which need to be addressed);
- allows you to go freely up and down levels of analysis without getting irretrievably lost down the rabbit holes;
- you can always ask yourself the question: 'What's the one big root cause that we have forgotten?'

Its potential disadvantages are that:

- it can reinforce the 'it's a problem' mindset;
- managers do tend to restrict themselves to solving the causes of the problem with fishbone analysis, rather than examining where they might be (the cunning plan);
- unless a fishbone is prioritized (which we will see later), it takes you only a limited way forward.

Fishbone analysis links with other techniques as follows:

- SWOT analysis – it helps to explore weaknesses and threats at a deeper level (the same can also be done for PEST problems, or for asking 'why is the bargaining power of buyers strong?' (seeing that as a symptom) or 'why are new entrants a threat?' (yet another symptom that might be highlighted by using Porter's five forces)).
- Gap analysis – to understand the causes of the gap.
- The GE grid: to explore why a market is attractive (or less attractive) and equally why competitive position is strong (or weak).
- Motivator-hygiene factor analysis – to explore the reasons for hygiene factors not being met.
- Competitor profiling – to analyse why a competitive gap exists.
- Uncertainty grid – fishbone analysis can tease out why an assumption is either a) very uncertain or b) very important.
- For the uncertainty tunnel (Chapter 8) – to analyse the precursors of change (as root causes), and also what causal factors may trigger future transitional events to take us into a new state of the world.

- For cost drivers – fishbone analysis can be used to explore the problem 'why are certain costs too high?' as an alternative format (to cost drivers).
- For force field analysis (coming later in this chapter) – to explore why a force is constraining.
- For stakeholder analysis (again coming later) – to explore why a key stakeholder is against.
- Once you have done it you can then lift out of this analysis and into the more creative space of the wishbone, which works on creating a more ideal space for the issue, seeing it as an opportunity as well.

It is also useful to highlight that fishbone analysis can be of considerable help in structuring problems. Generally many problems hide inside each other but are interrelated. This invites us to split them up, although they remain linked. We call this 'piranha analysis' – to highlight the fact that while smaller problems can appear to be more manageable, they can actually be deadly and ferocious (hence the piranha analogy). Figure 7.3 is a picture of a generic piranha analysis.

FIGURE 7.3   Piranha analysis

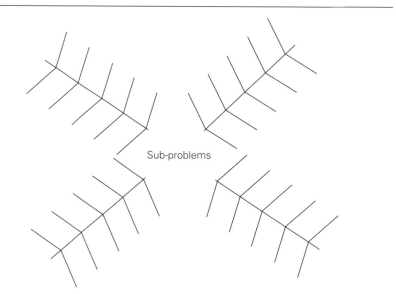

Sub-problems

One application of piranha analysis is to relationship difficulties, which are endemic in management and in complex, changing organizations (not to mention in personal lives), and strategic thinking is a vital tool in helping you deal with them.

Relationship difficulties typically occur with your boss, with a subordinate or with a close rival:

- what you yourself bring to it;
- what others bring to it;
- the current organizational context;
- the past organizational legacy.

These can be overlaid on top of the four core roots of the piranha analysis.

This useful four-themed structure forces you into assessing what you yourself brought to the situation. It also focuses on some things which you ought to have much more influence over – which is particularly beneficial for self-reflection.

The context should generate some thoughts about what is currently going on around the relationship context, for example any restructuring, performance pressures, inconsistent organizational priorities. The legacy can be very important as it helps to understand how the problem might have developed and how this might have been at least partially caused by past organizational mistakes.

Having used the piranha, it is common to witness a partial or even a complete turnaround of a relationship, especially if it has been shared openly between both sides. (It is also very helpful here to use the wishbone analysis to create a vision for a much better working relationship and the alignment factors for it to go well.)

One can see a piranha picture being helpful to re-cluster the root causes in Figure 7.2 – the angry manager fishbone – including a separate mini-fishbone for the manager to reflect on what he had done both before and during this encounter to cause the problem.

STRATEGIC EXERCISE 7.2 Fishbone analysis – 10 minutes

For one major strategic problem or constraint:

- What is the key symptom?
- What are the root causes (level 1)?
- What are the root causes behind these (level 2)?
- What options can you see from this analysis to start to build a strategy around?

Wishbone analysis

Wishbone analysis is a sister technique to fishbone analysis. Wishbone analysis is a way of dealing with an opportunity, as opposed to a problem. Here, instead of symptoms of essentially what has gone wrong, we start off with a vision or more ideal state of how we would like to see the world, and we then work backwards from this to identify what has to go right to deliver that.

That vision was once encapsulated in the British girl band the 'Spice Girls' who became world famous for singing 'What do we really-really-really want?'

Essentially we see the same structure as the fishbone, yet reversed to differentiate it – see Figure 7.4.

So here the wishbones are the 'necessary and sufficient conditions of success'. Note here that these go beyond the things that you plan for – in terms of being controllable – and include the key environmental and other uncertainties that need to be in alignment too.

In the case of the wishbone in Figure 7.4, when Dyson first launched his bagless carpet cleaner in the mid-1990s he had a number of mutually reinforcing competitive advantages, such as the fact that he had patented his design and had established premium pricing for his leading brand. But these competitive advantages were not necessarily easily sustainable, and Dyson was already being caught up around 2000 by some competitors who were imitating the company.

FIGURE 7.4   Wishbone analysis

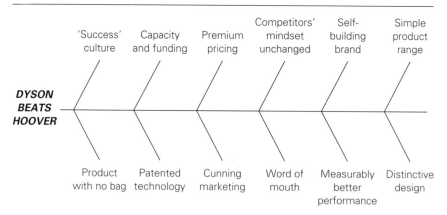

Also, there were a number of alignment factors that weren't necessarily permanent and weren't actually within his control, for instance 'competitors' mindset unchanged'. So the wishbone analysis is far from being merely about the content of the plan in order to achieve a goal or vision. Indeed, arguably we should have put a lot more alignment factors in the wishbone analysis to see how resilient it is. Each of these might then be analysed using the uncertainty grid – to get a sense of true resilience.

While wishbone analysis clearly has a role to play in competitive strategy, it also has a function in implementation as well, where it can play an imaginative role, for example:

- after doing a fishbone analysis so that we can now look at what might be needed to bring more positive success;
- in order to formulate a more cunning plan for implementation.

Wishbone analysis, like fishbone analysis, may be taken down to a second level of analysis. So, for example, we can look at all the necessary and sufficient conditions of cunning marketing in the future. Again, if this is criticized for being just a 'wish list', it needs to be said that you need something down on paper so that a group can have a common visualization of the issues, and also that none will get lost. Also, the wishbone is a structured thinking process and the wishbones and sub-bones are a pictorial and meaningful representation of that structure, which is important.

STRATEGIC EXERCISE 7.3 Wishbone analysis – 10 minutes

For an area of implementation:

- What is the implementation vision?
- What are the alignment factors?
- Are these both necessary and sufficient to achieve that goal?
- Is there a 'one big thing' or a 'two big things' we've forgotten?
- For one or more of the wishbones, what do you see when you go down another level?
- How do all these level 1 alignment factors appear on the uncertainty grid?

From–to (FT) analysis

FT analysis helps to scope the extent of the strategic project you are working on, in terms of its breadth and its degree of stretch.

FT analysis is another useful tool for scoping the extent of implementation, especially for organizational change or for operational development. When a development project has a significant impact on the 'paradigm' or on 'how we do things around here' (see Grundy, 1993), it is essential that at least a rudimentary FT analysis is conducted.

FIGURE 7.5   FT analysis

FROM ⟶ TO

Structures*

Goals*

Behaviours*

Cost base*

Responsiveness*

You need to identify shifts relevant to you

The 'paradigm' embraces a whole range of organizational processes, some of which are 'soft' and less tangible and some of which are 'hard' and tangible. See Figure 7.5 for a generic FT analysis.

For instance, managers within a financial services company once used an FT analysis based specifically on the paradigm to scope their organizational change project. This helped them to get their minds around the 'soft' as well as the 'hard' factors, as follows:

Paradigm	From	To
Power	Restricted	Resides at the lowest appropriate level
Structure	Hierarchical	Flatter
Controls	Instinctive and 'seat of pants'	Measured objectives
Routines	Retrospective-looking	Live and forward-looking
Rituals	Loose plans	Structured plans
Myths	The 'Mighty Pru', 'Life Administration is OK'	Real world
Stories	Our job well done	Delighted customers
Symbols	Status hierarchy	Rewards for performance
Management style	Aloof	Open

This type of analysis to explore shifts in organizational conditions and systems can also be used to monitor the progress of a strategic project, perhaps using a score of 1 to 5 with 1 being the 'From' and possibly 5 being the 'To'. (In some situations, however, we might well be starting off with better than 1, as we might already have made some progress towards our goals, prior to embarking on the project. Equally, we might wish to go all out for a 5, although a 4 or even 3 might be more realistic and acceptable, depending upon the situation.)

The example in the FT analysis is very much a more 'wholemeal' approach. We see a semi-structured approach being used to generate the key shifts which the strategic project is aimed at delivering. One approach is to quickly brainstorm the 'from's and to's' in a way much more specific to a particular project. The caveat here is the softer factors which are needed to shift, for example, behaviours, attitudes and mindset generally. Again, it may be helpful to draw from the Seven S's that we saw in the section on fishbone analysis earlier in this chapter, namely by thinking about:

- strategy;
- structure;
- style (or culture);
- skills;
- systems.

To carry out an FT analysis the following steps must be thought through:

- What are you trying to shift? (the critical categories).
- By how much are you trying to shift them? (the horizontal from and to shifts).

By now it may have become apparent to you that FT analysis is essentially an extended form of gap analysis. Because it breaks the gap down into a number of dimensions, it is generally more specific than gap analysis and is frequently the next step.

STRATEGIC EXERCISE 7.4 FT analysis – 10 minutes

For one area of strategy implementation of your choice and in particular one for which there is already an existing state of affairs which you are trying to change or shift:

- What are the key dimensions that you are trying to shift?
- What are the extremes of these shifts (from left to right), ie where have you started from originally, and where would you like to end up ultimately?
- Where you are actually now? (Note: this does not have to be a 1.)

- Where do you want to be as a result of this strategic project? (Note: this does not have to be a 5.)

- What specific actions or interventions might make each shift feasible?

The key benefits of FT analysis are:

- It gives a clear and more complete vision of the extent of the potential difficulty that achieving that vision may give rise to.
- It can be used to actually monitor strategic progress.
- It is a very useful technique for communicating what needs to be done, or for exploring the implications and for getting greater buy-in.
- More specifically, it is especially helpful in presenting business plans.

If it does have any drawback, however, it is that sometimes managers find it difficult, at least initially, to define their desired categories for development and change (because of antecedent lack of clarity and ownership).

FT analysis links into a number of other techniques as follows:

- It can be used to summarize changes in the external marketplace, for example by drawing from PEST factors, growth drivers, especially in the five competitive forces and also in the industry mindset.
- It can help to move from the starting point of a fishbone analysis for a programme of development and change.
- It can help give an overview of the more detailed 'how–how's (see next subsection).
- It helps break down any gap analysis.
- It can be used prior to AID analysis and stakeholder analysis to scope any likely implementation difficulty, and also the level of stakeholder support.

How–how analysis

How–how analysis is useful in planning the detail of implementation. It is also very helpful in finding a way forward which might not have been thought about before.

Figure 7.6 gives an example of a how–how analysis, where until this picture was drawn up managers perceived that there was no way that the cost of bought-in motors could be reduced.

While fishbone analysis works backwards from the current situation to find out how and why it exists, how–how works forwards to see how it can be resolved in the future.

FIGURE 7.6 How–how analysis

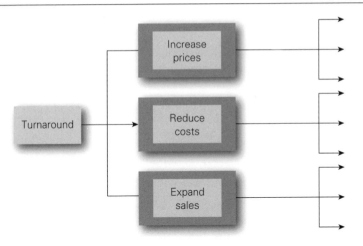

How–how analysis adds the most value when you have not really thought in much concrete detail about the implementation steps that will be needed to achieve something. But even when you have thought about this, it will also be useful just to help identify the less tangible as well as the tangible aspects of implementation, especially:

- positioning;
- communicating;
- influencing;
- team-building.

How–how analysis will also help to get some approximate order of the likely sequence in which things need to happen – and to help identify any potential critical paths (the longest time in a network of activities that the different steps will take to move through).

The major benefit of how–how analysis is that it exposes assumptions about what actually has to happen, reducing blind spots. A potential disadvantage is that it can tell you little more than you already know, if you have thought about something really well already.

How–how analysis links to other tools as follows:

- It may help to go from the fishbone's root causes to some potential implementation solutions.
- It can help to operationalize the various shifts which have been identified in the FT analysis.
- It can feed into the AID analysis (coming next).
- It can help scope the likely value and cost drivers (coming soon).

Attractiveness and implementation difficulty (AID) analysis

By looking at the relative attractiveness and its difficulty of implementation one can now begin to evaluate strategies at a micro level, from a number of perspectives:

- One can prioritize a portfolio of strategic activities, any one of which can be undertaken.
- Different options for implementing the concept can be evaluated.
- Mutually exclusive strategic activities can be prioritized.
- The different parts of activities within an activity can be prioritized.

The AID analysis grid combines both the strategic and financial attractiveness of the strategic option grid into single variable of attractiveness (the vertical axis). Implementation difficulty and stakeholder acceptability are thus brought together in the horizontal axis of 'implementation difficulty' (see Figure 7.7).

FIGURE 7.7   AID analysis

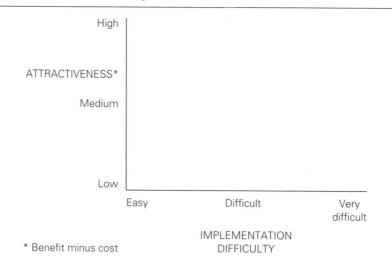

Beginning with the vertical dimension of attractiveness, one can now expand on the final bullet point above.

Only uncertainty is left out of the AID grid – a small limitation but one that is worth making unless that variable is hugely important – when we are dealing at the micro level of analysis. So we have a much simpler prioritization technique but one that does, however, omit uncertainty.

The strategic option grid and AID analysis are thus not mutually exclusive, by any means. The strategic option grid can be used first to evaluate different strategic options (either for different projects or for different ways of implementing a specific strategy at a macro level). Then the AID analysis might evaluate and prioritize sub-parts, at the micro level.

Sometimes some parts of a possible strategy can be undertaken without doing others. It can be unbundled. For example, buying a business is a project but the constituent parts of the business can be regarded as sub-projects to be retained or possibly disposed of.

Even where a strategy does consist of a number of discretionary sub-units, which are *not* discretionary (such as a training strategy), it is still possible to display their individual positioning on the AID grid. Some parts of any training may be more difficult to implement than others – and will thus have different positioning horizontally on the AID grid.

Thinking now about the vertical dimension of attractiveness, each part of a training strategy may vary in its relative benefits, and in its relative cost. For example, a training project might have the following profile:

	Benefits (B)	Costs (C)	Attractiveness (B) – (C)
Pre-diagnosis	High	Medium	Medium
Pre-work	Low	Low	Low
Main programme	High	Medium	High/Medium
Interim support	Medium	Low	Medium
Follow-up programme	High	Low	High
Ongoing support	High	Low	High

The AID grid can enable this trade-off to be made between different strategies. The vertical dimension of the picture focuses on the benefits less costs. The horizontal dimension represents the total difficulty over time. (See the difficulty-over-time curve coming very soon.) This time is the time up until delivery of results, and not of completion of earlier project phases. This tool enables a portfolio of possible projects to be prioritized. Figure 7.8 illustrates a hypothetical case.

Strategy A is seen as being both very attractive and relatively easy to implement. This project is non-contentious and will probably be given the go-ahead. Strategy C is relatively difficult – it will probably end up being zapped unless it can be reformulated to make it both a lot more attractive and easier.

Strategy D presents the biggest dilemma of all. Although it appears to be very attractive, it is also very difficult to implement. Yet managers will tend

FIGURE 7.8   AID analysis – example

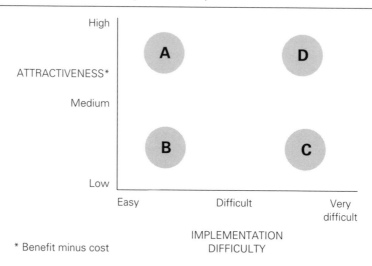

to focus on the attractiveness of the project rather than its actual difficulty. And that can occur even though they have gone through the force field and stakeholder analyses thoroughly.

When using the AID tool at HP, this happened on two occasions. Quite separately, two D-type strategies were identified and managers spent more time analysing them, and as a result of that their commitment to action levels built up.

Although neither of the projects went ahead, in their existing form, both the author and the (then) internal facilitator Stuart Reed had to be relatively strong to convince the teams that some further refinement was necessary. Stuart said at the time:

> I had gone through with them [the managers] both the implementation forces and the stakeholders. Although it did seem to be an attractive project, our two organizational tools were telling us 'it is not going to happen'. I think because the managers were going through the analysis tools for the first time (and hadn't actually tried to implement it), they hadn't quite realized that it really wasn't going to happen.

Strategies in the northeast zone do present us with some interesting management dilemmas. Following up one HP school of thought, one viewpoint is that it is unlikely to be worthwhile to do these projects – as realistically the organization will lack the commitment to drive them through. However, a second HP school of thought is that such projects merely represent a challenge for creative thinking – as long as they are potentially very attractive it may be very fruitful to do this.

At HP another senior manager re-examined a strategic project with which the author had been personally involved some 18 months earlier. This potential strategic project concerned a business process change and a restructuring. At the time the position of this strategic project was due east on the AID grid (ie medium, attractive and very difficult).

This strategic project went into suspended animation for around 18 months. On further contact with HP we discovered that the new senior manager had resolved the problem in a creative way by outsourcing the process, rather than by internal reorganization. The project had shifted from due east to northwest, that is: 'high attractiveness/low implementation difficulty'.

I also uncovered a third school of thought working with Pioneer UK, the hi-fi company. Its Japanese managing director said to us: 'Perhaps we should do that project *because* it is difficult.'

Initially, I wondered whether this was perhaps an example of the 'will to power' (Nietzsche) by management. On reflection, however, this philosophy fitted in well with the notion, which we have already explained, of break-through management, or *Hoshin*. Here a breakthrough is frequently something that is both highly attractive and very difficult to implement. (While breakthroughs do not have to be very difficult to implement – just hard for others to imitate – they frequently are.)

A cunning plan is to target projects which, while they are likely to be between very difficult to mission impossible for others to implement, we will find easier. Here mission impossible (MI) is just off the page to the east of the AID grid.

If one does decide to target projects which are very difficult, then following the *Hoshin* philosophy it is important to narrow the focus to a very small number of projects within a specific period of time. It is very unlikely that more than three can be undertaken simultaneously without distraction of organizational attention and loss of energy generally.

The positionings on the AID grid are thus likely to be relatively tentative unless tested out using other techniques. For example:

- The attractiveness of the project may require further analysis using value driver and cost driver analysis. (Ultimately, this attractiveness can be financially quantified, albeit perhaps approximately.)
- Implementation difficulty can be tested out using force field analysis and stakeholder analysis, and by the difficulty-over-time curve.

A useful heuristic for experienced users of the AID grid, or for those who have not used force field and stakeholder analysis to check out their horizontal positioning, is that:

- if you think the project is easy, it is probably difficult;
- if you think the project is difficult, it is probably very difficult;
- if you think the project is very difficult, it is probably MI.

Another technique is to tell scenario stories about the evolution of the project over time. This may help to tease out its likely trajectory on the AID grid. For example, many projects start out with an assumed northwest position (very attractive and easy), but then zigzag south and east to the southeast (low attractiveness and very difficult). Prioritize each of the bones of the fishbone (or, indeed, the wishbone.) This can be done either using a separate AID picture or – and this is neat – actually along the edges of the fishbone, as mini-AID pictures with a cross drawn of the positioning.

STRATEGIC EXERCISE 7.5 AID analysis – 10 minutes

- For a particular strategy, what does it entail?
- How do these elements appear on the AID analysis?
- How are these positionings underpinned by the value and cost drivers, and the difficulty-over-time curves etc?
- How might these implementation actions shift autonomously on the grid over time?

To summarize, AID analysis can be used:

- to prioritize strategic breakthroughs as a portfolio;
- to evaluate the sub-components of a strategic breakthrough or project;
- to track (in real time) an area of strategy implementation.

Its key benefits are that it is:

- a highly visual way of representing and debating priorities;
- a quick and easy technique to use.

Its potential disadvantages are that:

- it can just represent existing thinking on a breakthrough, rather than more creatively the cunning plan;
- it can be subjective, unless it is accompanied by further analysis – for example of value and cost drivers (for attractiveness) or of force field analysis (for implementation difficulty).

AID is linked to the following techniques:

- Value and cost drivers analysis help us to scope attractiveness.
- Force field analysis helps us with implementation difficulty.
- The root causes on the fishbone can be prioritized individually using the AID criteria.
- AID analysis helps to prioritize the from–to's of the FT analysis.

Force field analysis

Force field analysis (Lewin, 1935) is an invaluable technique which brings to the surface the underlying forces which may pull a particular change forward, which may prevent progress, or even move the change into reverse. These 'forces' can be separately identified as 'enablers' or 'constraints'. The enablers are all the internal and external forces that make implementation easier. The constraints are all of these things making it more difficult. But neither set of forces can be adequately identified without first specifying the objectives of the implementation.

When managers first come across force field analysis they often tend to look at it as being some form of extended cost–benefit or 'pros and cons' analysis, which it definitely is not. Force field analysis is simply concerned with the difficulty of the journey that a strategy is likely to make throughout its implementation.

The difficulty of this journey, like that of any other journey in life, has nothing to do with the attractiveness of reaching the destination. The only sense, therefore, where it is permissible to incorporate the perceived benefits of a strategy as a force field enabler is insofar as:

- there is actually a genuinely attractive business case for the strategy and one which has turned on key stakeholders;
- key stakeholders are attracted by the strategy for other reasons.

The most effective way of evaluating the forces enabling or constraining achievement of the strategy's objective is to represent this pictorially. This picture represents the relative strength of each individual enabling or constraining force by drawing an arrowed line whose length is in proportion to that relative strength: this is the 'vector'.

A horizontal version of force field analysis is depicted in Figure 7.9. This shows a very mixed bag and the balance of forces here probably represents everything from 'difficult' to 'very difficult'. Managers who have not already thought hard about the phases of difficulty and about options to get round potential hurdles (for example, push versus pull strategies) may be predestined to suffer a very difficult project.

Generally speaking, one would wish to see the enablers outweighing the constraints by a factor of at least 1.5 to 2 overall, in accordance with the principle of military dominance. Otherwise we should be concerned (and potentially worried) that implementation delay and droop will set in.

Also, many stoppers really must be addressed, otherwise implementation simply won't happen. Both during and before implementation the key implementation forces should be continually monitored to ensure that none threaten to become a 'stopper'.

The next issue is how to evaluate the relative strength of all of the various forces. Two ways of doing this are:

FIGURE 7.9   Force field analysis

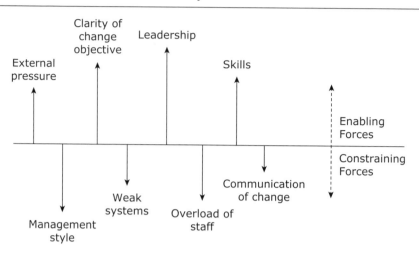

- score each force numerically on a scale of 1 to 5;
- score each force as having high, medium or low impact.

Most groups of managers work comfortably by using the high, medium or low scoring method (the second one). In exceptional cases (for example, where managers have scientific backgrounds or have an inherent love of quantification), the numerical 1 to 5 scale appears to fit more comfortably.

One of the common concerns people have with force field analysis is that the whole scoring exercise is felt to be highly subjective. (This normally occurs within the first 10 minutes or so of any analysis exercise.) It arises usually because all that managers have done is to identify that a force is an enabler or a constraint without exploring more fundamental questions, including:

- Why is it an enabler or a constraint?
- How important an influence is it on the change process (and when)?
- What underlying factors does it in turn depend upon?

This highlights that any force field analysis is dependent on many assumptions, many of which are explicit and need to be surfaced.

A number of drawbacks need to be avoided when using force field analysis, including:

- missing out major constraints because the team wishes to paint an 'ideal' rather than a realistic picture of the change (we return to these issues in a moment);
- focusing primarily on tangible (as opposed to less tangible) implementation forces;

- failing to identify a 'stopper': that is, a change which has such a powerful impact that it is likely to stop the change in its tracks. Stoppers should be drawn either as a thick black arrow or, alternatively, as an arrow which goes right to the bottom of the force field analysis and 'off the page'.

A stopper can be defined as being a constraint of sufficient influence that it will effectively put an end to the initiative – through either direct confrontation or passive resistance. Also, there may be cases where a specific enabling force can be made strong and prove decisive in moving the strategy forward. This kind of force may be described as a 'catalyst' and thus can be drawn as a very long (or thick) positive line upwards on the force field picture.

There may also be instances where a negative and constraining force can be reversed to make a positive force, and in doing so transform the picture completely. For instance, if a particularly influential stakeholder (who is currently negative) can be brought on board, this can provide a major driver in the strategic project's progress. Begin with the most presently limiting (or constraining) factor, in order to prioritize which force to focus on. This is the first key tenet of the theory of constraints (Goldratt, 1990).

A useful tip as well is to go beyond the existing enabling forces to the context of the implementation itself. Ask yourself here whether there are some latent enablers which, if brought to the surface, could be used to unlock organizational energy. For example, if staff feel overburdened with work then a restructuring which is targeted not so much on reducing cuts but on reducing organizational stress and strain is likely to be more gratefully received.

Or, using a 'pull' strategy to get staff's ideas on future organizational processes in advance of a restructuring might flush out some really good ideas for simplification. It might also get staff on board as they see these ideas already incorporated in the plans for the new structure.

This is another important theme in the theory of constraints, which is that within any really difficult situation there is invariably buried, somewhere, some latent, naturally enabling force.

Force field analysis can be used for implementation in virtually any context, including:

- strategic reviews (as a process);
- change projects;
- acquisition integration;
- business plans;
- organizational development.

The key benefits of force field analysis are that it:

- helps you to focus on the context and process for implementation, rather than its context;

- encourages you to think about difficulty as opposed merely to attractiveness;
- gives an early warning of MI projects.

The key disadvantages of force field analysis are that it:

- can be incomplete – which might give you the misleading impression that implementation is not too difficult really (this can be availed by asking the question again, 'What is the one big thing which we have forgotten?');
- is sometimes too much of a snapshot of the short and medium term. This can be remedied, however, by a later technique – the difficulty-over-time curve.

The key linkages with other techniques include:

- with AID analysis – to test out the assumed level of difficulty;
- with the strategic option grid – to help test out your views of implementation difficulty;
- with stakeholder analysis – to understand the context for change more deeply;
- with 'how–how' analysis – to analyse the difficulty of specific activities;
- with fishbone analysis – by using fishbone analysis to ask the question for major constraining forces, 'Why is this so difficult?';
- with the uncertainty grid – to tease out the most dubious implementation assumptions.

STRATEGIC EXERCISE 7.6 Force field analysis – 10 minutes

For one area of implementation in your organization generally, or a specific project, or in your role:

- What are the key enablers and constraints currently (represented as a vector picture)?
- What's the 'one big thing' that we have forgotten?
- How difficult does this look overall?
- How can these be reshaped with a better, or even a cunning implementation plan?
- How difficult does this now look?

Difficulty-over-time curves

While force field analysis is very good at tackling short- and medium-term difficulty, it may not cope well with the dynamics of implementation. To address this issue we need the difficulty-over-time curve (see Figure 7.10). This plots the precise degree of difficulty (easy, difficult, or very difficult) over time, thus effectively plotting the direction of the force field analysis through time.

FIGURE 7.10   Difficulty-over-time curve

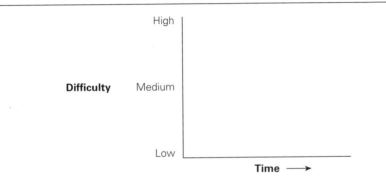

Sometimes implementation gets easier over time, but more commonly it gets more difficult. Increasing difficulties can occur at all kinds of different stages, perhaps as a steady incline or, alternatively, difficulty could climb a little, then fall back before getting really, really difficult.

This reminds me of one experience on a roller coaster in California. It appeared to be two roller coasters, one small and one enormous. I thought I had gone on the small one until I went over the first peak to see a huge upward incline right ahead. The experience was amplified by the fact that it was very quiet and early in the day. Indeed, I and my son accompanying me were the only two people on the ride! So we couldn't get solace or company from other people's screams. Nor would we probably have been missed had we fallen out – until our bodies were found!

Besides the difficulty-over-time curve, I was subsequently able to draw two new curves, the 'fear-over-time curve' and the 'excitement-and-pleasure-over-time curve'.

Fortunately the latter curve overtook the first one 60 seconds into the three rides! It is useful to be innovative with these kinds of curves as they curve a lot about the implementation experience.

Implementation can often feel very much like a roller coaster and there are more than a few parallels here in terms of a) anticipating the dynamics ahead, b) being able to interpret the experience and then to manage it and c) to get on the right roller coaster in the first instance!

The difficulty-over-time curve can be plotted either for the total difficulty of the implementation activity or project, or for just one constraining force. The difficulty-over-time curve is most helpful when creating scenario storylines for implementation.

The key benefits of the difficulty-over-time curve are that it:

- is dynamic, and helps to stretch our thinking about the future;
- is easy to visualize mentally.

The difficulty-over-time curve has the following linkages to other techniques:

- to force field analysis – it provides a visual way of thinking about the various forces through time;
- to AID analysis – it helps to think about where a strategic project might shift to;
- in conjunction with stakeholders – to examine how the difficulty of dealing with them is likely to change over time.

STRATEGIC EXERCISE 7.7 The difficulty-over-time curve
– 10 minutes

For the same area of implementation that you looked at in the last exercise, or a different one:

- Given what needs to happen over time, what does the aggregate difficulty-over-time curve look like?
- Where there are humps of difficulty, what can be done to smooth these out?

Revisiting stakeholder analysis

Stakeholder analysis is another major tool for analysing implementation (Piercy, 1989; Grundy, 2002b), which we introduced earlier on when dealing with the political perspective in Chapter 3. In this section we revisit that idea and amplify and expand on it further. It is for sure one of the most valuable of the tools of this book.

As a reminder, a stakeholder is an individual or group defined as being one who has:

- a decision-making role;
- an advisory role;

- an implementing role;
- a role as a user or as a victim.

It is very important to include all of these stakeholders in your analysis. Stakeholder analysis is performed as follows:

1 Identify *who* you believe the key stakeholders are at any phase of implementation.

2 Evaluate *whether* these stakeholders have a high, medium or low influence on the issue in question (you need to abstract this from their influence generally in the organization).

3 Evaluate *whether* at the current time they are for the project, against it, or idling in 'neutral' (see Figure 7.11).

FIGURE 7.11   Stakeholder analysis

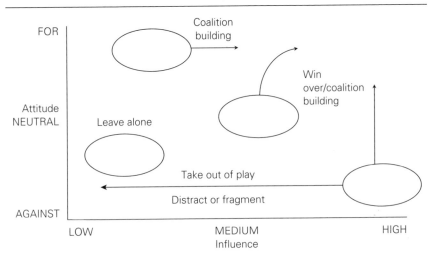

SOURCE: This tool is based on earlier versions by Piercy (1989)

In order to estimate where a stakeholder is positioned approximately, you will need to see the world from that particular stakeholder's perspective. From experience over the years we have found that the best way to convey this is to ask managers to have in effect an out-of-body experience – not quite literally, of course! (This was not gone into in depth when we first introduced it in Chapter 2.)

The out-of-body-experience also involves not merely trying to sense the surface attitudes of stakeholders to a particular issue but also the deeper-seated emotions, focus, anxieties and even prejudices. Figure 7.12 represents those levels which all need to be thought through. This is an 'iceberg' model of organizational agendas (Grundy, 1996).

FIGURE 7.12   Iceberg stakeholder agendas model

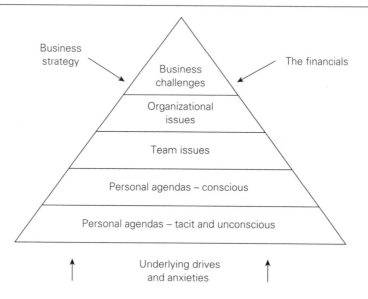

Later on we illustrate how a specific stakeholder's agenda can be mapped using stakeholder agenda analysis, which is another application of force field analysis.

To emphasize the point that stakeholder analysis really does involve having the out-of-body experience, we usually go as far as showing a picture of the two television stars of *The X Files*, Mulder and Scully! From experience, I have found that managers who literally do take the perspective that 'I am the stakeholder' are typically at least 50 per cent more accurate in their analysis.

The above-mentioned three steps give a good 'first cut' of the pattern of stakeholders. The cluster of stakeholders depicted on a stakeholder grid, which we saw earlier in the book (see Figure 3.1), should then be assessed to see what the overall picture looks like, particularly:

- Is implementation going to be relatively easy and straightforward?
- Or is it highlighting a long slog?
- Or does this seem as if it is going to be 'mission impossible'?

For instance, if most of the stakeholders are clustered towards the bottom part of the stakeholder grid, you have a mission impossible on your hands (unless the stakeholders can be radically repositioned somehow).

Another difficult solution you might find is where there is an equal number of supporting stakeholders (with lower influence), in the northwest of the picture, as those against (but having higher influence), in the southeast. This will again mean that implementation is likely to be very difficult.

Also, where you have a large number of stakeholders floating in neutral in the middle of the picture, that very neutrality can present major problems because of inertia.

It is essential to position yourself on the stakeholder grid, especially if you are project managing it. This helps you to re-examine your own position – and your underlying agendas, which may be mixed.

Following your initial, tentative, assessment, you should move on to the next phase:

1 Can new stakeholders be brought into play to shift the balance of influence or can existing players be withdrawn in some way (or be subtly distracted)?

2 Is it possible to boost the influence of stakeholders who are currently in favour of the project?

3 Is it possible to reduce the influence of any antagonistic stakeholders?

4 Can coalitions of stakeholders in favour be achieved so as to strengthen their combined influence?

5 Can coalitions of stakeholders antagonistic to the project be prevented?

6 Can the project change itself, in appearance or in substance, and be reformulated to diffuse hostility towards it?

7 Are there possibilities of 'bringing on board' any negative stakeholders by allowing them a role or in incorporating one or more of their prized ideas?

8 Is the pattern of influence of stakeholders sufficiently hostile to the project to warrant its redefinition?

This is a very rich process to follow.

Once you have done the stakeholder analysis it may well be worthwhile revisiting the force field analysis either to introduce one, or more, new forces or to revise earlier views. The force field analysis will now incorporate all of the enabling and constraining forces, including some of the more political and less tangible ones.

Often a particular stakeholder can be difficult to position. This may be because his or her agendas might be complex. It is quite common to find that it is only one specific negative agenda which has made a stakeholder into an influential antagonist. The micro-level stakeholder agenda analysis in the next section can be very helpful here.

Where there are very large numbers of stakeholders at play on a particular issue, this may invite some simplification of the implementation. For instance, the implementation project may need to be refined, perhaps even stopped and then restarted, in order to resolve an organizational mess.

In order to use stakeholder analysis effectively you may need to set some process arrangements in place where a team project is involved. First, the analysis may be usefully performed in a 'workshop' environment so as to give the analysis a 'reflective' or 'learning' feel. This will help to integrate managers' thinking on a key strategy. It may also be useful to devise code words for key stakeholders in order to make the outputs from this change tool feel 'safe'. On several occasions managers have decided to adopt nicknames for the key players. An element of humour will help to diffuse the potential seriousness of performing stakeholder analysis.

STRATEGIC EXERCISE 7.8 Stakeholder analysis – 10–15 minutes

For an implementation issue of your choice:

- Who are the key stakeholders?
- Who is the one big stakeholder that you have forgotten?
- What is on their agendas about this implementation plan?
- Where are they positioned on the grid?
- What is your most cunning implementation plan and how difficult, given their new positions, is it likely to be?

So far we have used stakeholder analysis in a relatively static manner. But obviously key stakeholders are likely to shift over time – and early support for the project may therefore evaporate. A number of things therefore need to be anticipated, namely:

- Senior managers' support is likely to be sensitive to the perceived ongoing success of the strategic project as it evolves. Any signs of failure are likely to be accompanied by suddenly diminishing support.
- New stakeholders may enter the scheme, and others might disappear.
- Certain stakeholders may increase in influence, or even decrease in influence.
- Where the project changes in its scope or in its focus significantly, stakeholders will then change their positions.
- Stakeholders' own agendas might change owing to external factors outside this particular project. For example, other projects might distract them or result in a re-prioritization of agendas and of this project in particular.

Owing to the above, it may be necessary to review stakeholder positions at least several times during the lifetime of the project.

As a final note, obviously the stakeholder tool should not be used for covert personal and political purposes. Its purpose is to help get things done in organizations and not to obtain personal advantage for its own sake.

For further analysis it is possible to examine how stakeholders may change over time (using a similar dynamic picture to the 'difficulty-over-time curve') by plotting:

- their attitude over time (ranging from 'against' through to 'for');
- their influence over time (ranging from 'for' through to 'against').

One thing to watch with stakeholder analysis is that you do not make fixed and rigid assumptions about stakeholders' attitudes. Using the grid over many years leads us to believe that often managers have a pessimistic bias – assuming that certain stakeholders will be against. In fact, they are often in neutral owing to overload of existing agendas or perceived resource constraints.

When confronted with the positioning of themselves as 'against' they are often slightly surprised. The lesson here is that often many organizational agendas are actually more fluid than is perceived. This is actually good news for strategic thinkers who may feel that there is little real chance of their ideas being actually implemented.

Stakeholder analysis is useful:

- at the very start of a strategic process, especially during the plan for the plan;
- at the strategic options stage;
- when performing detailed planning during mobilization of implementation;
- midway or at the latter stages of implementation;
- after implementation – to draw out the learning lessons.

Stakeholder analysis is also particularly useful in helping to develop an effective communication strategy. Here it will help, finally, to identify which stakeholders to communicate with, when, how and with what message.

The key benefits of stakeholder analysis are:

- It deals effectively with the political issues associated with strategy.
- It encourages mental agility and the ability to take a variety of perspectives on an issue (through the out-of-body experience) simultaneously.
- It defuses organizational politics and makes particularly sensitive issues discussible, sometimes called 'the zone of uncomfortable debate', or ZUDE.

Stakeholder analysis is linked with the other techniques as follows:

- Fishbone analysis can be used to ask: 'why is a particular stakeholder against this?'

- Wishbone analysis can be used to identify all the things that would have to line up to influence a key stakeholder.
- How–how analysis can break down the tactical steps required to influence either a collection of stakeholders or an individual stakeholder.
- The uncertainty grid can be used to rate your assumptions that a stakeholder is 'for' in terms of how important this is, and also how certain/uncertain.
- Stakeholder analysis can also be used to deal with political uncertainties.
- Stakeholder analysis helps you to arrive at a more accurate appraisal of 'stakeholder acceptability' per the strategic option grid (see Chapter 6).
- Stakeholder analysis (following) helps to go under the surface of these assumptions.
- AID analysis can prioritize which stakeholders to influence.
- Force field analysis can help to understand the overall difficulty and potential for influencing a stakeholder (what things make this easier, and what things make this more difficult).

Stakeholder agenda analysis

Stakeholder agenda analysis now helps you to go down a level deeper – to the agenda of a specific individual, distinguishing between positive agendas (or 'turn-ons') versus negative agendas (the 'turn-offs') – see Figure 7.13.

FIGURE 7.13   Stakeholder agenda analysis

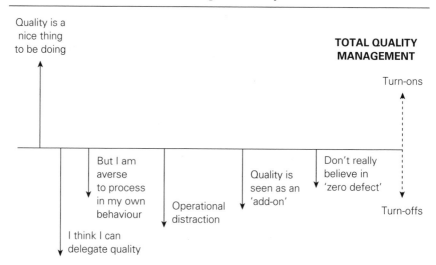

Besides being applied at a macro level on the bigger strategic issues, stakeholder agenda analysis can be used on projects, for meetings generally, and even for drafting a simple letter or e-mail, or making a telephone call.

The major benefits of stakeholder agenda analysis are:

- It helps you to make a business case or to make a strategic presentation.
- It can be used to help identify your own position on something and why you are in a dilemma.
- It can help you to get a new role – either inside or outside the organization.
- It can suggest what the deeper agendas of the organization are, so that you can target your activities in strategic thinking to the 'hotter spots' – thereby avoiding unnecessary frustration.

Stakeholder agenda analysis has the following linkages:

- for doing a deep dive on the positioning of key players on the overall stakeholder analysis, especially of ones in neutral or against;
- with the uncertainty grid: how attractive is it to persuade a particular individual to shift their agenda – and how difficult is this?
- with the strategic option grid: as an overview of the influences on one's thinking before scoring and prioritizing the key options;
- with the five competitive forces: to help understand the agendas of potential entrants, rivals, buyers and suppliers.

Interrelating the tools

The tools are highly interrelated and it is worthwhile examining briefly how they are intertwined. They can also be used very much in smaller combinations – as a 'pick and mix'). You are permitted to skip this section or go back to it on another read if you wish.

Some of their major linkages that we have looked at are between:

- fishbone analysis and AID analysis: to prioritize the possible solutions;
- FT analysis and gap analysis;
- competitor and fishbone analyses (why are we weak?);
- value and cost drivers and value-over-time curves: one is a dynamic of the other;
- customer value analysis and the value-over-time curve: value added and destroyed over profiling time;
- force field analysis and difficulty-over-time curves: one is a dynamic of the other;

- wishbone analysis and the uncertainty grid (to test alignment factors);
- force field enablers and mini-wishbone analyses (what has to line up);
- force field constraints and mini-fishbone analyses (what are the root causes of constraints);
- stakeholder analysis and stakeholder agenda analysis (a deep dive), or alternatively doing a fishbone on this;
- stakeholder analysis and the uncertainty grid (to do stakeholder analysis);
- how–how and AID analysis (for prioritizing implementation activities);
- FT analysis and how–how analysis, force field analysis, etc;
- fishbone analysis followed by wishbone analysis.

So there are many possible combinations of 'dishes' that can be served: it is a very flexible menu. It is really useful for dealing with implementation issues, or simply more localized management issues that you might wish to explore strategically in my 'mini strategy' process. This is shown in Figure 7.14 and has six key steps:

1 Fishbone the issue as a problem.

2 Vision what you really-really want (the vision of the wishbone).

3 What are the options (the wishbone's bones)?

4 Position these on the AID grid.

5 What is the implementation difficulty (force field/difficulty-over-time curves) for some or all of these?

6 What is the stakeholder support? Stakeholder analysis.

FIGURE 7.14   A process for managing mini strategies

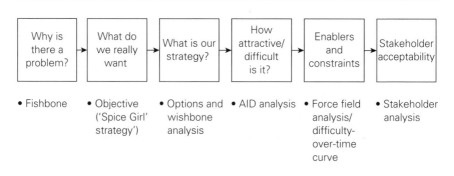

STRATEGIC EXERCISE 7.9 Using the mini strategy process
                                     – 15 minutes

Taking either a strategy implementation issue or just a more localized issue affecting you in your role that is complex:

- Why is there a problem? (Diagnosis – fishbone analysis)

- What do I 'really-really-really want?' (Your vision)

- What are the alignment factors to support that? (Wishbone analysis)

- How attractive and difficult are these? (AID analysis)

- What is the basis of that difficulty? (Difficulty-over-time curve or force field analysis)

- Who are the stakeholders and what is their pattern of influence? (Stakeholder analysis)

Note that the wishbone analysis here will have a very different cognitive feel to it: while fishbone is dealing with what factually already exists, wishbone analysis demands much more imaginative thinking.

Key insights from the chapter

- The five key stages of strategy implementation are: diagnosis, options, planning, implementation, learning and control.
- At each stage there are a number of tools that can be used. Some tools work for different stages – so they can be used more than once.
- Fishbone analysis can be very helpful in turnaround situations.
- Fishbone analysis can be used to diagnose problems with considerable complexity, and can be used to uncover the systems at work between root causes.
- Wishbone analysis can also be used for visualizing an opportunity and the alignment conditions that will help it to crystallize.
- FT analysis will help you to explore the scope of strategy implementation, to determine the level of desired stretch. It will also help you to communicate it within the organization and to monitor progress towards goals.
- How–how analysis then breaks down each shift within the FT analysis into manageable steps.

- AID analysis is needed to prioritize particular strategic actions.
- Force field analysis and the difficulty-over-time curve then tests out its difficulty.
- Stakeholder analysis identifies the key stakeholders, positions them, and also suggests new influencing strategies to accomplish with the cunning influencing plan.
- Stakeholder agenda analysis enables you to go another level deeper, to explore a particular stakeholder's ambitions and anxieties.
- Stakeholders can also be disaggregated into:
  - those who have greatest influence;
  - those we have greatest influence over; and
  - those who are least/most important.

Implementation is an absolutely critical part of the strategy process. It is much neglected in the vast majority of strategy books, perhaps because it isn't as conceptual or as sexy, and more mundane: I beg to disagree. Not only is the fact that this is about getting on and doing things something that shouldn't prevent it from getting the space that it deserves, but also I believe that it is often more complex than corporate strategy itself. There are actually more tools that are needed here, which tells you something.

In the next chapter we look in more depth at many aspects of the strategy process and how these can be managed more effectively. In the final chapter we take a look at how you might actually deploy these ideas at a practical level. We also take a look at an example – the Legal Complaints Service – for a model of how this can be done.

Managing the strategy process

08

Introduction

Besides gaining an understanding of the concepts of strategy and the tools, an equally important dimension is that of the strategy process itself. We can define the strategy process as being 'the step-by-step formulation, implementation, control and evaluation of strategies – as they move through the ideas, evaluation, decision-making and action phases'.

The strategy process is thus one which:

- is step-by step (and not all at once);
- is phased;
- is reflective and shared;
- is focused on making important decisions about the future;
- will change in its level of detail over time, beginning with a broader shape and direction, and then becoming more specific;
- is anchored in real action;
- we can see if it worked or not.

It is also an iterative process through which we are in a continuous state of refinement and creative work, rather than a hard and mechanistic slog. While the end product – the cunning plan – is very important, almost as important are the awareness and sensitivity gained by going through the process, and the quality of the learning that is being created and shared within the organization. Techniques like the strategic option grid (and of course its sister technique the optopus) lend themselves really well to that more intuitive and interpretative type of enquiry. The strategy process has many likenesses to detective work, where there is creative generation of 'lines of enquiry' that are then subjected to more rigorous work.

We have already covered a number of insights on managing the strategy process, which it is now opportune to synthesize here:

- Strategy is about saying 'no' as well as 'yes'.
- Strategy is thus about choice – and not spreading yourself too thinly.

- It is also about the creative definition of options.
- It has an important diagnostic phase, too.
- Strategy is about the how – it is tangible and actionable.
- It needs to be creative and cunning.
- We need to think about the environment, how it is changing, and how we can shape or even change it.
- So that invites the art of storytelling the future.
- And within that, the possible degrees of freedom, the possible intent, the agendas and behaviours of competitors and other players as well as ourselves.
- Timing is a critical issue, as well as capability.
- We need to manage the political dimension – eg with the 'P' behaviours.
- We need to influence stakeholders.
- In terms of all three of the points immediately above, this requires taking the perspective of others, through the out-of-body experience.
- Implementation is a second, and most important cycle of the process.

So we have already uncovered some very rich ideas as a foundation to add to. In this present chapter we now take these ideas further by examining the other key areas that need managing, and give many pointers to how one should tackle this.

We deal first with more on doing the plan for the plan, and also with asking the right questions. We then look at how you can begin by doing a strategic audit of your existing position and strategy, how to run strategic workshops and how to collect data in cunning ways. We do an overview of the tools that we have seen so far and how they map onto the process. We then turn to the more detailed aspects of project managing key strategic breakthroughs and doing the business case and strategic position papers. Our next port of call is to look at the management of uncertainties using scenarios, and fuzzier notions like 'contingent strategy'. We follow that by examining how intangibles can be managed.

The plan for the plan

In this section we give more specific guidance to how to actually create a plan for the plan. The plan for the plan, as we said earlier, is the blueprint for doing the plan. It gives the process an incisive focus as it guides managers to focus on the three things that really matter. These are 1) the key strategic issues, 2) the strategic options and 3) the strategic breakthroughs. It aims to move through the planning process in least time and with the maximum impact.

So the key ingredients of the plan for the plan should be:

- overview of current position and issues;
- any earlier and more tentative appreciation of the strategic gap;
- a quick statement of ambitions;
- the key areas for investigation and the activities needed to address these;
- with their inputs, any data requirements, outputs, processes and tools, who is going to be involved, how and when and any interdependencies with other planning activities;
- interim outputs such as strategic position papers;
- any common assumptions that need to be made: about the economy, the market, the competitive environment etc;
- a Gantt chart of what will be done, when and over what timescales – the project plan;
- an outline of the structure of the eventual plan;
- any issues affecting implementation: eg communication, roll-out, budgetary linkages and links to rewards and recognition systems, training requirements etc.

STRATEGIC EXERCISE 8.1 Evaluating your planning for the planning – 10 minutes

For your preparation for the planning process in the past, how well do you do in terms of the above headings, of which there are 10:

8 to 10	excellent!
6 to 7	more to be done
3 to 5	sounds like you should start again
1 to 2	how do you cope?

Typically the plan for the plan can be done in around half a day of intensive working with a small group (2 to 4), or a day with a larger gathering (over

5 or 6). The time spent will pay for itself many times over, as it will shorten the timescales and focus the work on the more crucial areas, and also leverage a better result at the end of the day.

Asking the right questions

Strategy is all about asking the right questions – a skill that many MBA students could do well to take on board. We will call these incisive questions 'helicopter questions' to symbolize the fact that they are taking a detached and objective view of the situation, as if we had a helicopter viewpoint looking down, Some examples of key strategic questions that I have asked in the past are:

- 'How many strategic projects do we actually have?' (to the CEO of an insurance company; answer – 'Forty-four'; it took a month to count them!).

- 'Why are you going to charge the same prices for petrol in your convenience stores as in your superstores, when in the former you have more convenient service?' (this led to successful premium pricing).

- 'What is it really worth to customers to have extra baggage and what can we charge for it without causing customers to switch?' (to a group of senior executives at a leading UK budget airline, which triggered the decision to go down that route – sorry everyone!).

- 'If we are really going to franchise one of our budget fitness clubs then is that going to be a problem if you ever want to exit the business?' (which led to a change in the legal agreement to provide for such a scenario).

- 'If we are struggling to find a smaller acquisition than ourselves, then are there any larger and sleepy players that we could do a reverse takeover of?' (to the board of a chain of caravan sites – there was actually just such an attractive target).

- 'Are we simply in just too many businesses?' (on learning from the CEO of the leasing division of a major bank that there were no fewer than 15 business units – two were later exited).

- 'How could we manage our water business if we were easyJet?' (to senior executives of a water company). 'How could we manage it if there had been a plague of bird flu?' (ditto – the answer to this resulted in identifying £40 million of potential cost savings).

- 'What is the one big thing we've forgotten?' (to the team of the direct channel of a major mobile company; answer: 'What competitors might do.') 'What is the second big thing we've forgotten?' – ditto; 'New substitute technologies.'

So is this all about intellectual training? I don't think that this is more than a small part of the picture. It is also about having the sensitivity, the intuition and the skills of a detective to hone in on the really important. Then it is about not just being judgemental and coming up with the perfect solution, but turning the issue into a slightly more open question. If one isn't terribly confident, a gentle way of posing the question is to ask it as: 'Do you mind if I think out aloud...?' so that you invite permission to pose it.

I have always said that asking the right question is often more powerful than suggesting the right solution. So, asking myself how I have managed to get it just about right in asking the right question in the above, on reflection this seems to come in one of two ways: 1) by spontaneously asking the question at the time that it occurs to me, and 2) by allowing it to evolve over a period of time.

An example of case 1 was an occasion where I had been asked to facilitate some work on self-managed teams at a very large insurance company. We got 10 minutes into the workshop and it turned out that they seemed very confused about what they thought a self-managed team actually was. So I asked the question: 'Have you defined what a "self-managed team" actually is?' They hadn't – which was a root cause of their problem. Once I had defined it for them, it was all downhill.

Case 1 situations are relatively straightforward, and I suspect that in those cases there is no big surprise when I have asked it, as it is quite clearly in context. But in the second case there seems to be a period of reflective digestion, as I normally go through the following kind of process:

- diagnosis: of a dilemma or a constraint that people are struggling with;
- modelling: what could be possibilities, in terms of both causality and future options;
- hypothesizing: thinking about the possible lines of enquiry that could help them become clearer;
- positioning: thinking about how best to frame the question;
- timing: feeling that 'the time to ask is now';
- framing it: deciding on how I will best ask it.

I found that an interesting exercise in uncovering tacit knowledge. So probably that gestation period is anything between 5 and 10 minutes – one doesn't just blurt it out.

A related theme is that of the strategic hypothesis. This can be defined as being 'a hypothetical causal relationship – either past, present or future, which explains particular patterns in the data'.

It can be useful to posit some strategic hypothesis that uncovers some causal relationship or pattern in a company's market, or strategic position. Usually this will be a response to identifying some kind of problem or un-explained pattern.

Examples of these might include, for example:

- a decline in year-on-year sales;
- a loss of market share;
- the decline of a particular product;
- a business turnaround situation;
- a possible new and unpredictable market.

For example, we may be experiencing a year-on-year decline in sales – either in all sales, or just in some areas of our sales. Using fishbone analysis (see Chapter 7) we may suspect that this might be due to:

- competitor activity;
- life-cycle effects;
- squeeze on consumer incomes;
- loss in our own relative competitive position;
- simply being too slow or not innovative or under-investing.

The strategic hypothesis may thus suggest that 'sales are declining by x per cent because of these above factors, and without radical change this is likely to accelerate'.

Both asking the right question and posing strategic hypotheses can add a lot of value to strategic thinking.

The strategy audit

A strategy audit is a process of taking an objective and detached look at the quality and completeness of the existing strategy and of the process that underpins its development. It proceeds by devising a number of key questions that need answering: the strategic health check.

The process of the strategy audit is pictured in Figure 8.1.

The idea of the strategy audit originally came out of a chance conversation on the second day of a strategy course which I was running in London. On that particular course was a most interesting guy – a very senior Inland Revenue tax inspector.

Now you may not know, but tax inspectors sometimes pay visits to businesses. When they do they have been trained to be microscopically observant, just like the US detective with the scruffy rain-mac – Lieutenant Colombo – in many TV films. This delegate told us over lunch that they have a very cunning training course to help them develop these observational and memory skills. Inspectors are taken out to somewhere like a public park and are asked to observe everything over about 20 minutes. They are then tested on what they observed and remembered, even down to how many sparrows got together to eat someone's sandwich etc.

FIGURE 8.1 The strategy audit process

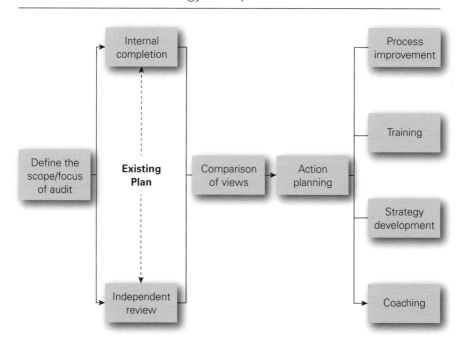

In effect, they are using the Buddhist concept of mindfulness to absorb what is going on around them, and then memorize it all photographically.

During the latter part of the conversation I realized a very close comparison with being a strategy facilitator. I said: 'That's a lot like what I do when I visit a company: everything is interesting data – the car park hierarchy, how friendly and helpful the receptionist is, the ambiance of the place, the expressions on people's faces, how they actually walk calmly about or rush around....' In effect I am like an anthropologist, I am doing a strategic audit. That was big idea No 1. Also, in the same breath almost, I realized that here there was vast potential for assisting clients with concerns about their existing strategy to do a 'resilience check' on its quality: the big idea No 2.

So I set to work to construct a series of structured questions – the strategic audit – which could form a more general starting point for tailoring to a particular organization. There were scores for these questions – and provided that the answers were given in a way that withstood independent testing and challenge, they would give at least some overall feel of the quality of the strategy. This proved to be an invaluable discovery for the many companies that have gone through this process with me.

While the practice of a financial audit is very well established, the idea that your company's strategy should be subjected to a similar strategic audit most certainly isn't. The concept of a strategic audit is rather like that of having a personal health check. But here a strategy audit takes a look at the wider environment in terms of competitive threats, at relative competitive positioning and at capability. It seeks to identify the gaps in thinking and the blind spots. Commissioning one is akin to buying insurance in some ways, although besides its 'protective value' it can also yield insights and options and thus add 'developmental value', too.

We can define a strategy audit as 'a systematic, structured and comprehensive review of your strategy and strategic processes, to identify weaknesses, blind spots and areas where potentially a lot more value can be added'. It can be conducted at the corporate or business level, or for things like an HR strategy.

To give you a feel of what kinds of strategic questions you can deploy, let's focus in on the area of competitive advantage, going back once again to the three C's (Chapter 5) of:

- customers;
- competitors;
- cost base.

Customers:

- To what extent do you know how customers perceive how much value you add to them and the characteristics within your products and services which distract from this, and by different segments?

- Do you have a very clear idea of what is most important to them (in terms of 'turn-ons' and 'turn-offs') and again by segment?

- To what level do you know what the buying criteria and buying process of your customers are, and what their buying psychology is?

- Do you understand your customers' external environment and pressures, their competitive position and their own strategic intent and options as well?

Competitors:

- Do you really know who your competitors are, and their relative size and resources?

- To what extent do you understand how your customers perceive your competitors' value added, especially in relation to what your value-added services give to them?

- To what extent do you understand your competitors' cost advantages/disadvantages relative to you?

- Do you know which of your competitors are the greatest threats to you, and how and why?

Cost base:

- To what extent do you have a very clear idea of the main drivers of your cost base (cost drivers), and how these can be managed optimally?

- To what extent have you targeted your unit costs medium and longer term (one to five years), rather than traditionally (one year), and to what degree are these supported by viable strategies to reach these?

STRATEGIC EXERCISE 8.2 Doing part of a strategic audit – 15 minutes

Using the above questions, rate them as follows:

score 8–10	criteria fully met/almost met
score 6–7	criteria met reasonably well
score 3–5	criteria very partially met
score 0–2	criteria hardly met, if at all

These questions are but a small sample of the total menu which, of course, should be tailored. There are well over a hundred others, and none of these are trivial.

In terms of the process, this can be done on a one-to-one basis for the CEO, or for two of the top management, eg the CEO and another director, or small group of senior managers, preferably with an outside facilitator. It can also be opened up to a larger number, perhaps in a workshop context.

Besides its role in being additive in terms of value added and in discovering blind spots, it can also be useful in giving more confidence that the strategy is going in the right direction. In an ideal world it would be used both before the plan for the plan and also to revisit it after the strategic process is finished: to see what shift has happened and also to see where there are still any gaps that need addressing. Besides its benefits in terms of strategic planning, it can also play a role in corporate governance, too.

The strategy audit checklists can be used on their own or alongside tools such as the strategic option grid, which can also be used to benchmark existing strategies. As with the strategic option grid, where there is an area that seems suspect on a rapid fly-over, a more detailed 'deep dive' can be done.

So, in conclusion, the strategy audit is a useful ancillary process that can also add a lot to the conduct of strategy.

Running strategy workshops

Strategic thinking is a lot harder to do both on your own and in conventional management meetings. So strategy workshops can help to share the strategic debate in a more structured and creative format, and provide enough time and space to do more thorough and wide-ranging thinking. These can be run for a very wide range of applications:

- acquisitions;
- alliances;
- change management;
- competitor analysis;
- cost management;
- distribution strategy;
- financial strategy;
- IT strategy;
- key account strategies;
- marketing strategy;
- organic business development;
- organizational and people strategy;
- organizational design;
- restructuring;
- scenarios;
- strategy development;
- strategy implementation;
- value-based strategy.

The list could go on.

Before we get into the processes that seem to be most effective, if you have been to a strategic workshop that didn't go so well, consider the following exercise.

STRATEGIC EXERCISE 8.3 Fishboning a strategic workshop that didn't go too well – 5 minutes

For that same workshop that could in your view have gone better, why was that the case? Draw a fishbone analysis of the root causes. What does this reveal?

In order to run a truly effective strategic workshop, 20 key questions may need to be addressed:

- Is there an adequate pre-planning process (the aims, the issues, process and outputs)?
- Should there be any pre-work, to warm up the thinking?
- Are expectations clearly set and managed (eg joining instructions)?
- Are there clear key questions to focus on in the exercises?
- Is there a good time plan and a realistic agenda?
- How is it going to be time managed?
- What facilities will be needed and will these be sufficient and suitable (eg maybe it needs to be off site)?
- What are the likely data requirements, if needed?
- What tools will be used and how will these be explained, and by whom?
- Are there measures in place to control or channel any politics and personal agendas?
- Is there adequate facilitation or equivalent?
- Is the facilitator suitably skilled and does he or she have an appropriate style?
- Are the right and suitable people being invited there?
- Are there strategies and tactics in place for dealing with anyone who might be difficult?
- Do we know anything about the cognitive, the team-working and political styles and the personalities of the participants – so we can take that into account during the session?
- Where there are more than five people attending, are you going to have some sub-group working?
- If the latter, will sub-groups work on different issues and options or in parallel in the same groups, and in the latter case, how will this be debated and integrated into a single final output?
- How will the output be recorded and when/will we have an administrator recording bullet points as they are generated/will there be a strategic position paper written out just on this workshop?
- What barriers and blockages could occur, what might trigger these, and how can they be avoided?
- Have you done any scenario storytelling for the process, the behaviours and the outcomes?

Returning now to the exercise that you just did now on a previous workshop:

STRATEGIC EXERCISE 8.4 Revisiting your workshop
diagnosis – 5 minutes

For the strategic workshop that you just analysed, using the above checklist, can you add any new things to your fishbone?

What are the interdependencies between these root causes, and what patterns emerged?

What are the lessons that you take away for the future?

The above account of organizing strategic workshops highlights the number of things that need to be thought through to ensure a safe trajectory for the event. It also highlights the extent of pre-thinking and planning that needs to happen so that it runs well, and also that its complexity warrants some project planning.

In terms of designing a strategic workshop, the following were used for a two-day session with the board of a mid-sized, privately owned retail company:

- What are the current strategic issues that we are facing externally and internally?
- Where do we want to be in the future and what do we think is our underlying 'strategic gap'?
- What is distinctive – from our customers' perspective – about what we do?
- What are our competitors' strengths and weaknesses, and how do we compare against these?
- Where are the biggest areas of market growth, and what is driving these?
- How is the competitive nature of the industry changing and what are the CSFs?
- What opportunities do we have in this context?
- What do the deep-dive techniques tell us about their attractiveness?
- What are our capability gaps and what internal strategic options do we need to consider?
- How attractive are these on the strategic option grid?
- What further questions do we now need to address and what data might we need to collect?

This is quite a full agenda for a two-day session.

Before we leave the issue of strategic workshops it would be useful to identify what is entailed in being a strategy facilitator. So that you can rate your own skills on this, it is included as a strategic exercise.

STRATEGIC EXERCISE 8.5 Your strategy facilitation skills
– 10–15 minutes

How do you rate in terms of:

	Very strong 5	Strong 4	Average 3	Weaker 2	Weak 1
Strategic analysis skills:					
Ability to generate strategic options:					
Ability to get others to generate them:					
Commercial knowledge:					
Organizational knowledge summarizing complex discussions:					
Challenging viewpoints:					
Managing conflict:					
Asking the right questions:					
Objectivity and detachment:					
Explaining processes and techniques:					
Interpersonal skills under pressure:					
Reading non-verbal behaviour:					

	Very strong 5	Strong 4	Average 3	Weaker 2	Weak 1
Very fast thinking speed:					
Self-confidence and resilience:					
Listening skills:					
Political skills:					
Time management:					
Anticipating future behavioural dynamics:					
Workshop design:					
Helicopter thinking:					

The maximum score possible here is 5 × 20 = 100.

Scores:	
80–100%	that's amazing!
60–80%	a lot of potential
40–60%	a lot to do
20–40%	best to shadow someone for a while

Before we leave that topic, it is worth just saying why some of these skills are very important. For instance, asking the right questions and at the right time requires an incisive mind and a lot of self-confidence. Being a strategy facilitator isn't just about being supportive and positive – a Mr Nice Guy, but also being able to cut through the mist and to penetrate some depth.

Also, I have mentioned very quick thinking speed. There will be those at workshops who are bright and want to show that they are – and will want to try to outsmart you, and those who are also bright, but are non-lucid in the way that they express themselves and one needs a fair amount of very fast thinking to puzzle them out, while at the same time preserving one's own core thinking stream. Then there are those who think they are very bright and want you to know that, but their thinking is disjointed. One can have to use a lot of thinking speed to go through all the options of dealing with that. In addition, usually as a facilitator one is well outnumbered, possibly 12 to 1, so if the group has taken a dislike to *anything you may have said whatsoever*, you may find yourself under simultaneous challenge from two or more people. That is an interesting experience, and one is thinking really fast then!

Not that I would ever want to put you off strategy facilitation: flying the Eurofighter is probably comparable, as both are highly unstable. With the Eurofighter the aircraft stays in the air only because of complex and continuous coordination of a number of variables, such as velocity, angle of turn, rate of ascent or descent, acceleration and engine power etc. This is achieved in a dynamic way through complex, fast-thinking computer coordination: without the computer the Eurofighter would simply go out of control if flown by a human, unaided. So likewise, as a strategic facilitator, one is constantly tracking the present dynamic of the team, and anticipating what manoeuvres it is going to get into next.

Again I would highlight that there are not only a large number of skills that are needed but also that many of them are quite soft ones. I have been facilitating for around 25 years now and there is always a sense of uncertainty about what is going to happen. One needs to be constantly thinking ahead and anticipating where it might go. Although a strategic workshop is similar on the surface to an executive strategy course in terms of some processes, not only is it very real and thus emotional but it is political, too. While it is quite taxing, time flies – a whole half-day can go by when everyone is in the flow, much can be accomplished, and it has seemed to have been only an hour or so.

Collecting the data in cunning ways

When using tools like the strategic option grid one frequently identifies more questions to ask – in order to firm up the scores. For example, in a retail and distribution clothes company there was a point where we were addressing the question: 'What is distinctive – from our customers' perspective – about what we do?', where we weren't really sure. So I suggested that it would be good to ask: 'What do some of our key accounts really think about us, in terms of distinctive turn-ons, and also turn-offs?'

Another 'best practice' idea is to ask: 'What is the most cunning way of collecting the right data to address these questions?'

In the above question we could then have launched into a major customer attitude survey, which would have been time-consuming and distracting. So instead I proposed that we collect some rich, qualitative data from three key accounts to explore not only what value we were adding and destroying, but also how we could add more value to them in the future.

So I called three of them up and their CEOs were most obliging. The average time was 30 minutes per conversation, and in that time they gave me very incisive diagnoses of where the company was going wrong, what risks that posed, and what they would like us to do much better or differently in the future. Not only did I get a very clear picture of what the company wasn't doing that well, but the CEOs were really pleased with the attention they got and the fact that my client had paid someone independent to listen to them, so there was goodwill created.

The whole exercise took just half a day, including review and feedback, and so was extremely effective: often diminishing returns set in quickly when collecting data, provided that it is rich and high quality.

Potential ways of seeing how you can collect rich data in cunning ways are to ask:

- Who might be the best person to ask to get this data?
- If we don't know, who is the best person to ask as to who we should talk to?
- Has someone, somewhere, actually got this data already?
- If we now know what to do, what is the most efficient and effective way of getting that data out?
- If we were to set about collecting data in a certain way, then given that process and those questions, what sorts of answers are likely to come out?

As we said in Chapter 5, the internet is a powerful way of collecting data on markets and competitors.

Overview of the tools

This is a quick section to just make sure that you know where the tools fit in best. Figure 8.2 now shows the five key stages of the strategy process as being:

- diagnosis: current position;
- option generation and evaluation;
- breakthrough planning;
- implementation;
- performance review – control and learning.

FIGURE 8.2 Strategy process with tools

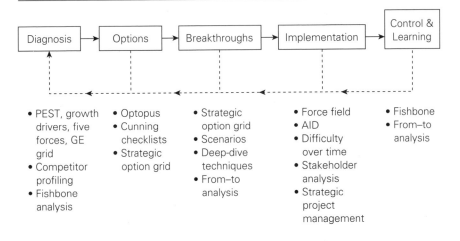

Figure 8.2 gives the tools that are most frequently chosen off the menu. That isn't to say that we will use them all, as we might only use, say, five for a particular strategic workshop. For example, we might use just a SWOT, the five forces, gap analysis, the optopus and the strategic option grid over a day. (Once I had a lady who had been going through my Cranfield Breakthrough Strategic Thinking programme trying to use six tools in a one-and-a-half-hour session with managers who were totally unfamiliar with them: that didn't come off at all well – it was too much. As a facilitator there is quite a lot of reflective thinking in the pre-planning of a workshop to decide what the best combination is likely to be – it needs to be very tailored.)

In terms of the other options for techniques that are feasible we have the following:

- In 'current position' we have fishbone analysis for diagnosing and problems or constraints.

- In 'future options' we have, within the cunning plan, the cunning checklists.

- In 'future options' we might also have the deep-dive techniques like the GE grid, value and cost drivers, force field analysis and the difficulty-over-time curve, the uncertainty grid, stakeholder analysis and stakeholder agenda analysis.

- We might also be iterating the scores of the strategic option grid in 'strategic breakthroughs'.

- We might see value and cost drivers being used to help position the more micro-level implementation options and actions on the attractiveness and implementation difficulty grid – or the AID analysis – in the implementation phase.

- In the implementation phase we may decide to do some further strategic option grid work for a variety of implementation options for a particular strategic decision.

- In the implementation phase we might also have value and cost drivers, force field analysis and the difficulty-over-time curve, the uncertainty grid, stakeholder analysis and stakeholder agenda analysis.

- We might see scenario storytelling coming into the future options, the strategic options or the implementation phase, and also being used to develop influencing strategies throughout.

- We might well draw some project management tools such as how–how analysis, Gantt charts and critical path analysis into the strategic breakthrough or the implementation phases – see the next section.

- In the learning and control phase we might see the strategic option grid scores being used to track the attractiveness that has been actually realized, and we can then compare that to previous and anticipated scores – to see if the strategies are on track. We might also be considering what further action or adjustments we might need to get them back on track.

- In the learning and control phase we may also be revisiting the gap analysis and also the uncertainty grid – for assessing what factors turned out to be more important or more uncertain than we thought, or both. We might also revisit the difficulty-over-time curve and the value-over-time curve.

Scenarios can also be used as a separate process from the main one. For example, if it turns out during the diagnosis of current position that we need to take a closer look at some aspect of the environment, for example economic, regulatory or competitive threat, or where there is a quite new and emergent area of market opportunity, scenarios of the future could be helpful.

We might then wish to test some options that we have already thought of in terms of addressing these different future worlds, and to have a number of columns for the emergent scores for these different scenarios across the page.

So, all in all, the strategy process is a very flexible process in terms of what tools we actually select, and in what combination. There is also flexibility in the sequence in which we use the tools and even potentially in the order in which we do the work. For example, one might decide that there are likely to be quite critical constraints in internal capability. This might suggest that we should fishbone these first, as these will frame how ambitious we can be in terms of objective setting and in our stance to exploiting the growth drivers: there is no point being very ambitious if there is a lot to fix first! (We need to understand what the most limiting constraint is here.)

Also, we might decide to do some rough positioning, and then generate some strategic options before returning to the 'current position' stage to understand more of where we are now. Then after some competitive bench-marking we return to evaluate the strategic options that we have come up with in a more informed way. Or we might do the competitive benchmark-ing first and then look at the external environment second. The earlier case study of the clothing retailer and wholesaler workshop question reflects the latter.

Regarding strategic objectives, their role may be different, depending on the situation. For instance, they may be quite well articulated at the very start, to help frame the kind of stretch that we are looking to deliver on. This can help to generate more radical and creative thinking, but it might result in options being too unrealistic or ones which might be achievable but because of resources or other constraints this is going to be very difficult.

Or one might let the strategic objectives emerge out of our thought-through appraisal of the strategic options. Generally speaking I would nor-mally prefer this route as it is more likely to result in a realistic appraisal and one which is grounded on the competitive analysis rather than on wishful thinking: it all depends. In that case one can always try to take the managers through the optopus or the cunning checklists to get a better and more re-fined result.

STRATEGIC EXERCISE 8.6 Prioritizing and choosing some
strategic tools – 5–10 minutes

From Figure 8.2, which tools would you now see as adding to your planning process that are currently not in use?

Project managing the strategic breakthroughs

Project management is a key part of the strategy process. I am a big fan of project management provided that it is both kept simple and maintained at a strategic level. A project can be defined here as 'a complex set of inter-related activities that are intended to achieve a specific result in a certain time and cost'.

The 'result' breaks down into two things: the quality of the result and the quantity. Sometimes we achieve the quantity but not the quality, or vice versa.

These three types of goal are often in tension with one another. For instance, one might well find that:

- we achieve the result but not in the time nor the cost targets;
- we achieve the cost targets but the result is unsatisfactory and it takes longer to get there;
- we achieve results in the time we hoped for but not the full result and this then costs more.

This is sometimes called the 'project triangle' (Grundy, 2002a).

A strategic project is one which 'has a major role in terms of achieving the strategy at a particular level, and has to be managed within its environment. It is a project that will have a big impact on either competitive edge, on financial performance, on capability, or two or all three of these.' It has its own environment within the organization in that it will be affected by changing organizational conditions and influences and also compete for attention and resources with other projects.

Figure 8.3 illustrates the symbiotic relationship between the core strategy process itself and the strategic project management process. Here we see the two processes inextricably intertwined. So there might, for example, be projects that are driven out of the strategy. Or there might be strategic projects which evolve such that they actually frame the strategy to a considerable extent. Here we see project management as being at least in part a vehicle for emergent strategies and their transformation into deliberate strategies. Where there is a very well-thought-out strategic project process, the strategy process can become less central as it is more of a direction-setting context diagnosis, and acts as an overall umbrella for the project strategies.

FIGURE 8.3 Strategic management and project management process

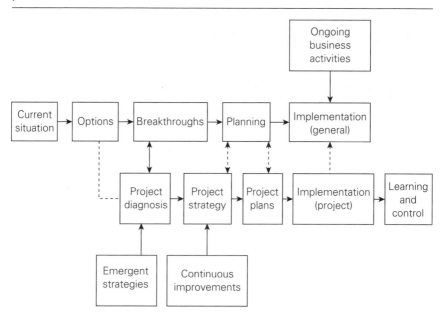

In the latter event there might well be extensive strategic thinking in the project plans and this will be summarized in the somewhat shorter strategic plan, with the project plans in appendices.

Project management might seem to be a less than obvious framework relative to strategy. This is perhaps because it is usually considered as being operational. However, not only does strategy invariably entail some change in the business but it also requires implementation of new strategic options and thus, projects. As these need to be broken down into action plans, they require detailed project management.

Also, the very process of developing the strategy and mobilizing it is one which occurs over time, is complex and has predefined results, so that too is a project.

Finally a third reason for considering project management as a core strategic framework is that the strategic breakthroughs often themselves break down into large and complex projects. These projects are of a 'strategic' nature and have their own strategic goals, complex environments, implementation needs and stakeholders. So where an organization is very comfortable with project managing its main strategies, the resulting strategy is often as much a product of this project process as the planning process itself.

For the latter to be effective, though, project management must be a sophisticated process that not only uses traditional ideas such as activity analysis, critical paths etc but also many of the tools that we have seen earlier in this book, such as the strategic option grid, difficulty-over-time curves and stakeholder analysis. Microsoft project manager software or a 'Prince 2' qualification on project management won't do that for you alone, sorry.

Project management is a useful process which helps to structure the strategy implementation phase and particularly the management of change and any specific projects. This process takes us through the stages of:

- diagnosis of the project's scope and key objectives, and rationale;
- creation of strategic options for the project, and their evaluation;
- detailed planning of activities and resources, timings and deliverables;
- project mobilization;
- control and learning.

Doing a business or 'economic case' is often a product of both the second phase, evaluation of options, and the third, detailed planning.

How much use of project management has been made in your organization in terms of developing and implementing the strategy, and could this be more/different?

Figure 8.4 now takes you through the strategic project management process. Here we see many of the more general strategic tools being used alongside ones like Gantt analysis and how–how analysis. Again, this is a menu and not a very fixed and prescriptive process.

FIGURE 8.4 Strategic project management process

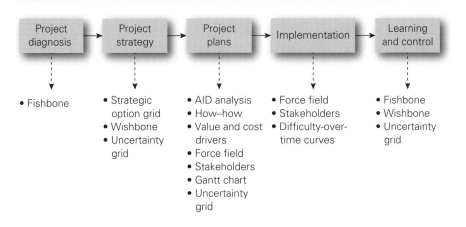

Also, we may well see some of these tools being intermingled. For example, we might see AID analysis being used to evaluate the activities in the how–how analysis, and to prioritize these. We might see, too, the uncertainty grid being used on particular elements of activities to identify which milestones we are hoping to achieve are most important and most uncertain, especially those on any critical path. This may seem a lot of work but it doesn't take really very long and it is pretty important to do.

In the simplest of approaches a project plan can be quite short but it should contain:

- key strategic goals and any gap analysis;
- project options and their appraisal;
- an implementation plan with the key activities and their milestones;
- a business case and uncertainty analysis;
- communication and stakeholders;
- appendices.

STRATEGIC EXERCISE 8.7 Assessing past project plans –
10 minutes

For a past strategy:

- What were the key strategic projects that delivered it?
- What were their key interdependencies?
- How well were these managed?

- For one project that didn't quite work out as planned, why was this (fishbone analysis)?
- For that project that didn't quite work out as planned, how could this be project managed in a better way?

Examples of strategic projects might include:

- acquisitions;
- alliances;
- brand development;
- divestment;
- market development;
- organizational development interventions;
- outsourcing;
- product development;
- relocations;
- restructurings;
- systems.

So, in conclusion, project management should play a key role in the break-through and implementation parts of the process.

The business case

Where there is either a large strategic project or a particular strategic decision requiring substantial investment (a strategic investment decision), this will necessitate some kind of a business case as follows:

- its key strategic and financial objectives;
- some value and cost driver analysis;
- some quantification of economic value added incrementally in the form of future net cash flows and a discounted cash flow/payback/future present value divided by the outlay;
- a listing of the key assumptions – with some testing on the uncertainty grid;
- a sensitivity analysis based on the evaluation of the most critical assumptions.

It is important to emphasize here that the numbers must follow the strategic analysis very closely and are only as good as the quality of the assumptions that we are making.

STRATEGIC EXERCISE 8.8 Doing a business case in your own company – 10 minutes

- For a project or decision in your own company, what would an outline business case look like using the above headings?

- What value is being targeted and how might that be improved with the cunning plan?

- What do the value and cost driver tools reveal, and the value-over-time curve?

- What are the most critical assumptions (using the uncertainty grid) and what might be their impact in broad terms on the numbers?

The business case is thus a useful piece of thinking both to target the value of the decision and to assess this value after the event.

Doing a strategic position paper

A strategic position paper is a draft document which is there for discussion. It is not intended as a strategic plan. Its purpose is to identify and debate the key strategic issues, to diagnose these, to identify some options and to come up with some initial thoughts of their attractiveness. One would not normally expect to see very detailed strategic plans here, nor detailed and definitive strategic objectives, nor detailed financials and business cases.

A strategic position paper enables a number of things to happen:

- Get some first thoughts and reflections down.
- Do initial work on the options.
- Help provide an agenda for the plan for the plan.
- Gain stakeholder views.
- Provide a health check on the thinking as part of the 'challenge and build' process.
- Record the output from a strategic workshop – and develop it further.
- Accelerate the process for arriving at a strategic plan.

On the latter point, while the strategic position paper doesn't strive to produce a plan, paradoxically it often goes a long way there.

A strategic position paper will usually contain:

- present situation and diagnosis;
- key strategic issues;
- potential strategic options;
- overview of implementation implications;
- stakeholder views;
- a list of the key strategic questions that need to be answered still;
- any input to the plan for the plan.

Strategic position papers can be done on many topics, for instance:

- corporate strategy;
- business strategy;
- possible acquisitions;
- turnaround;
- functional strategies like IT and HR;
- competitive scenarios;
- market development;
- regulatory scenarios;
- strategic cost breakthroughs;
- restructurings;
- organizational development.

Typically it shouldn't take a lot of time to produce a strategic position paper: as a rule of thumb it takes about three-quarters of a day to do this for a day's workshop output, if that is rich. Ideally this should be written up freshly – within two days, otherwise some of the detail will begin to fade in the memory. Also, ideally you want to get it to the attendees as soon as possible. The draft is then circulated around attendees and other stakeholders to check accuracy and further thoughts – this can be done by e-mail unless there is a lot for controversy.

STRATEGIC EXERCISE 8.9 Targeting a position paper – 10 minutes

Identify an area where it might be useful to do a strategic position paper:

- What are the issues that it should focus on?
- What are the likely dilemmas and options?
- What are the really key strategic questions it should address?
- Who might get involved in providing input to it?

- How would a workshop be useful?

- What would its likely value be?

Scenarios and uncertainty

We have already looked at some role playing (with the London riots) in Chapter 1 and also the uncertainty grid in Chapter 6. In this short section we will round off that discussion with a review of the scenario process.

A scenario can be defined as 'a story of the future where there is cause and effect stream of events that lead to a shift or change in some state of the world'. Scenarios are thus a series of pictures of the future rather like that of a film or a novel. They are internally consistent and have some plausibility. But they are not the same thing as projections and shouldn't be confused with those.

Figure 8.5 describes the scenario process and shows that this should go through a number of activities, namely:

- inputs on economic assumptions, eg GDP growth;

- understanding the key systems that impact on the strategy;

- looking at the underlying driving forces and the key shifts;

- identifying the most important interdependencies;

- scenario development itself.

FIGURE 8.5   Scenarios – the process

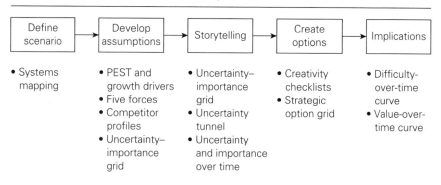

The uncertainty grid (see Figure 6.5) comes in here in terms of identifying, out of the driving forces and interdependencies, the most critical group of assumptions. This can be done on its own to generate the storylines, or from the transitional events, or using the two in unison. Doing some role playing of the key players and having the out-of-body experience of being them will also bring this to life.

In terms of the number of scenarios, these would normally be between two and four. These shouldn't necessarily be of a polar nature: for example, optimistic and pessimistic. Likewise, where there are three scenarios the middle one can become the average of the other two.

Personally, I feel that it is generally better to frame the scenarios around a particular pattern of events. That said, if only for resilience – or stress-testing – it can be a good idea to do a doomsday scenario.

The duration of a scenario can be quite variable, depending on the time-scales for decision making and also the period of foreseeability, beyond which it becomes hard to be realistic, because of compounding uncertainty. Using the techniques at our disposal, such as the uncertainty tunnel, this can be further into the future than you perhaps think. I have often said that 'uncertainty' is more often than not a label for those things that we haven't bothered thinking about deeply enough.

A scenario can be as long as 20 years, for example of the global decline of the United States as a superpower, or as short as an hour, for example of an important meeting. Indeed, I recalled today the time when I took my daughter and son out for a pub lunch when they were about 11 and 9. In my scenario I foresaw that, after a while, they would start to argue as they often did. We got to the pub and went in, and before we had sat down they were arguing over 'where are we going to sit? and whether it was a nice pub or not. Having done my scenario storytelling I was ready for it.

This process was originally developed for British Telecom in the 1990s and was used, for example, to look at the prospects for the internet – out of which was ultimately born BT's strategy for the internet.

Other applications of scenarios were for:

- Amerada Hess's entry to the North Sea gas market;
- Tesco's strategy for Express and Extra formats and Non Food;
- Standard Life's strategy for dealing with regulatory change;
- HSBC's strategy for mobile telephone banking;

and many others.

The main problem with scenario storytelling is that managers struggle to be imaginative in their telling of those stories. I believe that this is a function of the fact that much of their job is very operational and generally reactive, so they often underuse their imagination in their day-to-day roles. In one case I had to take over some of the creative process as they couldn't get into the storytelling. I did say at the time, 'Just imagine that you are making up a story to tell your kids', but they still couldn't do it. On another occasion I had the head of group strategy say to me: 'Tony, I think that the trouble with us is that we think in bullet points.'

I developed a very useful framework to help with this difficulty: the 'uncertainty tunnel' – see Figure 8.6. Here we have to imagine that we are transitioning between two different states of the world (the second one un-known or just sensed in part). This begins with the antecedents of change. Often the germs of the change are latent in the existing situation. Then we have those things in the system that might amplify it: make it more extreme or more volatile. Also, we have the dampeners – things like market or organizational inertia, recognition delays etc.

FIGURE 8.6   The uncertainty tunnel

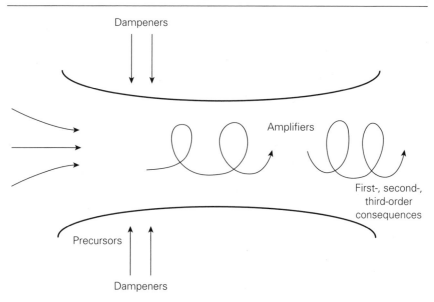

Finally the consequences can unfold over time in sequences, so we have the first-, second- and third-order consequences.

The pivotal parts of the storytelling are thus around:

- the initiation of the change;
- the dynamics as it shifts;
- the sequence of consequences.

Within that storyline there need to be some 'transitional events' which are tipping points that make the system we are looking at begin to behave in a new way. So, for example, there were transitional events in the credit crunch of: the seizing up of the wholesale money markets; the run on deposits at Northern Rock building society in the UK which then had to be nationalized by the Bank of England.

In terms of actually writing a scenario it is thus essential to make up very specific events and to set them inside the time dimension. For example, at the time of writing – October 2011, we are facing great economic turbu-lence. A possible scenario would be:

In late October 2011 there is an agreed bailout of Greece with support to Spain, too. This is based on tighter lending than these countries actually need and by late 2012 it is apparent that an even bigger round of funding is needed. Also, a number of Spanish banks are looking jittery. World recovery has stalled and the Chinese begin first to slow their purchase of US government securities because of sluggish global demand and as these securities are downgraded, too. This means that there are simultaneous financial pressures on both sides of the Atlantic. International efforts to shore up funding gaps collapse and shares drop in price. Speculators then gamble that shares will fall even more, causing a stock market collapse. Governments are unable to reflate the world economy and a second Great Depression ensues.

Implausible? I do hope so! (Of course, the 2011 bailout didn't happen!)

The storyline here was generated by working the future causal chain back and forth: looking at an outcome and then imagining an event sufficient to cause it, or starting with one or more plausible events and seeing what these could lead on to. The other ingredients in my head are things like assumed lead times, for example that the marginal states might begin to start the process of refinancing only a year away, and the trends already discernible, such as the Chinese appetite for US debt, which may well be unsustainable.

Obviously, were Greece to be well funded and be able to turn itself around, the United States to become less dependent on overseas funding and the euro saved, that scenario would be averted. I hope that gives you a working example of what a scenario looks like and how you might arrive at it.

Such scenarios are not unthinkable and appear plausible. As reported in *The Daily Telegraph* (19 October 2011): 'The root cause of the debt crisis (according to the Governor of the Bank of England) was a long period of "unsustainably high consumption" in which governments, companies and individuals spent more than they earned.' That spending was made possible because fast-growing emerging economies such as China spent much less than they earned, and used the surpluses to lend to the West. 'All the emergency measures had done was to simply buy time for world leaders to address that imbalance. So far that time has not been used to deal with the underlying imbalances... time is running out', said Sir Mervyn King.

Additional help in providing context for externally focused scenarios like the above can come from two tools we have already mentioned, one of them at length – PEST analysis and Porter's five forces (Figure 4.1) and also from an additional framework – the strategy onion. In addition, we have the last missing piece of the jigsaw puzzle – my own contribution of growth drivers (Grundy, 1995, 2002b), which models the dynamics of market growth at the macro-market level.

The strategy onion depicts the five main systems of environmental and competitive analysis that underpin strategic attractiveness – our first criterion of the strategic option grid (Figure 6.1). In Figure 8.7 we see the impact of life-cycle effects, the wider PEST factors, then the growth drivers and, last but not least, competitive position. This is rather like a radar picture – strategic radar – for the systems that are around you.

FIGURE 8.7   The strategy onion

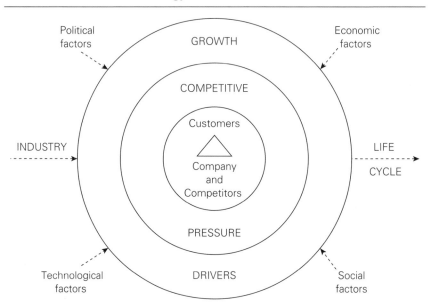

Figure 8.7 is not only visually powerful and relatively easy to remember but it reminds us to see these five elements as merely aspects of a single, dynamic system – and not as very separate techniques. They are all highly interdependent. For example:

- PEST factors will have a big and direct impact on the growth drivers of a particular market.
- And also have an indirect impact on the behaviour of Porter's five competitive forces, eg on buyer power and on competitive rivalry (as we saw during the credit crunch across many markets).
- Porter's five forces will be shaped by life-cycle effects, as will growth drivers.
- Porter's five forces will shape the immediate competitive environment and thus have great relevance to how we look at competitive position.

For completeness I include at this point a model of PEST – see Figure 8.8. This shows the interdependencies which may need to be thought about when exploring this model and the environment more deeply than producing a brainstormed list.

In the immediate context of scenarios we use the strategy onion to start to develop storylines of how the business model of the entire industry can shift. For example, a meltdown in the euro and the southern European countries' financing in late 2011/12 could upset the growth and stability of the banking industry, intensify rivalry and weaken margins.

FIGURE 8.8 PEST analysis

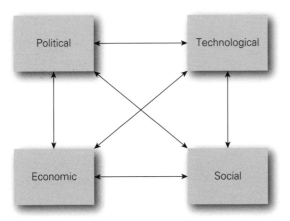

NOTE: PEST factors may also be considered in evaluating growth drivers, particularly to test sustainability of growth

We ought also to include here the growth driver picture to satisfy any curiosity. This is done again as a vector picture representing the forces within a particular market which are enabling or constraining its annual rate of percentage growth: see Figure 8.9 for the dotcom market for its share prices at a historic period of boom in 1990. Figure 8.10 shows the same market in a dramatic reversal in 1991. Growth driver analysis can thus be helpful not only in dissecting the dynamics of market growth but also in sensing potential turning points. The latter is especially useful in scenario work.

FIGURE 8.9 Growth driver analysis – 1

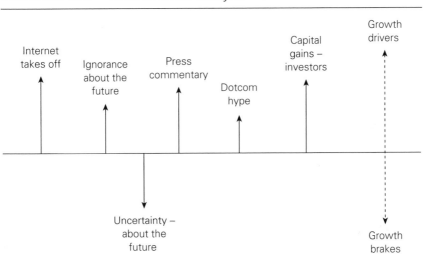

FIGURE 8.10   Growth driver analysis – 2

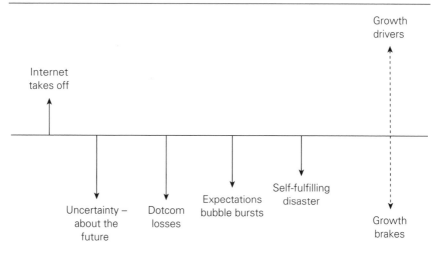

STRATEGIC EXERCISE 8.10 Using scenario storytelling –
15 minutes

For either an uncertain market opportunity that you are facing or an issue of an organizational nature:

● What systems of change does this involve thinking about?

● How might these behave in future?

● What specific transitional events might occur that prove to be tipping points, eg an economic slowdown, the entry of a new form of competitor to the market, a sudden surge of market growth or reversal in this, the appointment of a new CEO from outside the organization etc?

● How might change develop as a dynamic – using the uncertainty tunnel?

● What might the 'end game' look like?

In doing this you might well do some role playing of key players or stakeholders – such as the regulator, competitors, customers, new owners or new leadership – using the out-of-body experience.

This might be done for each of the players and presented in a forum attended by senior and informed managers for debating the interdependencies and knock-on effects. It might be helpful at this point to draw the environment as a systems diagram as we now see in Figure 8.11. This was drawn for the DIY market in the UK just after a period of slump. This suggested that the fact that many homeowners were putting off moving owing to stagnant house prices meant that there was a high possibility of a turnaround in market growth, which actually occurred.

FIGURE 8.11   Scenario systems

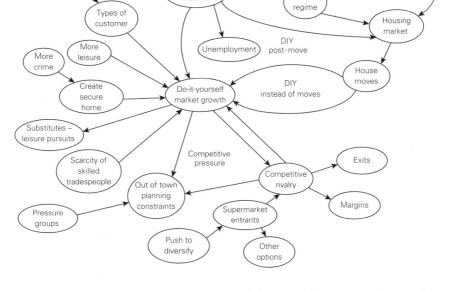

Finally scenario storytelling can be used for a wide variety of uses, for example:

- competitive strategy;
- cost management scenarios;
- change programmes;
- M&A;
- choosing an alliance partner;
- regulatory change;
- change of government;
- any project;
- taking a new job;
- any challenge in everyday life.

In the next section on contingent strategy we explore some ways of dealing with situations of high uncertainty.

Contingent strategy

Contingent strategy is a way of coping with alternative scenarios. It can be defined as 'a strategy which will be initiated, pursued and committed to only when certain external and internal conditions are in alignment and which is communicated within the organization as such.'

Contingent strategy is thus:

a) fluid and extremely flexible;

b) one that holds commitments in suspense;

c) one that requires that its fluidity, flexibility and open commitment is in itself communicated explicitly within the organization.

This is illustrated well in the next case study from military strategy. Here is a quote from coverage of the 2003 Iraqi war, being a reflection of Day 4 when US troops got bogged down in the south:

> The broad thrust of the strategy will be largely unaffected [by the problems of taking Umm Qasr] except that they might want to use these troops somewhere else.
>
> But their strategic intention is to take Umm Qasr, to clear it and to use the port. But they haven't been able to use this yet.
>
> Now General Tommy Franks will say that this is 'No problem' for... it is a reactive plan, a multifaceted, multi-levelled plan, a very complicated plan. And it is rather like going into a fish mongers to buy fish... they will pick up that [particular] fish when they want to have that fish, and are... letting it [run on until that fish is actually there].
>
> Mission command [still] works on, so that mission commanders get on with their work [in parallel].
>
> But equally... at the operational level of war, between the tactical, low-level stuff and the strategic stuff, the generals are planning what 'happens next'. They will have a whole range of options to select from. They will have other options to get back to what they do want to do without using these people [at Umm Qasr].
>
> Inflexible is not the word, which you would use. A principle of war is flexibility, flexibility is the key to planning. Plans don't last, plans are just there, plans are something in the future, and once you start you adapt as necessary.
> (Source: ITV News Channel, 2 March 2003, 09.43)

The above suggests that a contingent approach to strategy – so often applied by the military – has perhaps been forgotten by many business managers.

Strategy is about managing the future, as we saw in the above example – and a future which is frequently uncertain. All of strategy is thus a bet about the future – and the conventional response is to try to absorb this uncertainty through some form of business or strategic plan.

An entrepreneurial approach to strategy recognizes that all strategies and business plans are bets – but how can we improve the odds of strategic success? And how do we manage strategies which are essentially contingent on aligned future states of the world? Perhaps through having a contingent strategy. With a contingent strategy, instead of making a single relatively irrevocable commitment to a course of action, the commitment is held in as fluid a form as possible – reducing exposure to increase its return and also reduce its risk.

Contingent strategy, it is argued, offers a more open and flexible way of managing strategy than the perhaps simplistic terms of 'deliberate' and 'emergent'.

While existing theory makes reference to strategic management concepts such as contingency theory, scenarios, game theory and options, these still appear relatively remote from many managers' experience. Contingent strategy (by contrast) offers a way of crystallizing these ideas effectively, just as the forms of deliberate and emergent strategy previously achieved a similar condition. Also, in a more relatively uncertain world, contingent strategy may be a more frequent form of, or appropriate model of, strategy than deliberate or emergent strategy.

Within a contingent scenario context we are effectively looking at a multitude of possible futures, which we can represent as being at the top of the page on the strategic option grid. This allows us to judge the appropriateness and resilience of a particular strategy or strategic option against a variety of future states of the world. So in it we make decisions on commitment when it is perceived that a particular state of the world, and one in which the strategy is attractive, is likely to hold or materialize. So, like a predator, we wait to pounce until conditions are right.

Contingent strategy (as above) can manifest itself in two ways: either as a potential strategy or as an actual strategy (ie that one is actually embarked upon). In both cases it has the distinctive feature of preserving maximum flexibility. This is achieved by managing senior management's commitment to the strategy – through not making commitment prematurely, and not making commitment either virtually unconditional or hard to change (Ghemawat, 1991).

Underlying this concept of commitment is perhaps also the fact that deliberate strategy makes it easier and more comfortable in dealing with its emotional aspects. More open-ended or contingent approaches may prolong ambiguity and uncertainty, perhaps leading to anxiety.

The two main traditional forms of strategy – deliberate and emergent – are far too polar and simplistic, and not sufficiently flexible. Contingent strategy is an intermediate form lying between these two extremes. Where the originating external and/or internal environment is even modestly uncertain, a contingent strategy form may be preferable to the two more extreme typologies from Mintzberg. Also, were an organization to adopt a mere contingent mode of strategy for its main business strategies, this will have far-reaching implications for management processes – including business plans, budgets, control and reward systems, and communications systems.

Contingent strategy potentially transforms the substance of strategic plans and their optimal communication style throughout the organization, as senior management now need to put caveats on 'we intend to do this, and this is how' by also specifying the conditions under which this may, or may not, happen. It also frees up strategic thinking to be less focused on a single-world view – something which to date has only been on offer via scenario development. It also means that where managers are muddling through – 'logical incrementalism' (Quinn, 1980), strategies can become more thought through, while still preserving flexibility in managers' strategic mindsets.

So in practical terms, with a contingent strategy the modus operandi is:

- Where there are great uncertainties in the world, it makes sense to press home a strategy if and only if all the factors, both internal and external, are well aligned.

- Even if we don't describe a strategy explicitly as contingent, we can still ascribe conditionality to it.

- This also means that where a strategy is in the 'contingent zone', a meeting should be held before commitment is more or less irresistible.

STRATEGIC EXERCISE 8.11 Contingent strategy – 10 minutes

For one area of uncertainty:

- What are its key drivers and possible dynamics?

- What are the possible strategies?

- Under what conditions do any of these line up to give the necessary and sufficient conditions for success?

- What triggers do you see as needing to be there to take advantage of that?

- How are you going to position the contingent nature of any plan to key stakeholders and accommodate for this in the management process, eg in budgets and in communication and expectations management?

Managing intangibles

Intangibles are areas of value that are inherently hard to value economically. These are important to get to grips with in the strategy process because they frustrate the assessment of financial attractiveness, value-based management, business cases and also the strategic management of costs. They make it particularly hard to evaluate brand strategies, synergies, investment in organizational capability and in change.

Traditionally, intangibles were regarded as a fringe area of difficulty that meant that no quantified estimates of economic value could be made. But some have suggested that there are usually ways of assessing utility and thus what value a customer will generally attribute to an intangible (Roberts, 2008). Indeed in Roberts' view almost anything can be valued economically, even for example in the case of an individual worshipper investing in a religion. In effect, Roberts argues, one can put a value on this as a subjective probabilistic view of the outcomes given devotion versus non-devotion and even the levels of giving financially to the church. He suggests that religions which offer more extreme paybacks can generate proportionately higher levels of charitable giving! – an entertaining book.

I first met this problem in the late 1980s when I was doing my PhD into the links between strategy and value. I found in my research (Grundy, 1998b) that a lot of the problem was that quantification wasn't forthcoming as the numbers couldn't be assessed on an accurate or reliable basis. But that didn't mean that it was impossible to estimate value on a 'what if?' basis.

A second problem is that 'intangibles' is a broad label to cover many different phenomena. For instance, there are all kinds of different types of intangibles:

- Protective value – if we don't do it, competitive advantage will erode and cash flows will go down: this can be assessed by doing 'what if?' scenarios of decline in competitive position.

- Insurance value – a special kind of value of protection against unlikely events: these can be valued in a similar way to an insurance risk/policy.

- Contingent value – value which is highly interdependent with other things: this can be assessed through probabilistic assumptions and pay-offs, multiplying these to get 'expected values'. If these are considered too fuzzy or of too low probability and we are risk averse, we can use the idea of 'regret value', ie what would we pay to have that possibility (or real options pricing – for the gourmet financial types)?

- Value is intangible because it is only part of a bigger set of things (which I call the 'strategic project set').

- Value comes in many ways: here the value driver trees are invaluable for dissecting the different aspects of value generation.

In the latter case this can give rise to some fascinating analyses. For instance, I was asked to see whether it was possible to do an economic value of the value of investment in police training, by West Midlands Police. This proved something of a challenge, partly because of the lack of a price mechanism. Also, it was naturally somewhat difficult to get police officers to think in a more commercial way about this investment.

We had three shots at it: training to drive with sirens on fast, advanced interviewing skills, and training to do physical arrests. We had progress on the first one, a fuller business case for the second, and a very detailed one for the third.

The third, physical arrest training, had a wide range of value drivers:

- Costs of injury to the police avoided.
- Costs of injury to the public avoided.
- The fact was that if there is no or little training, officers would be more reticent in arresting as they would be more fearful of getting hurt.
- More problems in arresting people could lead to some loss of confidence in the force.
- Cost of complaints avoided.
- Adverse media coverage.
- Risk of serious injury or death and the attendant legal and other costs avoided.

By doing 'what ifs?' on these I was able to painstakingly assess the minimum realistic value of the aggregate intangibles. A couple were left out as they were softer. I put some assessments on the 'with' and 'without' investment cases, such as that it would be likely that injuries would double without training. I assumed that the lifetime of benefit would be about three years, as after that the officer might move on. Based on these reasoned assumptions we came out with a value of the training over its cost – as a ratio – of around 7 times, which was very healthy.

This was a tough one to crack but it showed that one can push the frontier of putting a value on intangibles back a great deal. I have had similar and even greater success with things like putting a value on culture change at BP and valuing strategic thinking etc.

STRATEGIC EXERCISE 8.12 Putting a value on intangibles
– 10 minutes

For one area of intangibles:

- What types of value does it generate?

- For each segment of value, what are the conditions under which it will crystallize?

- If you were to lose that value, what would you pay to get it back (its 'regret' value)?

- What other clues do you get about how to value it from the valuation recipes that I have mentioned above?

Managing implementation

We have already spent a whole chapter on implementation tools. In this chapter and also in Chapter 3 we have also looked at things like project management and change management. The important message here is that there should be just as much strategic thinking here as there is in the core of the process to arrive at the strategic plan. So we will limit what we say here to covering the control mechanisms.

The major controls are:

- the strategic audit and the ongoing use of the strategic option grid and other techniques to monitor strategy implementation;
- budgets: to control investment and costs;
- the balanced score card – see Chapter 3;
- KPIs – see Chapter 3;
- more strategically orientated review of results and performance, and board meetings.

Key insights from the chapter

- Strategy is about saying 'no' as well as 'yes'.
- Strategy is thus about choice – and not spreading yourself too thinly.
- And is about the creative definition of options.
- And has an important diagnostic phase, too.
- Strategy is about the how – it is tangible and actionable.

- And needs to be creative and cunning.
- We need to think about the environment, how it is changing, and how we can shape or even change that.
- So that invites the art of storytelling the future.
- And within that, the possible degrees of freedom, the possible intent, the agendas and behaviours of competitors and other players as well as ourselves.
- Timing is a critical issue, as well as capability.
- We need to manage the political dimension – eg with the 'P' behaviours.
- And influencing stakeholders.
- In terms of all three of the points immediately above, this requires taking the perspective of others, through the out-of-body experience.
- The plan for the plan is an essential preliminary step in the preparation process that will make it quicker and more effective and gain buy-in.
- More important than the quality of analysis is the ability to ask the right 'helicopter' questions.
- And at the right time and in the best way: this involves a lot of digestion and framing the question to open up thinking in a particular direction.
- Where are you likely to shift on the basis of current changes and current strategies?
- The strategic audit can be a helpful mechanism to do a more detached and objective evaluation of existing strategies and of the performance of the strategy, ongoing.
- This can be performed at a variety of levels and areas.
- Strategic workshops are an essential vehicle for opening up the debate and for making much better progress and for more informed and structured decision making.
- They do need quite a lot of preparation.
- Their agenda needs to take the form of a number of well-articulated strategic questions.
- And work in subgroups, preferably with some facilitation.
- The skills to be an effective strategic facilitator are many, diverse and challenging.
- A strategic position paper is an excellent vehicle for capturing the output of the debate, for generating more ideas, for encouraging the challenge and build process, for getting buy-in, for input to the plan for the plan, and to accelerate the process for writing the final strategic plan.

- Data is most important to get really solid justification, but it should be collected economically and from rich sources in least time, and in cunning ways.

- Scenario storytelling can also be a very useful way of dealing with uncertainty, for sensing the future and for anticipating what others will do.

- This again can be applied to a varied range of strategic issues and topics, either as a separate exercise or as a main part of the core, strategic process.

- This isn't easy to do, so that offers very real potential for gaining competitive advantage – as others will find that very difficult, too.

- Project management is also essential, both as part of detailed planning of strategic breakthroughs and also for steering and controlling the implementation process.

- Strategic projects demand a rather different approach, through strategic project management – to ensure that the project has a vision, a strategy and looks at the project fully in the round.

- While conventional project management techniques such as activity analysis are necessary, they are insufficient: also needed are many of the strategic tools, such as the strategic option grid and stakeholder analysis, scenario storytelling etc.

- Business cases are another helpful management process and provide a much-needed financial focus to gain attention and commitment and for influencing purposes.

- These need to make full use of value and cost driver analysis, value-over-time curves and the uncertainty grid, and also stress-testing and sensitivity analysis.

- Where there is much uncertainty, framing a strategy as a contingent one can help you to manage the commitment levels and to help to deploy decisions in such a way and timing as to optimize economic value added.

- Where there is intangible value, much of this can be captured through value and cost driver analysis, through data collection from a variety of sources, and this doesn't mean that you have to quantify with precision – they can be supported by reasoned estimates, and even 'what ifs?'.

Implementation is thus a key part of the strategic process and needs project management, change management, appropriate choice of management metrics, and indicators.

In this important and wide-ranging chapter I hope that I have given you a wealth of practical tips that will help to transform your strategy process going forward. Bet one of your colleagues to read this as well to see what he or she believes could be really helpful to enhance and upgrade your current process.

STRATEGIC EXERCISE 8.13 Prioritizing the improvements
to make

From the extensive menu of strategic processes within this chapter, identify a number of candidates for introducing these:

- For a number of these, what is your cunning plan for introducing it and how might you set about influencing key stakeholders to encourage this?

- For these improvements, where are they positioned on the AID grid?

In the next and final chapter we will be looking at how you might set about ensuring that you do more strategic thinking in your everyday management activity. We look at how you can now think and do things differently, having read, digested, worked with and internalized the thoughts and messages of this book – and at a deep level. The objective of this is to raise your game as a strategic thinker and as a strategic manager.

Bringing it all together

09

Introduction

In this final and shorter chapter we will sweep up a number of final things before we finally draw to a close, looking at:

- a final case of implementing the strategy process at the Legal Complaints Service;
- enhanced influencing;
- managing your own cognitive processes and emotions;
- tips for applying strategic thinking to the everyday;
- summary of insights;
- concluding story.

The initial case study is of interest at this point, particularly as it highlights the added value that strategic thinking at an organizational and team level can provide.

Case study: Implementing the process at the Legal Complaints Service

The Legal Complaints Service dealt with complaints against solicitors from members of the public across England and Wales. Quite often, clients were not completely satisfied with their legal service and the Legal Complaints Service helped them resolve their complaints. The Legal Complaints Service was set up in 2006 and was finally wound down and replaced by an ombudsman scheme in late 2010.

I first began my involvement with this company around 2008 and worked with them through to closedown in 2010. Its CEO, Deborah Evans, asked me to run a tailored version of my Cranfield programme, Breakthrough Strategic Thinking, for her senior team and herself. This was an initial two-day practical workshop followed by remotely facilitated group project work.

During these workshops we worked on the many real strategic issues concerning an organization facing closedown, at the same time as training the team in the techniques and getting them to think differently, and also handing the process over to them. Much was accomplished in that first cycle.

Deborah was prescient, as the organization was about to be faced with some major strategic change:

> The management of the organization was undoubtedly a challenge – there
> was first the issue of maximizing performance in a complaint-handling body
> under significant challenge from the regulator to perform at increasingly high
> levels. On top of this, we had to deal with any organizational demotivation that
> inevitably comes with impending closure and redundancies.

In 2009 we followed this up with further away days to focus on particular topics, such as scenario development around closure and change management (in particular, developing process efficiencies to enable the organization to do the same amount of work, to the same high standard, with a diminishing number of staff over time). Further live strategic issues and current challenges were dealt with as they came up.

On one particular occasion the organization was faced with a very large fine from the regulator for narrowly missing KPIs. We not only role played the regulator to see what arguments would be most persuasive but also looked at the possible negotiation tactics on both sides and modelled how these might pan out. Using the various techniques such as the strategic option grid and stakeholder agenda analysis, Deborah and her team turned their original and more defensive and pessimistic perceptions to become more confident that their story and argument (and tactics) might just work – the result, no fine of £250,000:

> There is a tendency to think as a management team that you know what works
> and what is best. The strategic options grid is an essential tool as it changes
> the angles from which you think, and makes the analysis more thorough and
> grounded. It regularly opened our eyes as to different approaches and changed
> the decisions we took for the better.

In 2009 a repeat of the earlier Breakthrough Strategic Thinking course was done for some new people on the team. Deborah wisely wanted to build a common language, mindset and shared process. The new senior managers were very eager and enthusiastic, no doubt encouraged by the fact that the rest of the team had clearly found the process very useful.

While it had been known since 2006 that the service would be replaced, the date was never set. However, in late 2009 it was apparent that closure would occur during 2010. No firm date was given, which made planning difficult. A further away day was done to help the managers begin to think about their own future career strategies, and to reflect on how the entire team was working together under the stress of impending redundancy. This was quite a deep session and gave even more of a sense of team cohesion and unity, as well as allowing all those present to process what their thoughts and feelings were about the whole thing. We had a touching session where individuals fed back to each other their perceptions of the distinctive strengths of each other: it was very inspiring. Truly we reached a point where they deepened shared culture – very important when dealing with the fact that external stakeholders had decided to take away its role. This could have been damaging to shared and individual self-esteem.

> As a management team we prioritized the needs of the organization and the staff before our own needs. We all knew that the only way to successful closure was through stability of leadership and team in a time of stress. There was a great deal of loyalty. However, we were able to work out that it wasn't all or nothing – that the team could (and should) shrink, and that if some managers were able to secure employment quickly staff would benefit from opportunities for internal promotions for the remaining period. It was important to take time out to consider our own futures and to support each other through this period, and to find ways of celebrating each other's successes in job hunting, and to support each other when things weren't going so well. I wanted to build a culture where the managers could be open with each other about their job hunting without feeling like traitors, and that those staff committed to staying to the end could be happy in their decision.

Our final workshop was around the Election in May 2010 when it was still emerging as to who would call the political shots which would determine when and how the organization would be wound up. We again used scenario techniques to storytell the future, and found that as we were actually doing that, news broke which some were monitoring on their BlackBerry smartphones – a first!

Deborah continued in role until the very end, which I do admire: she always seemed to put Legal Complaints first and left finding a new career role largely until later so that there would be continuity of leadership:

> Closing down an organization successfully in such a managed and planned way was a beneficial experience for the whole team. We did it respectfully, looking after both the customers and the staff in the process. Unusually for an organization in closedown, we maintained performance at very high standards until the end. The demotivation we had feared became feelings of great satisfaction for managers and all staff as we rode the storm so successfully. We closed on a high.

This case study captures a number of pointers in any situation where the organization and the senior team are facing strategic change. These include:

- Training in strategic thinking can really shift organizational capability, as well as helping tackle some very challenging strategic issues in a creative and constructive way.
- There can be some very direct value wins indeed from this.
- Ideally this should be mobilized by a sufficiently in-depth intervention.
- Far from being a scenario of diminishing returns, further and periodic sessions help to spiral that capability to even higher levels.

- Other benefits are strategic team building and also the adoption of a new and much more effective set of processes and techniques.
- These aren't intrusive at all, and after a little while don't feel unnatural.
- These sessions can also help deal with behavioural issues.
- Its success will obviously have a lot to do with the leadership style and the culture, which were clearly very supportive here.
- Strategic thinking at the organizational, the team and the individual level can reduce anxieties and stress greatly.

Enhanced influencing

A continual theme throughout this book has been the application of strategic thinking to the influencing process. We have already dealt with many aspects of this in earlier chapters, particularly in Chapter 7 on implementation. Here we will focus on some very specific and practical thoughts that will help you gain a little more control over your stakeholder environment than hitherto.

One of the key problems frequently faced by managers here is 'saying no'. There are many ways of saying 'no' and these can be generated by the thinking prompts implicit in our strategy tools. To say 'no', the following list in the form of key questions might well be helpful:

1 What are the objectives of our doing X?
2 What are the benefits that you see?
3 What are the options we have for achieving these objectives?
4 How attractive are these?
5 What do you see as the problem and what are the causes?
6 What do you think might be the opportunity costs of doing that?
7 What do you think a successful outcome will depend on?
8 How uncertain are those things?
9 Can we get sufficient stakeholder support to make it happen?
10 How much time do you think it might take?
11 What are the hidden costs?
12 Who might be for it and against it?
13 What are the options for how we will do it?
14 Do you think there is a risk of spreading ourselves too thinly?
15 Who besides myself might be well placed to do it?
16 Is it a really important part of our strategy?
17 How complex do you see this and is this really a 'project'?

18 What is your feeling on its scope?

19 What are the main constraints as you see them?

20 What might be the 'one big thing we forgot?'

21 Do you think we need a 'cunning plan' for this?

22 How much time input will it absorb from you as we get into it?

23 Do you suspect there might be change management issues at all?

24 Do you think it will get sufficient attention and priority at this time?

25 In the unlikely event that we begin to get bogged down in this, for instance when XYZ is going on, what do you think we might have to do to dig our way out of that?

I feel that I could go on, but I will stop at 25 questions.

Obviously, one needs to show some spontaneity and sensitivity in using this list in order to avoid doing things which aren't particularly strategic or indeed value added; such things take the right kind of positioning and the right kind of tone of voice and eye contact. They will also depend a lot on your relationship with your boss and the political context and the history around it.

You might recognize in the above the use of fishbone and stakeholder analysis, the strategic option grid, force field analysis, the uncertainty grid etc.

Managing your own cognitive processes and emotions

The book has made extensive reference to psychological factors throughout and I felt that it would be worthwhile just drawing these together. The main elements of self-management of cognitive and emotional processes that we have looked at are:

- helicopter thinking – for cultivating a sense of detachment, objectivity and agility of cognitive processes;
- fishbone analysis for making a problem more 'out there' rather than enmeshed in lots of thoughts and emotions and anxieties – and thus gaining more mental flow and freedom from turbulent feelings about issues;
- stakeholder agenda analysis for reflecting on one's own agendas on a particular issue – especially where some of these might be contradictory;
- where one has negative agendas to be able to dig down into their drivers through root cause analysis (fishbones) on these at an individual level;

- mindset detachment – as we saw in some of the cunning checklists;
- monitoring one's emotional states through, for example, the anxiety-over-time curve, the excitement-over-time curve etc;
- taking on board the practice of mindfulness so that one doesn't miss strategic signals in everyday experiences – keeping one's strategic radar actively scanning.

Another, more general factor is that as you progress to spend more time doing strategic thinking and get better and better at it, the more relaxed, calm and confident you will be, and feeling on top of things. This, I hope, will bring you to a state of 'strategic mindfulness'. Practical tips for this are to:

- maintain a strategic notebook or diary;
- book regular slots for meetings with yourself just do some strategic thinking, or 'white space' – half an hour to an hour;
- focus on a small number of issues at a time;
- use the tools for making presentations;
- put your favourite cunning checklists on the wall;
- put the key tools onto your computer for regular use;
- continually practise the out-of-body experience;
- identify a specific strategic project to which you are going to apply the strategic thinking tools;
- consider the benefits of having a strategic mentor or coach.

On the last note, and briefly, for many years I have acted as a strategic coach myself and know all too well that this can be a very powerful catalyst for upgrading the capability and potential of very senior managers – sometimes at CEO level. This gives them a confidentially safe space to reflect on their thoughts and on themselves, and to lift them outside of mindsets, assumptions and even patterns of behaviour. This can even be effective during two- to three-hour sessions. One huge benefit of this is that virtually no one else need be aware of it – and there is no need for a long executive course with diluted relevance.

As I was finishing this book I asked myself whether there had been any big things that I forgot. The answer was acquisitions and divestment. This is well catered for in my previous book, *Be Your Own Strategy Consultant* (2002b), and even more fully in *Mergers and Acquisitions* (2003a). Suffice it to say that acquisitions must be managed through strategic tools and strategic thinking, as we have seen in this book, particularly evaluation, doing the deal and integration (the implementation techniques).

Indeed, an obvious port of call in planning further work to do is to read the sister and complementary books on *Mergers and Acquisitions* (2003a), *Shareholder Value* (2002c), *Value-Based Human Resource Strategy* (2003b), *Strategic Project Management* (2002a) and *Harnessing Strategic Behaviour* (1998a). (Don't ask how these were all done so close together.)

Tips for applying strategic thinking to the everyday

In this book I have made quite frequent reference to events and issues that I have faced in everyday life. I assure the reader that this is something that is a deep habit – and I hope that you can borrow from that example. For example, as I write I have a very big personal project on the go – a family-related contact case. In this I have made extensive use of, for example:

- SWOT analysis: of the two sides in the dispute;
- out-of-body experiences: the judge, the social worker and also the party that I am up against – and their agendas;
- innumerable imaginary role-playing simulations;
- considering my most powerful strategic assets;
- scenarios reaching years into the future;
- difficulty- and value-over-time curves;
- frequently revisiting my strategic objectives and the attractiveness of the options;
- identifying new options as they come up;
- asking myself the question 'what's the one big thing that I missed';
- thinking deeply about the cunning checklists;
- not ruling out unpalatable options;
- thinking about the criteria which the court will use in making its final decision;
- looking for the sweet spot that I can argue;
- questioning my assumptions about the case;
- preparing a range of contingent strategies to deal with different scenarios;
- seeking independent opinion from a wide variety of people who I knew would give me different perspectives etc.

Without that, I think that I would be in rehab by now. Indeed, writing these down makes me conscious of some gaps and that I could do more. By the time this book is published the final hearing will have been done, so it will be too late for the opposition to read the above!

Looking forward again, as we will see in the turkey story with which we close, it seems foolish to not use these tools and processes as much in your personal life as in your business life. As some suggestions, you can choose from things like:

- holidays;
- new relationships;
- breaking up existing ones;

- friendships;
- social events such as dinner parties;
- house moves;
- buying a car;
- doing an MBA;
- doing a strategic audit of an area of your life;
- managing major life changes;
- applying for a new job;
- exiting your existing one;
- starting up a business etc;
- major cases in family courts.

STRATEGIC EXERCISE 9.1 Applying strategic thinking to everyday life – 10–15 minutes

For one of the above areas of your life:

- Where there are problems or difficulties, why do these exist?
- What are the key options?
- How attractive are these on the strategic option grid?
- What is your cunning plan?
- Is that 'what you really-really want?'
- What's the 'one big thing that you have forgotten?'

To judge where you now are in terms of your strategic thinking, complete the following exercise.

STRATEGIC EXERCISE 9.2 How competent is your strategic thinking? – 10 minutes

For yourself, how would you judge your capability in terms of strategic thinking?
Rate these as:

| 5 = Very strong |
| 4 = Strong |
| 3 = Moderate |
| 2 = Weaker |
| 1 = Weak |

Complete this both for where you saw yourself before you read this book and for where you see yourself now:

	Before reading	After reading
	Add scores	Add scores
Diagnosis:		
Option generation:		
Option evaluation:		
Cunning/innovative thinking:		
Stakeholder awareness:		
Ability to think future:		
Questioning ability:		
Ability to think about implementation:		
Knowledge of strategic concepts:		
Knowledge of strategic tools:		

How was this originally? What shifts may have already occurred in the process of reading this book? What further work and reinforcement do you now need to consider? (By doubling your results you can arrive at a percentage, as there are 10 criteria times a possible top score of 5, or 50 in all.)

And for a very final one:

STRATEGIC EXERCISE 9.3 Reflecting on what you have
                           learnt – 5–10 minutes

What are the 10 biggest insights that you have gained from this book, eg about:

- The existing business's position (eg from the strategy audit etc)?

- The changing nature of your markets and of the competition?

- The options that it has available?

- The barriers to implementation and change?

- The form of strategy most suitable for the business: deliberate, emergent, detergent, contingent etc?

- The influence of stakeholders on this?

- How the strategy process is currently, and should be, conducted?

- The effectiveness and value added of particular tools – particularly in the context of your own organization?

- What you might be advised to stop doing strategically?

- Applying the tools to more everyday issues?

- What your own strengths and weaknesses are – cognitively, emotionally and behaviourally, and how you can become a more effective strategic thinker, facilitator and influencer in the future, and on the need to invest the time in this?

Summary of insights

There are many insights that I hope that you will have taken from this book, listed in the strategic learnings at the end of each chapter. Taking these chapters one at a time, in Chapter 1 we looked at the nature of strategy and strategic thinking. The most important insights from that were:

- Strategy should be kept as simple and as practical as possible, at all times, without unnecessarily complex language.
- Beware using strategy tools too naively and avoid the traps.
- Strategy entails knowing where you are now, where you want to be in the future and how to get there with real competitive advantage.

- Gaining real competitive advantage isn't easy, as you need to be doing something that others would find it hard to do well.
- Think about 'what you really-really-really want', in determining where you want to go.
- The future can have a range of time horizons and strategies can be short and medium term – so we have to be a time traveller.
- A strategy mustn't be just average, it must be cunning.
- Cunning can be discovered both in what you choose to analyse and thus its content and in how you set about thinking from it – ie in the process.
- Always ask: 'what is the one big question we forgot?' – and 'what is the second big question we forgot to ask?'
- Often in strategy the process is more important than the content.

In Chapter 2 on the first three perspectives, the conceptual, the cognitive and the emotional, we looked at how these have an influence on the strategy process and on strategic thinking:

- Narrow down your strategies to just a few to really give sufficient focus: ideally no more than three breakthroughs, and decide your 'strategic don'ts'.
- RBT tells us to minimize exposure to being copied.
- Costs need to be managed more strategically and in a way that never neglects economic value.
- Costs must be managed using gap analysis.
- Change is often complex and requires many strategic tools – and much strategic thinking.
- Strategic planning processes need to be designed in a bespoke way, depending on the issues and context.
- We need to be strategically inventive and this requires an agile mindset and skills.
- Mindsets play a very big role in shaping strategic decisions – and need managing.
- Strategy discussions often generate a lot of anxiety, which affects behaviours and the process.
- Strategy is a very emotional thing and this emotion will be experienced by different team members in different ways.
- Non-verbal communication is very influential and can shape the outcomes of interactive behaviour greatly.
- Emotional and cognitive states are conditioned by the energies of an individual or group or their climate and you can be mindful and intuitive in sensing and recognizing these.

Chapter 3 then looked at the influencing and political, the process and the implementation perspectives. This yielded the following key insights:

- Stakeholder analysis is a 'must-do' but to do it properly you must have the out-of-body experience.
- Stakeholders may change positions over time, and this needs tracking.
- Influencing strategies should not be average but cunning.
- The buying-in process in organizations is complex and can be tortuous – be patient.
- Business and personal agendas often get mixed up and need untangling, using stakeholder analysis.
- Use the 'P's to help channel the politics of strategic debate, or suggest a 'politics-free zone'.
- Too much emergent strategy is often a bad thing.
- Often the strategy seems to move around a cycle – the strategy mix, and go through more chaotic phases before being re-formed.
- When in a state of flux, contingent strategies can be helpful.
- Performance = (quality of strategy) × (quality of implementation) × (timing).
- There isn't a simplistic recipe for change generally – it needs to be tailored to the context.
- The change management process has many phases, including gestation, diagnosis, options, planning, mobilization, consolidation, control and learning.

Chapter 4 on economic analysis looked at how we need to employ a lot of essentially economic thinking as we go on to understand the conditions that create successful strategies. Key insights were:

- Different markets have different degrees of inherent economic attractiveness – due to Porter's five forces, and this attractiveness changes over time, with the forces.
- This can have a huge impact on prices, margins, profit and economic returns.
- Companies can use different strategic recipes or styles for competing: eg differentiation, cost leadership, but beware trying to be many things – choose.
- Strategic resources which are special – strategic assets – can be sources of ideas in creating a sustainable advantage, from the inside out.
- But check that this is 'sufficient, transcendent (a cut above?), rare, important, protectable, evolutionary' (ie offers dynamic potential).

- Time (or speed – especially of implementation) can be a key source of competitive advantage.
- 'Blue ocean' strategies suggest that we should try to find uncontested competitive space, but this may be not sustainable – perhaps it is more useful to discern blue, green, brown, red and black ones – to be less simplistic.

More specifically, on Porter's five forces from Chapter 4:

- Porter's forces aren't fixed constraints: they offer opportunities for getting around them.
- In many industries the existence of high entry barriers is the key to its superior attractiveness: this is a strategic clue – how can entry barriers be raised?
- Also, where there is potentially a lot of emotional value, this can suggest ways of achieving high customer value capture (higher prices/ selling more products).
- There might even be 'blue ocean' possibilities beyond the existing patterns of competition to be explored – industry attractiveness is not necessarily a given.
- The forces will vary over the 'strategic landscape' of different products/market segments/geographies – industries have different levels of attractiveness within them.
- These forces will change over the industry life cycle, the economic life cycle, the transaction life cycle and the relationship life cycle, and this can be represented as 'curves of competitive pressure' over time.
- In addition to the five forces, there is a sixth, the industry mindset, which is the shared perceptions, expectations and assumptions that shape competitive behaviour – understanding this can lead to spotting opportunities for identifying uncontested competitive space.

In Chapter 5 we looked at the more dynamic models of competitive strategy, where we learnt, for example, that:

- The three C's model is a useful framework for thinking about competitive advantage.
- The hidden or fourth 'C' is often equally important: costs.
- Comparisons of relative competitive advantage can be too simplistic and require deeper thing about segmentation and the competitive context.
- It is often more important to think of how the three C's will be in the future.
- The three C's is too much of a static model.
- The sweet spot is a useful concept as long as one does not delude oneself over its size and zone of applicability – and it decays over time usually, unless this is attended to.

- More dynamic models, such as competitive-pressure-over-time and competitive-advantage-over-time curves and the time window and speed to realize an opportunity, are important in a dynamic context.
- We must also ensure that no areas of value destruction that undermine the sweet spot come up.
- Life-cycle effects need to be tracked and anticipated, as in the Bikram yoga case, and the business model refreshed.

In Chapter 6 on strategic options we met a very powerful way of processing complex and ambiguous choices and dilemmas. Key insights were:

- To make strategic choices we need to have some comprehensive and consistent criteria.
- Strategic attractiveness is the external market attractiveness and the relative competitive position. Market attractiveness is based on the growth drivers, Porter's five forces and perhaps PEST analysis. 'Competitive positioning' is a quite separate thing from this but is also a key part of strategic attractiveness.
- Financial attractiveness: these are the long- and short-term returns from the option – which depend on the value and cost drivers, and the financial model.
- Implementation difficulty: this is the sum of difficulty over time.
- Uncertainty and risk: this is the extent of the volatility of the assumptions.
- Stakeholder acceptability: this is the extent to which stakeholders favour, disfavour, or are neutral – have the out-of-body experience to get this.
- The scores on the option grid are only as good as the cunning plan.
- Besides its use on more deliberate strategies, it can also be used for more emergent and detergent strategies within the strategy mix.
- The scores can be tested through the deep-dive techniques, or through scenario storytelling.
- The options can be scored not only from your own perspective but from the perspective of other players, too (the double option grid), and can be used to simulate their possible behaviours.
- Judgements on financial attractiveness should also be accompanied by some detailed financial modelling as well as modelling of the uncertainties and risks.
- The options should be made as specific as possible and should have clear parameters.
- In terms of option generation, there are options for what you do, how you do it and when you do it.
- The grid can be used to appraise not only new options but also existing strategies, eg as part of any strategic audit.

- Using the optopus will get a much broader range of options than brainstorming.
- The dimensions of the optopus can be adapted and added to: for example with brand and pricing options.
- The ideas can be further developed and enriched by the 'pick and mix' of different combinations of ideas.
- The cunning checklists can be used to generate new options as well as to refine option grid scores.
- The option grid can also be used for making presentations, for position papers, for influencing, defusing politics and for identifying key questions and data needs.

Next, in Chapter 7 we examined implementation where, once again, there were many lessons. The five key stages of strategy implementation are: diagnosis, options, planning, implementation, learning and control:

- At each stage there are a number of tools that can be used – so they can be used more than once.
- Fishbone analysis can be used to diagnose problems with considerable complexity, such as turnarounds, and can be used to uncover the systems at work between the root causes.
- Wishbone analysis can be used for visualizing an opportunity and the alignment of the necessary and sufficient conditions that will help it to crystallize.
- FT analysis will help you to explore the scope of strategy implementation, to determine the level of desired stretch, to communicate it and to monitor progress towards goals.
- How–how analysis then breaks down each shift within the FT analysis into manageable steps.
- AID analysis is needed to prioritize particular strategic actions.
- Value and cost driver analysis then helps test out your assumed attractiveness in more depth.
- Force field analysis and the difficulty-over-time curve then test out its difficulty.
- Stakeholder analysis identifies the key stakeholders, positions them, and also suggests new influencing strategies to accomplish with the cunning influencing plan.
- Stakeholder agenda analysis enables you to explore a particular stakeholder's ambitions and anxieties.
- Stakeholders can also be disaggregated into:
  - those who have greatest influence;
  - those we have greatest influence over; and
  - those who are least/most important.

In Chapter 8 we looked at the need to have a tailored strategy process in which:

- There is a creative and cunning definition of options.
- It has an important diagnostic phase, too.
- Strategy is about the how – it is tangible and actionable.
- We need to think about the environment, how it is changing, and how we can shape or even change that.
- So that invites the art of storytelling the future.
- And within that, the possible degrees of freedom, the possible intent, the agendas and behaviours of competitors and other players as well as ourselves.
- Timing is a critical issue, as well as capability.
- We need to manage the political dimension (eg with the 'P' behaviours) and the stakeholders.
- The plan for the plan is an essential preliminary step in the preparation process that will make it quicker and more effective and gain buy-in.
- More important than the quality of analysis is the ability to ask the right 'helicopter' questions in the right way, and at the right time.
- The strategic audit can help you to do a more detached and objective evaluation of existing strategies and of the performance of the strategy, ongoing.
- Strategic workshops open up the debate and help you make much better and quicker progress.
- Their agenda needs to take the form of a number of well-articulated strategic questions, and requires subgroups and sufficient preparation and planning, possibly with facilitation.
- A strategic position paper is an excellent vehicle for capturing the output of the debate, for generating more ideas, for getting buy-in and to accelerate the delivery of the strategic plan.
- Data should be collected economically and from rich sources in least time, and in cunning ways.
- Scenario storytelling can also be a very useful way of dealing with uncertainty, for sensing the future and for anticipating what others will do.
- Strategic project management, using many of the strategic thinking tools, is also essential both as part of detailed planning of strategic breakthroughs and for steering and controlling the implementation process.
- Business cases provide a much-needed financial focus to gain attention and commitment and for influencing purposes.

- Where there is much uncertainty, framing a strategy as a 'contingent' one can help you to manage commitment levels.
- Intangible value can be captured through value and cost driver analysis, and through data collection from a variety of sources; this doesn't mean that you have to quantify with precision.

In the present chapter the key insights are that:

- The optimal way of introducing strategic thinking as a central management process in an organization is to teach all the key managers the tools and the process, to reinforce that learning, to apply this to real and challenging strategic issues, and to embed that language and thought process in the culture and management processes.
- The techniques are especially useful for influencing and particularly for 'saying no'.
- The techniques also allow you to manage your cognitive and emotional states more effectively so that management feels less turbulent and anxiety provoking, and you feel on top of things – practise strategic mindfulness.
- There are many opportunities to practise the techniques at an everyday level – be constantly alert to these.

In turning these insights into action you should remember the strategic principles of extending your strategic radar – not just to the competitive but to the influencing and stakeholder dimensions. You should practise strategic mindfulness – and ideally carry a strategic notebook to capture your ideas and insights. You should always practise the art of detachment and that of 'helicopter thinking'.

You will never again jump straight from diagnosis to conclusions: you will always think options. You will no longer believe that you can develop successful strategies without writing your thoughts down – and using the tools to help to structure them.

You will always try to be cunning, and to come up with new ways of looking at things. You will seek out dominance in the areas where you have greatest advantage – and will ruthlessly choose *not* to do things. You will, when it is important and necessary, reserve commitment through the contingent strategy and will strike only when both the timing and the conditions are right.

Above all, you will see yourself as a confident, strategic thinker.

Conclusion: a final story

I will finish with a short story that I often tell at the end of workshops. It goes like this:

> Once upon a time there were some turkeys walking across London's Hyde Park. They stopped where there were a lot of people exercising. A man came up to them and said: 'I am a flying instructor, here for the afternoon – if you like, I will teach you to fly.'
>
> The turkeys were feeling unusually adventurous that afternoon and said that they would quite like to try that. The flying instructor got in a microlite and asked the turkeys just to do as he did and to follow him. They all took off and soared above the park, over Kensington Palace and west along the Thames. They flew over the Queen's 'other big house' at Windsor, then headed east again over Richmond Park and Chelsea football ground.
>
> They all landed safely after a lovely afternoon where they had seen London from a different perspective.
>
> The flying instructor got out of his microlite and asked them: 'How was that for you?'
>
> They said that it had been fantastic and that they had really enjoyed it – and then walked home happily...

So, what was the one big thing they failed to do? Fly?

The moral of this story is that unless you have a proactive mindset to use all this knowledge of strategy and strategic thinking as much as is possible, you will never gain the full benefit – like Bikram yoga, it requires focus and effort.

I do hope that for you this is just the start of a journey, and not just the end of the book, and that you continue to use this guide throughout your management career. I will be glad to hear from your experiences (contact details below).

Tony
www.tonygrundy.com
tony.grundy1@virginmedia.co.uk

REFERENCES

Barney, J B (2001) Is the resource based theory a useful perspective for strategic management research? Yes, *Academy of Management Review*, **26** (1) pp 41–56

Barney, J B and Hesterly, W S (2002) *Strategic Management and Competitive Advantage*, Prentice Hall, Englewood Cliffs, NJ

Carnall, C (1990) *Managing Change in Organizations*, Financial Times/Prentice Hall, London

Ghemawat, P (1991) *Commitment: The dynamic of strategy*, The Free Press, New York

Goldratt, E M (1990) *Theory of Constraints*, North River Press, Great Barrington, MA

Grant, R (1991) The resource based theory of competitive advantage, *California Business Review*, Spring, pp 114–35

Grundy, A N (1993) *Implementing Strategic Change*, Kogan Page, London

Grundy, A N (1995) *Breakthrough Strategies for Growth*, Pitman, London

Grundy, A N (1996) Cost is a strategic issue, *Long Range Planning*, **29** (1), pp 58–68

Grundy, A N (1998a) *Harnessing Strategic Behaviour*, FT, London

Grundy, A N, Scholes, T and Johnson, G (1998b) *Exploring Strategic Financial Management*, Prentice Hall, London

Grundy, A N (2002a) *Strategic Project Management*, Thomson Learning, London

Grundy, A N (2002b) *Be Your Own Strategy Consultant*, Thomson Learning, London

Grundy, A N (2002c) *Shareholder Value*, Capstone, Oxford

Grundy, A N (2003a) *Mergers and Acquisitions*, Capstone, Oxford

Grundy, A N (2003b) *Value-Based Human Resource Strategy*, Butterworth-Heinemann, Oxford

Grundy, A N (2004) Rejuvenating strategic management: the strategic option grid, *Strategic Change*, **13** (3), pp 111–23

Grundy, A N (2006) Rethinking and reinventing Porter's five forces model, *Strategic Change*, **15**, pp 213–29

Hamel, G and Prahalad, C K (1994) *Competing For the Future*, Harvard Business School Press, Boston, MA

Janis, L L (1982) *Groupthink: Psychological studies of policy decisions and fiascos*, Houghton-Mifflin, Boston, MA

Johnson, G and Scholes, K (1987) *Exploring Corporate Strategy*, Prentice Hall, London

Kim, W C and Mauborgne, R (2005) *Blue Ocean Strategy*, Harvard Business School Press, Boston, MA

Lewin, K (1935) *A Dynamic Theory of Personality*, McGraw Book Co, New York

Miles, R E and Snow, M C (1978) *Organizational Strategy*, McGraw-Hill, New York

Mintzberg, H (1994) *The Rise and Fall of Strategic Planning*, The Free Press, New York

Mintzberg, H, Ahlsrand, B and Lampel, J (1998) *Strategy Safari*, Simon & Schuster, New York

Mitroff, I I and Linstone, H A (1993) *The Unbounded Mind*, Oxford University Press, Oxford

Ohmae, K (1982) *The Mind of the Strategist*, McGraw-Hill, New York

Peters, T and Waterman, R H (1982) *In Search of Excellence*, Harper and Row, New York

Piercy, N (1989) Diagnosing and solving implementation problems in strategic planning, *Journal of General Management*, **15** (1), pp 19–38

Porter, E M (1980) *Competitive Strategy*, The Free Press, New York

Porter, E M (1985) *Competitive Advantage*, The Free Press, New York

Quinn, J B (1980) *Strategies for Change: Logical incrementalism*, Richard D Urwin, Homewood, IL

Roberts, R (2008) *The Price of Everything*, Princeton University Press, Princeton, NJ

Rumelt, R (1991) How much does industry matter? *Strategic Management Journal*, **12** (3), pp 167–85

Stalk, E (1991) *Competing Against Time*, The Free Press, New York

Tovstiga, G (2010) *Strategy in Practice*, John Wiley & Sons, Chichester

Warren, K (2008) *Strategic Management Dynamics*, John Wiley & Sons, Chichester

INDEX

NB page numbers in *italic* indicate figures or tables

With over 1,000 titles in printed and digital format, **Kogan Page** offers affordable, sound business advice

www.koganpage.com